# DC
## by Metro

# DC

## by Metro

### A HISTORY & GUIDE

MICHELLE GOLDCHAIN

THE
History
PRESS

Published by The History Press
Charleston, SC
www.historypress.com

All images courtesy of the author.
Maps by Anna Burrous.

First published 2019

Manufactured in the United States

ISBN 9781467140140

Library of Congress Control Number: 2018966267

# Contents

PART I. THE RED LINE

1. Shady Grove                             11
2. Rockville                               14
3. Twinbrook                               18
4. White Flint                             19
5. Grosvenor-Strathmore                    21
6. Medical Center                          24
7. Bethesda                                27
8. Friendship Heights                      28
9. Tenleytown-AU                           33
10. Van Ness–UDC                           36
11. Cleveland Park                         39
12. Woodley Park                           44
13. Dupont Circle                          48
14. Farragut North                         61
15. Metro Center                           62
16. Gallery Place–Chinatown                67
17. Judiciary Square                       72
18. Union Station                          76
19. NoMa–Gallaudet U                       82
20. Rhode Island Avenue                    88
21. Brookland-CUA                          92
22. Fort Totten                            97
23. Takoma                                 100
24. Silver Spring                          104
25. Forest Glen                            106
26. Wheaton                                108
27. Glenmont                               109

## PART II. THE BLUE LINE

1. Franconia-Springfield 113
2. Van Dorn Street 115
3. King Street–Old Town 116
4. Braddock Road 126
5. Ronald Reagan Washington National Airport 128
6. Crystal City 131
7. Pentagon City 132
8. Pentagon 133
9. Arlington Cemetery 135
10. Rosslyn 141
11. Foggy Bottom–GWU 145
12. Farragut West 157
13. McPherson Square 167
14. Federal Triangle 170
15. Smithsonian 172
16. L'Enfant Plaza 190
17. Federal Center SW 192
18. Capitol South 196
19. Eastern Market 199
20. Potomac Avenue 206
21. Stadium-Armory 208
22. Benning Road 212
23. Capitol Heights 214
24. Addison Road 215
25. Morgan Boulevard 216
26. Largo Town Center 218

## PART III. THE ORANGE LINE

1. Vienna 221
2. Dunn Loring 225
3. West Falls Church 227
4. East Falls Church 228
5. Ballston-MU 231
6. Virginia Square–GMU 233
7. Clarendon 235
8. Courthouse 237
9. Minnesota Avenue 238
10. Deanwood 240

11. Cheverly     242
12. Landover     244
13. New Carrollton     245

## PART IV. THE YELLOW LINE

1. Huntington     249
2. Eisenhower Avenue     250
3. Mount Vernon Square     252
4. Shaw–Howard U     256
5. U Street     262
6. Columbia Heights     269
7. Georgia Avenue–Petworth     271

## PART V. THE GREEN LINE

1. Greenbelt     277
2. College Park–University of Maryland     279
3. Prince George's Plaza     282
4. West Hyattsville     285
5. Archives     286
6. Waterfront     288
7. Navy Yard–Ballpark     292
8. Anacostia     296
9. Congress Heights     299
10. Southern Avenue     300
11. Naylor Road     302
12. Suitland     303
13. Branch Avenue     304

## PART VI. THE SILVER LINE

1. Wiehle–Reston East     307
2. Spring Hill     310
3. Greensboro     311
4. Tysons Corner     312
5. McLean     313

Further Reading     315
Index     317
About the Author     331

# Part I

# The Red Line

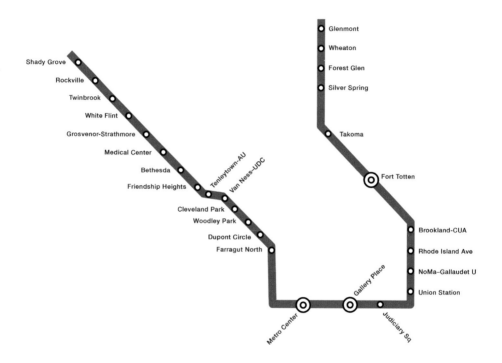

## HIGHLIGHTS ON THE RED LINE:

> Uptown Theater at Cleveland Park
> National Zoo at Woodley Park
> Ford's Theater at Metro Center
> National Building Museum at Judiciary Square
> U.S. Capitol at Union Station
> Union Market at NoMa—Gallaudet U

# 1

# Shady Grove

## KENTLANDS MANSION

320 Kent Square Road
Approximate distance to Metro: 6 miles

This historic Gaithersburg, Maryland mansion is a popular venue for weddings, bar or bat mitzvahs and other special private events. It is also an art gallery and a notable landmark in the area, dating all the way back to 1901, when it was constructed by D.C.-born wholesale pharmaceutical distributor Frederick Tschiffely. Inside, there are twenty-two-foot-high ceilings, hardwood flooring and myriad crystal chandeliers.

Designed in the Georgian Revival style, this two-and-a-half-story manor didn't receive its current moniker until wealthy tax attorney and conservationist Otis Beall Kent purchased the property and renamed it in 1942. The mansion also goes by the name of the Tschiffely-Kent property as a reference to these past two owners. The City of Gaithersburg eventually purchased the mansion in the 1960s and currently operates it.

Kent is also responsible for the nearby circa 1959–built Kentlands firehouse, a structure that harks back to the days when the area was mostly farmland. The firehouse has undergone myriad changes over the decades due to its conversion into a single-family home around the year 2013. During the approximately $800,000 conversion, cinder-block walls inside were demolished to make space for an open floor plan with a dining area and kitchen. This private residence is located at 321 Firehouse Lane.

## GAITHERSBURG COMMUNITY MUSEUM

9 South Summit Avenue
Approximate distance to Metro: 2.5 miles

Located in a restored Baltimore & Ohio (B&O) Railroad Station complex, this property still includes a 1950s-era caboose and a 1910s-era steam locomotive. Along with exhibiting railroad artifacts and equipment, the Gaithersburg Community Museum focuses on the city's history as well.

The property was designed by B&O Railroad's appointed architect Ephraim Francis Baldwin in 1884 and later placed in the National Register of Historic Places in 1978. The building reopened as a museum in 1988 thanks to the City of Gaithersburg.

## THE MOOSEUM AT KING FARM BARN

18028 Central Park Circle
Approximate distance to Metro: 10.5 miles

At one point, the majority of Montgomery County, Maryland, was farmland. In order to preserve and celebrate this history, the Mooseum serves as a dairy heritage museum with interactive exhibits and events. The museum is located in a restored dairy barn formerly owned by James and Macie King, who owned 350 acres of farmland between Germantown and Boyds, Maryland, in the early twentieth century.

This Boyds, Maryland museum is only open seasonally.

# WASHINGTON GROVE/EMORY GROVE

Montgomery County, Maryland
Approximate distance to Metro: 2.5 miles

Montgomery County, Maryland, was once the site of two popular Methodist summer camps, dating back to the 1860s and 1870s. Due to the area's proximity to Washington, D.C., the Washington Grove and Emory Grove communities became popular summer retreats, especially due to the B&O Railroad Metropolitan Line train station that opened in 1873.

When Washington Grove was chosen for a Methodist camp meeting in 1874, it was praised for its elevation and lush forests. Eventually, the community constructed a tabernacle with a belfry for meetings, while camp-goers swapped from tents to smaller cottages. These cottages were designed in the Gothic Revival style with steep roofs, pointed windows and finials. As the Washington Grove camp meetings grew, so, too, did these cottages, with large-scale houses on more spacious lots being constructed in the 1880s.

Eventually, the 500-person tabernacle met capacity. Circa 1901, an assembly hall was constructed, today known as McCathran Hall, named in honor of retiring Montgomery Grove mayor Roy McCathran. As the community expanded, an auditorium with a capacity of 1,400 was constructed in 1905 and eventually razed in 1963. The tabernacle also was eventually demolished.

It wasn't until the 1910s that Washington Grove finally had an established year-round community. Approximately ten years later, Methodist summer camp meetings met their end. The Town of Washington Grove was finally incorporated in 1937 before becoming listed in the National Register of Historic Places in 1979.

Predating Washington Grove is the nearby Emory Grove community. It was founded in 1868 by newly freed African American slaves who hoped to also host their own Methodist summer camps. The town is named after Methodist bishop, lawyer and publisher John Emory. It now consists of forty-seven privately owned cottages, an 1880s-era tabernacle that was used as a farmers' market and a former hotel that dates back to 1887 and is now used for receptions. There is also a temple, built in 1909, that once held children's church school classes but is now a recreation area.

Methodist summer camps in Emory Grove ended around the same time that those in Washington Grove ceased, in 1967.

# 2

# Rockville

## GLENVIEW MANSION

603 Edmonston Drive
Approximate distance to Metro: 1.5 miles

The first "Glenview" home that was built on this site was rather modest, but visitors of today's Glenview Mansion wouldn't be able to tell. The home didn't become the fashionable country estate it is now known as until 1923, when a firm including architects James A. Lockie and Irwin Stevens Porter was hired to incorporate the original home on the land into a T-shaped, five-section, Neoclassical Revival–style building. The construction did not complete until 1926.

The original two-story home was built in 1838 for Richard and Catherine Bowie, who used the land for farming. Richard was the son of Colonel Washington Bowie, a godson of U.S. president George Washington. Richard eventually was elected to the U.S. House of Representatives in 1848 and 1850 before being elected chief judge of the Second Judicial Circuit in 1861 and then a member of the Maryland Court of Appeals in 1863 and 1871.

The property changed hands several times, but the house wasn't expanded until the ownership was under Irene and J. Alexander Lyon, who owned the property until 1953. Before eventually selling the property, the Lyon family had a "doll house cottage" constructed in 1936 for their daughter. This one-story structure was designed as a full-size replica of a typical doll house.

For approximately three years, starting in 1953, the Montgomery County Historical Society owned the Glenview Mansion and twenty-eight of its acres with the hope of having a space for the organization's events, memorabilia and research library. After financial burden, the society sold the property and much of its land to the City of Rockville in 1957.

Nowadays, the building's facilities are used as a cultural and civic center. The historic significance of the property has been recognized since 2007, when the mansion was listed in the National Register of Historic Places.

## RED BRICK COURTHOUSE

29 Courthouse Square
Approximate distance to Metro: 0.3 miles

Before this courthouse was constructed in 1891, there was another nearby courthouse completed in 1840 and expanded in 1872. After the opening of the Metropolitan Branch of the B&O Railroad through Montgomery County in 1873, the area's population swiftly grew. From 1880 to 1890, the population increased from 588 to 1,568. With this, the need for a new courthouse became apparent, leading to Baltimore-based architect Frank E. Davis designing the Red Brick Courthouse, which still stands in Rockville, Maryland, today. While this is not the first courthouse in the county, it is currently the oldest. It is also the last Romanesque Revival-style building constructed in Montgomery County.

After its completion, the Red Brick Courthouse became a staple in Rockville and Montgomery Counties, with as many as 150 couples married each month. Many ceremonial events were also hosted here, including "Court Day," when various government agencies, including the County Commissioners and Orphans' Court, held their regular sessions together.

After World War I, the need for a larger courthouse was once again a priority, thanks to a dramatically rising population. In 1931, a new courthouse was designed by Delos H. Smith and Thomas H. Edwards in the Neoclassical style. With the new courthouse, Montgomery County planned to raze the 1891-constructed building in the late 1960s, but public protests reversed that decision.

In 1965, the Montgomery County Historical Society, Inc. designated the building as historic. During the 1970s and 1980s, the building was renovated, and the courtroom was restored to its original appearance. Still, it serves as a working courthouse for the county with an exterior that is virtually unaltered. Community-based organization Peerless Rockville Historic Preservation, Ltd. is also located here with the mission to preserve buildings, objects and information relevant to Rockville's history.

## STONESTREET MUSEUM

103 West Montgomery Avenue
Approximate distance to Metro: 0.5 miles

Visitors of this 1850-constructed, one-room doctor's office are able to learn about medical practices of the 1800s. The office was originally constructed for Dr. Edward Elisha Stonestreet, a graduate of the University of Maryland who served as one of Rockville, Maryland's doctors for over fifty years.

Originally, the office was located at Stonestreet's home property in Rockville, at the intersection of Monroe Street and Montgomery Avenue, but it was later relocated to where Richard Montgomery High School is today after World War II. To save it from demolition, the office was donated to the Montgomery County Historical Society and moved to its current location at the City of Rockville's Beall-Dawson Historic Park.

## BEALL-DAWSON MUSEUM

103 West Montgomery Avenue
Approximate distance to Metro: 0.5 miles

This historic Federal-style house dates back to 1815. It was constructed for Upton Beall, a prominent clerk of the court for the Montgomery County Court who hoped to impress with the architecture of his newly built home.

One notable guest of this property was French aristocrat and military officer Marquis de Lafayette, who visited the home during his 1824 tour of the United States.

The building's ownership was eventually passed down to John L. Dawson, a local farmer, and Amelia Somervell, a relative of Beall. Over time, over one hundred people resided there, including family members, slaves, servants and boarders. In 1946, Edwin L. Davis purchased the site in order to restore it to its original appearance and build an addition of what was once servant/slave quarters.

The building now serves as the headquarters of the Montgomery County Historical Society as well as a period historic house museum with two changing exhibit areas. Inside, there are more than ten thousand historic artifacts, including artworks, ceramics and furniture.

In 1973, this museum was listed in the National Register of Historic Places.

## LATVIAN MUSEUM

400 Hurley Avenue
Approximate distance to Metro: 3 miles

In the lower level of the Latvian Evangelical Lutheran Church, this museum celebrates Latvian culture through educational, performance and visual arts programs, as well as the maintenance of several culture collections. The items in these collections, most of which are textiles and jewelry, have been donated by Latvian immigrants. Exhibits also often highlight famous Latvians, such as opera singers, musicians, athletes and artists.

The American Latvian Association, which hosts the museum, was founded in February 1951.

This museum is only open by appointment.

# 3

# Twinbrook

## THE TWINBROOK COMMUNITY

### Between Maryland Route 355,
### Viers Mill Road and Twinbrook Parkway

While there are few tourist destinations near the Twinbrook Metro station, Twinbrook itself is a prime example of a typical post–World War II neighborhood that was developed in response to the housing shortage. After the war, Rockville experienced a population growth spurt, leading to four builders—Joseph L. Geeraert, Roland Simmon, Wesley Sauter and Donald Gingery—purchasing the 202-acre Walnut Hill Farm in 1946 to meet the housing demand.

By December 1948, the first families of Twinbrook had moved in. Each two-bedroom home was designed in the Cape Cod style. The earliest houses were designed loosely after American architect Frank Lloyd Wright's Usonian homes. Many of the new residents were veterans, and because of this, myriad streets in the community are named after World War II generals, battles and sites.

By 1951, newer homes were constructed on larger lots with additional bedrooms. New schools soon followed, and a community pool and an A&P supermarket opened in the mid-1950s. A shopping center and other retailers were developed in the late 1950s.

The name *Twinbrook* is a reference to two streams that passed through the area.

Twinbrook Metro station.

# 4

# White Flint

## JOSIAH HENSON PARK

11420 Old Georgetown Road
Approximate distance to Metro: 0.8 miles

This Montgomery County site is focused on educating the public about a slave who previously lived on this land and eventually inspired Harriet Beecher Stowe's famous novel *Uncle Tom's Cabin*.

Here, from 1795 to 1830, Reverend Josiah Henson was enslaved on Isaac Riley's plantation. Still on this site is the slave-owning family's home, dubbed Riley House, dating back to circa 1800. In the 1930s, the Riley House was greatly altered with Colonial Revival restorations in order to reflect an idealized image of the colonial era. A log kitchen, dating back to circa 1850, is also attached.

By 1830, Henson was able to escape to Canada, where he established a fugitive slave community, called Dawn. He also successfully led 118 people from enslavement in the United States to freedom in Canada.

Henson's 1849 autobiography, *The Life of Josiah Henson, Formerly a Slave, Now an Inhabitant of Canada*, became the third most popular slave narrative in the nation when it was published and the third most frequently studied slave narrative among scholars. His autobiography also later became a model for Stowe's novel, one of the most important publications in the abolitionist movement.

The Josiah Henson Park is part of the National Park Service National Underground Railroad Network to Freedom.

# BETHESDA TROLLEY TRAIL

### Approximate distance to Metro: 0.5 miles

This six-mile-long trail was once a right-of-way of the Tennallytown and Rockville Railroad's streetcar line, but today it serves as a low-impact pedestrian and bicycle path. The streetcar line operated from 1890 until 1935.

Since it opened, this trail has undergone a variety of changes, including the installation of a protected cycle track along Woodglen Drive in 2014.

At the Bethesda Trolley Trail, otherwise known as the North Bethesda Trail, expect a quiet, tree-lined path covered in pavement. Dogs are allowed on the trail but must be leashed at all times. No gas-powered motorized vehicles are allowed, though electric bikes and scooters are accepted.

# 5

# Grosvenor-Strathmore

## THE DENNIS AND PHILLIP RATNER MUSEUM

10001 Old Georgetown Road
Approximate distance to Metro: 2 miles

While often exhibiting a variety of established and emerging artists, this museum is mostly focused on showcasing a permanent collection of sculptures, drawings, paintings and other graphics from museum co-founder Phillip Ratner. Overall, the artworks found in this museum are devoted to portraying characters from the Bible.

The museum is composed of three buildings: one that houses a library, conference space and children's art and literature museum; a second devoted to exhibition space; and a final one that houses Ratner's studio and museum offices.

Ratner is known for exhibiting his works in locations that include the Supreme Court, Library of Congress, Statue of Liberty, Ellis Island and Smithsonian. In 1984, he also founded the Israel Bible Museum in Safad, Israel. His educational background is from Pratt Institute and American University.

Museum co-founder Dennis Ratner works as the CEO of Ratner Companies, which operates Hair Cuttery.

There is no admission charge for this museum.

# STRATHMORE

5301 Tuckerman Lane
Approximate distance to Metro: 0.2 miles

Here, there are two visual and performing arts venues worth searching for: the Strathmore Mansion and the Music Center.

Completed circa 1900, the mansion was designed by Appleton P. Clark Jr., an architect who is responsible for hundreds of buildings in the D.C. area, from the Embassy of Syria to the Christian Heurich Mansion. When the Strathmore Mansion was completed, it was a summer home for Captain James Frederick Oyster and his wife, who later sold the property and ninety-nine acres in 1908 to Charles I. Corby and his wife, Hattie. Corby was known as a business professional who patented machinery and techniques.

After the death of Hattie in 1941, the St. Mary's Academy purchased the home in 1943, utilizing it as a convent and school, known as St. Angela Hall. Decades later, in

TOP The Mansion at Strathmore.

BOTTOM The Music Center at Strathmore.

1977, the American Speech-Language-Hearing Association purchased the home before selling it to Montgomery County two years later. The mansion officially opened as a home for the arts in 1983.

Contrasting with the Neo-Georgian mansion is the limestone-covered Music Center at Strathmore, whose undulating roof is meant to mimic the rolling hills of the nearby landscape. The Music Center opened in February 2005 with 1,976 seats and a six-story, sixty-four-foot-high, glass walled lobby. There is also an Education Center with rehearsal spaces, a dance studio and a children's music classroom.

Along with a sculpture garden, the sixteen-acre grounds also feature over twenty commissioned and donated sculptures by artists like Stefan Saal and Wendy Ross.

# CARLTON R. SICKLES MEMORIAL SKY BRIDGE

5301 Tuckerman Lane
Approximate distance to Metro: 0 miles

Connecting the Strathmore Music Center and the Grosvenor-Strathmore Metro station is this 330-foot-long walkway, named after late Congressman Carlton R. Sickles. Born in Connecticut, Sickles was a lawyer, World War II army infantry officer and at-large delegate, representing the State of Maryland in the House of Representatives from 1963 through 1967. He unsuccessfully ran for governor of Maryland in 1966 and attempted to return to Congress in 1968.

With the moniker "father of Metro," Sickles is most known for helping bring the Metrorail system to Washington, D.C. From 1967 to 1974, he served on the Washington Metropolitan Area Transit Authority Board for Prince George's County, Maryland, and was an alternate board member from Montgomery County from 1981 to 2004.

Sickles graduated from Georgetown University in Washington, D.C. He lived from June 1921 to January 2004.

This bridge was dedicated in December 2004.

# CABIN JOHN REGIONAL PARK

7400 Tuckerman Lane
Approximate distance to Metro: 3 miles

With 528 acres of land, this nicely shaded park is a popular, family-friendly getaway from the city. Here, Montgomery County offers softball and baseball fields, a volleyball area, horseshoe pits, picnic spots, a playground and a trail reaching the edge of Rockville, Maryland. Nearby, there is also the Cabin John Ice Rink, located at 10610 Westlake Drive.

One aspect of this park that makes it so memorable is the miniature train that chugs through a scenic, two-mile-long section of the park. The train is only open during the spring, summer and fall months.

The park is open from sunrise to sunset, year round.

# 6

# Medical Center

## THE NATIONAL INSTITUTES OF HEALTH

9000 Center Drive
Approximate distance to Metro: 0.6 miles

Certainly, this is not much of a tourist destination, but it's one of the few historical sites located closest to this Metro station that is worth knowing about. The National Institutes of Health (NIH) is one of the world's foremost medical research centers, formed in 1887. This government agency comprises over twenty-five institutes and centers, focused on disciplines that include cancer, alcoholism, mental health and information technology.

Originally, the NIH was a one-room lab in the Marine Hospital on Staten Island, New York. It didn't relocate to its current site until 1938. At this point, there are over fifty buildings on the campus.

Since it was formed, the NIH has accomplished a remarkable number of studies, discovering insights into cholesterol control; licensing MRI; and developing vaccines against infections, HIV/AIDS and typhoid fever. More than eighty Nobel prizes have been awarded for NIH-supported research.

# U.S. NATIONAL LIBRARY OF MEDICINE

8600 Rockville Pike
Approximate distance to Metro: 0.3 miles

Located on the campus of the National Institutes of Health, this is the world's largest biomedical library, founded in 1836. The library allows millions across the nation to have access to health research, both in person and online. The library covers genomic, chemical, toxicological and environmental subjects, covered in books, journals, manuscripts, images and multimedia forms.

When the library began, it was located in the office of the U.S. Army surgeon general. It didn't move to its current location until 1962. Before then, it was located in the Riggs Bank Building, later Ford's Theatre, before moving once again to the Army Medical Museum and Library Building at 7th Street SW and Independence Avenue SW in Washington, D.C. This latter site now houses the Hirshhorn Museum.

The collection was once very humble, encompassing only a few books, before expanding to 25,000 books and 15,000 pamphlets by 1873. Thanks to Lieutenant John Shaw Billings, the collection soared by 1895 to 116,847 books and 191,598 pamphlets. By 2015, the full collection encompassed over 27.8 million publications.

# THE WALTER REED NATIONAL MILITARY MEDICAL CENTER

4494 North Palmer Road
Approximate distance to Metro: 0.5 miles

With 243 acres of land and over 2.4 million square feet of clinical space, this is the world's largest military medical center. This medical center is named after Walter Reed, a U.S. Army physician who is credited for having confirmed that yellow fever is transmitted by mosquitoes.

At one point, this one center was home to two different organizations, the Walter Reed General Hospital, which first opened in 1909 and closed in 2011, and the National Naval Medical Center, which was founded in

1940. The original Naval Medical Center tower was designated a historical landmark in 1977.

When the National Naval Medical Center opened in 1940, it was meant to house navy medical training, navy research and a medical library. Since then, it has served the president of the United States as well as members of Congress and the Supreme Court.

# 7

# Bethesda

## BETHESDA THEATRE

7719 Wisconsin Avenue
Approximate distance to Metro: 0.2 miles

This historic movie theater was constructed in 1938 and later listed in the National Register of Historic Places in 1999. Designed by "Dean of American Theater Architects" John Eberson, this Art Deco property still retains its original theater entrance with a marquee, marquee tower and central ticket booth. Much of the interior, especially the murals, remains intact, though the seating has been reconfigured.

The Bethesda Theater has undergone many owner changes and name revisions over the years. It was first named the Boro Theater, then reopened as the Bethesda Cinema and Drafthouse in 1983, and later renamed Bethesda Theater Cafe in 1990.

In 2007, Greenbelt, Maryland–based developer The Bozzuto Group

renovated the approximately seven-hundred-seat theater for $12 million. After opening a blues and jazz supper club in the space in 2013, the club ended up in the red, resulting in the property listing for sale two years later for $8.5 million. The foreclosure auction was later called off after the venue's owner came to an agreement with an investor.

8

# Friendship Heights

## CLARA BARTON NATIONAL HISTORIC SITE

5801 Oxford Road
Approximate distance to Metro: 4 miles

In 1975, this Glen Echo home became the first national historic site dedicated to the accomplishments of a woman. Here, the life of the founder of the American Red Cross, Clara Barton, is preserved. When the property was constructed circa 1891, it was designed by Dr. Julian B. Hubbell, the first field agent of the American Red Cross, with many of the original furnishings preserved.

Barton was born in Massachusetts and lived from 1821 to 1912. At the age of eighteen, she began teaching in schools near Oxford, Massachusetts, later establishing a school of her own for the children of her brother's mill workers in 1845 before opening a free public school in Bordentown, New Jersey, in 1852.

After working as a recording clerk at the U.S. Patent Office, she later gained permission to transport supplies to battlefields, assisting the wounded at battles that included the Battle of Cedar Mountain in Culpeper, Virginia, in August 1862 and the Battle of Antietam, Maryland, in September 1862.

In order to address the problem of missing soldiers during the Civil War, Barton established the Office of Correspondence with Friends of the Missing

Men of the United States Army in 1865, continuing her search for four years. During this time, she was able to identify twenty-two thousand missing men.

Her work didn't stop there. After the American Association of the Red Cross was formed in 1881, Barton was elected president. Through her work as president, she directed American Red Cross relief work during flooding along the Mississippi River and its tributaries in 1882 and 1883; directed relief work to flood victims in Johnstown, Pennsylvania, in 1889; and delivered numerous lectures promoting the organization from 1884 through 1890. She didn't resign as president until 1904.

## CAPITAL CRESCENT TRAIL

Approximate distance to Metro: 2.5 miles

This is not necessarily the best Metro station for heading to this shared-use off-road trail, but it is certainly one of many options. This eleven-mile rail-trail connects Washington, D.C.'s Georgetown neighborhood to Silver Spring, Maryland. It was built on the former railbed of the Georgetown branch of the Baltimore and Ohio Railroad, used exclusively as a freight line from 1910 to 1985.

One year after the line discontinued, the Coalition for the Capital Crescent Trail was formed in order to redevelop the line as a first-class trail. No longer is it used for trains. Today, the hard-surface trail is commonly utilized by walkers, joggers and bicyclists.

The Capital Crescent Trail is not only one of the most popular trails in the D.C. area, but it is also one of the most heavily used trails in the nation.

## GLEN ECHO PARK

7300 MacArthur Boulevard
Approximate distance to Metro: 3 miles

Formerly known as Glen Echo Amusement Park, this arts and culture center offers a variety of classes, workshops, performances and festivals throughout the year. While offering a space for artists in the D.C. area, the property also features a long history, dating back to the early 1900s.

It all started in 1891, when Philadelphia-based real estate promoter Edward Baltzley and his brother Edwin purchased over five hundred acres of land, naming it Glen Echo on the Potomac. Their goal was to bring the culture of the well-to-do to the masses by incorporating the National Chautauqua of Glen Echo in 1891, the fifty-third such assembly to be established. Here, the brothers offered arts and culture programs, including lectures and concerts, Bible study classes and physical training regimens.

By 1903, the Chautauqua grounds were foreclosed, later to be sold to the Washington Railway and Electric Company in 1911.

At this point, the site was significantly expanded to become Glen Echo Amusement Park, which operated continuously until its closure in 1968. The federal government then acquired the defunct amusement park with administrative responsibility given to the National Park Service.

While many of the rides and amusements are gone by this point, many of the major original buildings and structures remain. Most notably, guests will be able to discover a 1921-constructed, Gustav and William Dentzel–designed menagerie carousel with fifty-two carved wooden animals and vehicles, including horses, chariots, rabbits, ostriches, lions, tigers, giraffes and deer. The carousel was listed in the National Register of Historic Places in 1980. Also worth seeing is the 1933-built Spanish Ballroom with its 7,500-square-foot dance floor.

# ROBERT LLEWELLYN WRIGHT HOUSE

7927 Deepwell Drive
Approximate distance to Metro: 7 miles

This private residence is one of only two residences in the state of Maryland designed by prolific American architect Frank Lloyd Wright; the second is located in Baltimore. Wright designed this home in 1953 for his sixth child, Robert Llewellyn Wright, who worked at the Justice Department. The original design never ended up getting constructed as it was too costly.

The final product ended up being an 1,800-square-foot, two-story, concrete-block structure, completed in 1957, one year before the architect's death. The home is composed of intersecting and concentric segments of a circle, or "hemicycles," with a semicircular terrace and two second-floor balconies. Many of the furnishings are also designed by Wright, such as the built-in desks and trundle beds.

This single-family home was added to the National Register of Historic Places in 1986.

## PEPCO'S FRIENDSHIP HEIGHTS SUBSTATION

5210 Wisconsin Avenue NW
Approximate distance to Metro: 500 feet

Dating back to 1940, this art modern–style building offers a look into the past. According to the National Register of Historic Places application, the building reflects the area's evolution from farmland into a bustling community in the decades before World War II. The building is one story, L-shaped and covered in limestone.

Truthfully, this is not much of a tourist destination. In fact, for many locals, it's a blight on the neighborhood due to its neglected appearance. When local organizations pushed for this property to attain a landmark status, there were many who opposed the application. One argument was that some preservationists were simply attempting to prevent redevelopment of the site into something bigger and possibly less congruous with the neighborhood.

Despite opposition, the D.C. Historic Preservation Review Board voted for the property to become a historic landmark in November 2017.

## FORT BAYARD PARK

River Road NW and Western Avenue NW
Approximate distance to Metro: 0.6 miles

On this site, during the Civil War, was an earthwork fort, created in 1861. The shape was round, consisting of two twelve-pound howitzers and four twenty-pound Parrott guns mounted on platforms in embrasures. After the surrender of Robert E. Lee, the fort was decommissioned. It never faced major opposition, though it did come under attack once during the Battle of Fort Stevens in July 1864. The fort is no longer located at this site, but there is a marker commemorating its existence.

Since 1919, the Commissioners of the District planned on creating fort parks, but these plans were delayed for many decades, partially due to budget cuts and eventually World War II. Currently, the six-and-a-half-acre park contains a softball field and soccer field.

The fort was named after George Dashiell Bayard, a general in the Union army who was wounded and killed in the 1862 Battle of Fredericksburg.

## TAIT-TRUSSELL HOUSE

4900 Western Avenue
Approximate distance to Metro: 0.7 miles

This Maryland home once housed an infamous politician and later a Pulitzer Prize winner. It was constructed in 1901 by land developer, lawyer and collector of internal revenue Galen L. Tait. Described in a 1953 obit in the *Washington Evening Star* as "one of the most controversial figures in Maryland political history," Tait's work can be seen as Maryland's Republican chairman from 1914 to 1934 and then again from 1942 to 1948. He also invested heavily in the redevelopment of Massachusetts Avenue from Rock Creek Park to the Maryland boundary.

Tait's daughter, Beatrice, took ownership of the property after his death. Her husband, C.P. "Peck" Trussell, was a Pulitzer Prize–winning reporter for the *New York Times*. From 1946 to 1949, Trussell also worked as governor of the National Press Club.

# 9

# Tenleytown-AU

## KATZEN ARTS CENTER

4400 Massachusetts Avenue NW
Approximate distance to Metro: 1 mile

At American University, art lovers can discover one of the city's lesser-known arts spaces, known as the Katzen Arts Center. This 130,000-square-foot space features exhibition and performance spaces with a 30,000-square-foot museum and a 6,000-square-foot sculpture garden. While one of the more underrated arts spaces in the city, it is one of Washington, D.C.'s largest university facilities for art exhibitions.

Here, some of the famed artists featured are Pablo Picasso, Andy Warhol, Willem de Kooning and Roy Lichtenstein. Not only are the art

pieces worth taking a peek at, but so is the architecture. Designed by EYP Architecture & Engineering, this three-story, limestone- and concrete-covered center has been praised by the American Institute of Architects as a well-done architectural concept with a splendid location at the top of Embassy Row.

# FORT RENO PARK

## 3800 Donaldson Place NW
## Approximate distance to Metro: 0.5 miles

In this park, there was once a Civil War fort, constructed in 1862 to defend against the Confederates. At the time it was built, it was known as Fort Pennsylvania. A year later, it was renamed Fort Reno in honor of Major General Jesse Lee Reno, who died at the 1862 Battle of South Mountain. It was the largest of the Civil War circle forts that defended Washington, D.C. After the Civil War, the area became a home for freed slaves and, eventually, a reservoir.

The park is now managed by the National Park Service. As the highest natural elevation in the city, at 409 feet, Fort Reno Park is popular for those looking for sledding, sky-high views of the District and even an annual concert series.

# WESTERN UNION TOWER

## 4623 41st Street NW
## Approximate distance to Metro: 0.2 miles

This seventy-three-foot-tall octagonal tower, whose full title is the Western Union Telegraph Company Tenley Radio Terminal, finished construction in 1947. It was built in Tenleytown due to the neighborhood's high point in the city. When this tower was in use, it operated as a transmission and receiving station. Connecting D.C. with New York, Pittsburgh and Philadelphia, this was the first commercial network of microwave-radio relay stations.

The architect behind this national landmark was Leon Chatelain Jr., who served as the president of the American Institute of Architects and a founder of the Washington Building Congress. President John F. Kennedy also appointed Chatelain chairman of the National Commission on Architectural Barriers. Another of this architect's past designs is the Suffridge Building at 1755 K Street NW.

# IMMACULATA SEMINARY

4340 Nebraska Avenue NW
Approximate distance to Metro: 0.3 miles

In 1905, this seminary opened its doors to eighteen female pupils. The original building was designed by architect A.O. Von Herbulis. Many changes came within the coming decades. By 1935, the school needed more room for its students, leading to a new wing being built to the south of Dunblane Hall. In twenty years' time, another hall, known as Marian Hall, was constructed as a dormitory and classroom building. Dunblane was renovated with an extension built by 1974.

In 1978, the college closed due to declining enrollment and rising costs before being leased to American University. The university eventually purchased the property, officially closing the elementary and high schools in 1986. Regina, Marian and Loretta Halls were later demolished in 2013, with only the original Immaculata building and Dunblane Hall remaining, standing as protected landmarks

Still, the original buildings serve as an embodiment of the Catholic Church's role in educating the public, especially girls.

# 10

# Van Ness–UDC

## PEIRCE MILL

2401 Tilden Street NW
Approximate distance to Metro: 0.8 miles

At one point, Rock Creek had a flourishing milling industry. This mill is the last extant gristmill that remains in the District. Built in 1820 or 1829, this rectangular, gabled roof structure was constructed for a Pennsylvania-born pioneer miller, Isaac Peirce (sometimes spelled Pearce or Pierce). Over time, Peirce owned up to two thousand acres of land along Rock Creek, hiring workers to mill corn, wheat and rye.

For approximately thirty years, starting in 1906, the property was turned into a teahouse, popular among President William Howard Taft and members of "Washington's smart set." Minor changes were made during a 1936 restoration after the property was transferred to the National Park Service. By 1970, the mill was running again before operations stopped again in 1981. After the main shaft from the water wheel broke in 1993 due to decay, a multi-phased restoration effort began four years later to repair the mill. The latest grand reopening of the restored mill was in October 2011. Still, the original board floors remain, and the walls are the same stone as the exterior, made from stone granite taken from a nearby quarry on Broad Branch Road NW.

The milling machinery found inside the mill was installed circa 1934 as a reproduction of the 1897 equipment.

# HILLWOOD ESTATE, MUSEUM AND GARDENS

### 4155 Linnean Avenue NW
### Approximate distance to Metro: 0.8 miles

Overlooking Rock Creek Park, this twenty-five-acre estate is open to the public for visitors to get an inside look at the former home of cereal heiress Marjorie Merriweather Post. While constructed in 1926, it wasn't until 1955, when Post purchased the property, that it received its name, Hillwood. Before that, the neo-Georgian mansion was known as Abremont. Once she moved in, Post renovated the house in order to allow space for her large collection of imperial Russian and eighteenth-century French decorative art. The cost of this refurbishing totaled $680,000, comprising thirty-six rooms remade in the eighteenth-century French Rococo and Neoclassical styles.

To complement the artworks, Innocenti and Webel designed a French-style garden, while Perry Wheeler designed a circular rose garden with a curving pergola. As an added bonus, a Japanese-influenced garden, built in miniature, was refined by Shogo J. Myaida.

After her death in 1973, Post bequeathed Hillwood to the Smithsonian.

# EMBASSY OF CHINA

### 3505 International Place NW
### Approximate distance to Metro: 0.3 miles

Constructed in 2008, the Embassy of China is the largest embassy in the nation's capital, spanning 250,000 square feet. The multimillion-dollar complex was designed by Chien Chung and Li Chung Pei of Pei Partnership Architects, the latter of whose father is famed architect I.M. Pei. When designing this structure, the architects had the task to design something that would convey the importance of China and its role in the world.

In total, the complex is composed of five buildings on ten acres of land. Inside, there are multiple skylights, a two-hundred-seat auditorium and an all-purpose hall. In the surrounding land, there are traditional Chinese rock gardens.

When it was constructed, this embassy had its share of critics. President of the U.S.-China Policy Foundation Chi Wang told the *New York Times* that he felt the size was too much like a "fortress."

Since 2017, there have been efforts to change the address of the embassy to "1 Liu Xiaobo Plaza," named after Chinese pro-democracy activist and Nobel Peace Prize laureate Liu Xiaobo.

## UNIVERSITY OF THE DISTRICT OF COLUMBIA (UDC) STUDENT CENTER

4200 Connecticut Avenue NW
Approximate distance to Metro: 0.3 miles

This $63 million building is one of the most eco-friendly student unions in the nation. Constructed to LEED Platinum standards in 2016, this building offers a green roof, carpets composed of recycled fibers, reclaimed wood panels and storm drains that catch rainwater for use in restroom toilets. That's not all. The building also boasts a yoga studio and a lounge with video games and a pool table. The Student Center served as the centerpiece of a ten-year, campus-wide renovation.

In an interview with the *Washington Post* in 2015, UDC president Ronald Mason Jr. said that the building "is a symbol of where we want to be."

Behind the project is African American architect and UDC alumnus Michael Marshall of Marshall Moya Design. He is also behind the renovation of the Howard Theater and served as the associate architect for Audi Field in Buzzard Point.

# 11

# Cleveland Park

## PIERCE-KLINGLE MANSION

3545 Williamsburg Lane NW
Approximate distance to Metro: 1 mile

This three-story, ten-room Pennsylvania Dutch farmhouse-style mansion dates all the way back to 1823, when it was built by Joshua Pierce, a horticulturist who supplied the first ornamental plantings for the White House, the U.S. Capitol and other government buildings and parks. Originally, Pierce named the property Linnaean Hill in honor of Swedish botanist Karl Van Linnaeus.

The property received a west-side addition in 1843. East of the main house is a two-story barn and carriage house. There is also a two-story utility house and a potting shed. After Pierce's death, he left his estate to his nephew Joshua Pierce Klingle, who lived in the home until 1890.

By 1890, the U.S. government had purchased the property as part of Rock Creek Park. Despite efforts by Pierce's grandnephew Louis P. Shoemaker to convert the mansion into a reception hall, these plans were never adopted, and it remained a residence. In 1933, the property was transferred to the National Park Service, and four years later, the house and its grounds were restored.

Several times over the coming years, the Children's Museum of Washington sought to obtain the property for its museum, but these requests were repeatedly turned down. Instead, it was leased as a private residence before the Junior Nature Center leased the mansion in 1959. Afterward, the Junior League of Washington used the mansion for its administrative offices.

Since 1972, the National Park Service has been in control of the mansion, using it for a horticultural outreach program known as Green Scene, as well as other natural resource program activities and administrative purposes. In 1973, the Pierce-Klingle Mansion was listed in the National Register of Historic Places.

## WASHINGTON NATIONAL CATHEDRAL (CATHEDRAL OF SAINT PETER AND SAINT PAUL)

3101 Wisconsin Avenue NW
Approximate distance to Metro: 1.5 miles

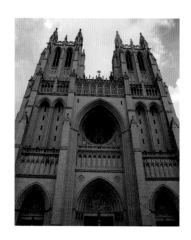

This Neo-Gothic Episcopal cathedral is the fourth-tallest structure in the nation's capital, the second-largest church in the United States and the sixth-largest cathedral in the world. Over the years, this church has hosted the funeral services of several U.S. presidents, as well as the final sermon of Martin Luther King Jr. Additionally, this site is the burial place of myriad well-known figures, such as Helen Keller.

The construction of this building cost $65 million and took over eighty years. Construction began in 1907 before being halted by World War I and resumed in 1922. The building was not complete until 1990 with the placement of the final finial laid in the presence of President George H.W. Bush.

While construction is completed, the structure continues to be altered every so often. In September 2017, the National Cathedral removed stained-glass windows honoring Confederate generals Robert E. Lee and Thomas "Stonewall" Jackson that were installed in 1953. These stained-glass windows were sponsored by the United Daughters of the Confederacy.

Throughout the 518-foot-long property, there are a total of 112 gargoyles, 215 stained-glass windows, a 10,000-piece "Creation" rose window and, most surprisingly, a sculpture of the fictional sci-fi villain Darth Vader. There is also a crypt floor with three chapels and a museum.

The architect behind this iconic cathedral was George Frederick Bodley, who was England's leading Anglican church architect in the late nineteenth and early twentieth centuries. The structure was inspired by Pierre Charles L'Enfant's plan for a national cathedral that would have been bounded by F and G and 7th and 9th Streets NW. The final product most closely resembles England's Wells Cathedral, with a façade similar to the Notre Dame in Paris, though rendered in an English gothic vocabulary.

The National Cathedral was listed in the National Register of Historic Places in 1974.

## TWIN OAKS

### 3225 Woodley Road NW
### Approximate distance to Metro: 0.8 miles

This is the largest privately owned estate in Washington, D.C., that does not house the U.S. president. It is also the only remaining example of a New England frame summer house in the city.

Named after two oak trees that fronted the property when it was built, this historic seventeen-acre estate was constructed in 1888 by Boston-based architect Francis Richmond Allen. The summer house was designed for Gardiner Green Hubbard, founder and first president of the National Geographic Society and father-in-law of Alexander Graham Bell. When Hubbard purchased the land, he intended to construct a cooler summer residence than his Dupont Circle home. The twenty-six-room Twin Oaks ended up utilizing a mixture of Queen Anne and Colonial Revival styles.

After ten years of the home being rented to the ambassador of the Republic of China, the Chinese government purchased the property in 1947. Each successive ambassador made Twin Oaks his residence until 1979, when it was sold to the nonprofit Friends of Free China Association. The Taiwan government later purchased Twin Oaks in 1982.

Four years later, Twin Oaks was listed in the National Register of Historic Places.

## UPTOWN THEATER

3426 Connecticut Avenue NW
Approximate distance to Metro: 300 feet

Opened in 1936, this 1,500-seat theater was designed by Baltimore-based firm Zink, Atkins and Craycroft in the Art Deco style. The building is composed of vertical limestone planes, a central cantilevered marquee and a large rectangular street façade with etched-glass windows and neon lights.

The firm later went on to build over two hundred movie theaters.

One notable film premiere hosted at the Uptown Theater was the June 1993 world premiere of Steven Spielberg's dinosaur thriller film *Jurassic Park*.

## THE KENNEDY-WARREN

3133 Connecticut Avenue NW
Approximate distance to Metro: 0.3 miles

Listed in the National Register of Historic Places in 1994, this Art Deco property is one of the most respected apartment buildings in Washington, D.C. According to Pamela Scott and Antoinette J. Lee in their 1993 publication *Buildings of the District of Columbia*, the Kennedy-Warren is "one of the city's finest buildings from this era," while James M. Goode in his esteemed 1988 publication *Best Addresses* described the development as "easily…among the top 10 apartment houses" and "the finest Art Deco apartment house ever built" in D.C.

Designed by Washington, D.C.–based architect Joseph Younger, this property opened in 1931 with the nation's first forced natural air cooling system. It was also the first building in the city to use aluminum extensively both inside and outside. When it was built, the finished product ended up using only a portion of Younger's original design, with two planned wings missing. By 1935, a left rear wing was added, designed by supervising architect Alexander H. Sonnemann.

The design of this 317-unit apartment building offers an Aztec motif on the exterior and in many of the interior spaces.

## ROSEDALE (URIAH FORREST HOME)

3501 Newark Street NW
Approximate distance to Metro: 0.8 miles

Here, in Cleveland Park, visitors can find one of Washington, D.C.'s oldest remaining residences. This private property was built circa 1793 for Maryland-born Uriah Forrest, one of the nineteen original proprietors of the District of Columbia, a Revolutionary War leader and a prominent civic leader who served as mayor of Georgetown and later a representative from Maryland.

In its history, this home was host to many well-known figures, including President John Adams and Assistant Secretary of Defense John N. Irwin II. In the parlor of this home, in June 1855, Agustín Cosme Damián de Iturbide y Arámburu, a Mexican army general, politician and the original designer of the first Mexican flag, married Alice Green, whose family occupied the home at the time.

After Forrest's death in 1805, Rosedale switched hands many times before the National Cathedral purchased the property to use it as a boarding facility for students attending the National Cathedral School for girls. An exchange student organization, known as Youth for Understanding, later used the site as its headquarters before a neighborhood-wide effort led to a Cleveland Park local neighborhood land trust purchasing the property in September 2002.

Still, this three-acre farmhouse retains its original floor plan.

# 12

# Woodley Park

## SMITHSONIAN NATIONAL ZOOLOGICAL PARK

3001 Connecticut Avenue NW
Approximate distance to Metro: 0.4 miles

It was thanks to William Temple Hornaday, chief taxidermist at the Smithsonian from 1882 to 1887, that the Smithsonian's ever-popular zoo came into existence. Disheartened by the dwindling numbers of American bison, Hornaday went on a quest to save it and other endangered species from extinction, later becoming the first head of the Department of Living Animals at the Smithsonian.

After bringing fifteen North American species to live on the National Mall—species that included prairie dogs, lynx and deer—President Grover Cleveland signed an act of Congress in 1889 that created the National Zoological Park.

The zoo, which finished completion two years later, was designed by the father of American landscape architecture, Frederick Law Olmsted. Since it opened, the National Zoological Park has prospered, with roughly 2.7 million visitors in 2016. Today, there are approximately 1,800 animals representing 300 species cared for by the Smithsonian's National Zoo and Conservation Biology Institute.

Some of the scientific initiatives that the Smithsonian has succeeded in have included the first kiwi chick to be born outside New Zealand, the first Komodo dragon to hatch outside of Indonesia and the establishment of the first genome repository for Great Barrier Reef coral. The National Zoo also became the first zoo or aquarium to successfully grow two species of anemones.

## UNITED STATES NAVAL OBSERVATORY (USNO)

3450 Massachusetts Avenue NW
Approximate distance to Metro: 1.5 miles

Established in 1842, USNO is one of the oldest scientific agencies in the nation, acting as America's timekeeper and observer of stars, planets and moons. Originally, the observatory was located in Foggy Bottom, but it relocated to its present site in 1893.

Here, visitors will find the telescope used for the discovery of Mars's moons, as well as the largest astronomy library in the nation and the largest astrophysical periodicals collection in the world.

It wasn't until 1974 that the USNO became the official residence for the U.S. vice president. The home, located at Number One Observatory Circle, dates back to 1893, with a refurbishment in 1974.

## WASHINGTON MARRIOTT WARDMAN PARK

2660 Woodley Road NW
Approximate distance to Metro: 300 feet

Since this development opened in 1918, it has been the home of congressmen, government officials and diplomats. Some of the tenants have included Vice President Spiro Agnew, Secretary of the Interior Walter Hickel, Chief Justice Earl Warren and Senators Barry Goldwater and Spessard Holland.

When it opened, it was the largest hotel in the city, with 1,200 rooms included. Ten years later, the project's builder, Harry Wardman, broke ground on a 350-room residential annex, known as the Wardman Tower, located east of the main hotel. At the time, an article from the *Washington Post* described the annex as "the most fashionable apartment address" in the city. Thereafter, construction of apartment-hotel projects became popular in the District, thanks to Wardman's influence.

Still, the building continues to make history. In 2015, developer JBG SMITH renovated floors three through eight into thirty-two luxury condominiums. Two years later, an anonymous buyer purchased a penthouse condominium for $8.4 million, making it the second-most expensive condominium sold in D.C. so far.

The architect behind the eight-story, red-brick hotel was Mihran Mesrobian, who later went on to design the Carlton Hotel (now known as the St. Regis) and the Hay-Adams Hotel. In 1926, the American Institute of Architects gave him an award for excellence for this project.

## HOLT HOUSE (JACKSON HILL)

Approximate distance to Metro: 0.7 miles

Inside the Smithsonian National Zoological Park, this once-grand summer villa is hidden on a corner of the grounds, derelict. Dating back to circa 1810, this building is the oldest structure owned by the Smithsonian. It once served as an administrative office for the park, thanks to father of American landscape architecture Frederick Law Olmsted. After the house's interior was gutted and rebuilt, it remained as office space for approximately one century before the zoo abandoned the structure in the late 1980s.

By 2002, the National Trust for Historic Preservation reported that the house was at risk of a massive collapse due to termite damage to its structural walls. While abandoned and neglected, it remains standing with no wrecking ball to tear it down, in part thanks to the structure being listed in the National Register of Historic Places.

The name Holt House is attributed to one of the property's former owners, Dr. Henry C. Holt, who acquired the Palladian-style villa in 1844. He later sold it to the National Zoological Park in 1890. The home is also known as Jackson Hill because the tract of land on which it was built was known as that by 1841, though it was earlier known as Pretty Prospect.

# MARILYN MONROE MURAL

2604 Connecticut Avenue NW
Approximate distance to Metro: 400 feet

This is one of the most famous murals in Washington, D.C., featured in various publications, including the *New York Times*, the *Washington Post* and the local alternative newspaper, *Washington City Paper*. In 2014, a poll conducted by *Washington City Paper* dubbed this mural as the first runner-up for best mural in the city.

Here, Marilyn Monroe's face is located on the upper outside wall of Salon Roi. Salon Roi co-founders Roi Barnard and Charles Stinson commissioned artist John Bailey to paint the celebrity on the location in 1981. Barnard chose Monroe for the space because she is "my altar ego."

The painting was restored in 2001, thanks to funds contributed by the Woodley Park neighborhood.

# 13

# Dupont Circle

## DUPONT CIRCLE FOUNTAIN

1 Dupont Circle NW
Approximate distance to Metro: 0 miles

Originally, this circle, once known as Pacific Circle, was host to a statue. When it was installed in 1884, this statue was so unpopular that in 1919 a *Washington Times* article described it as both "an eye-sore" and "rather awkward-looking." It was meant to memorialize Rear Admiral Samuel Francis Du Pont, a naval officer who served in the Mexican and Civil Wars and who also helped draw up the curriculum and regulations for the Naval Academy in Annapolis, Maryland.

After the Du Pont family spoke up against the statue, they worked to replace it with a fountain. Henry Bacon, the same architect behind the Lincoln Memorial, and Daniel Chester French, the same sculptor behind the statue of Abraham Lincoln in the Lincoln Memorial, were hired to create a two-tiered marble fountain with three allegorical sculptures (representing the Sea, the Stars and the Wind) with maritime details on a concrete base surrounded by an open plaza. When the fountain was dedicated in 1921, prominent guests at the dedication ceremony included First Lady Florence Harding, Secretary of War John W. Weeks and Secretary of the Navy Edwin Denby.

The statue that was formerly located here is now located in Wilmington, Delaware's Rockford Park.

## THE SOCIETY OF THE CINCINNATI
## (LARZ ANDERSON HOUSE)

2118 Massachusetts Avenue NW
Approximate distance to Metro: 0.2 miles

This is one of Washington, D.C.'s largest and costliest homes, dating back to 1905. Since it was built, it has hosted a multitude of notable guests, including the King and Queen of Siam in 1931, as well as Presidents William Howard Taft and Calvin Coolidge.

This Renaissance Revival–style home is covered in limestone, spanning four stories with fifty total rooms. When designing this home, Boston-based architects Arthur Little and Herbert W.C. Browne of the firm Little & Browne based the look on eighteenth-century French and English country houses. The building costs totaled approximately $800,000.

The first owners were Ambassador Larz and heiress Isabel Anderson, who lived in the home until 1937. Larz served in the Spanish-American War and allowed his home to be used for Belgian Relief work, Red Cross work for the blind and as housing for French officers. By 1937, it was turned over to the Society of Cincinnati, the nation's oldest patriotic order, founded in 1783.

The structure features a two-story ballroom, walled garden, tennis court and three-story carriage house and stable. Several of the first-floor rooms have been converted to a National Museum of Relics of the American Revolution, while the basement is the society's Research Library, with over forty thousand titles on the art of warfare in the eighteenth century and the American Revolution.

## THE PRESIDENT WOODROW WILSON HOUSE

2340 S Street NW
Approximate distance to Metro: 0.7 miles

After President Woodrow Wilson left office, he resided in this three-story Embassy Row home. This red brick structure was designed in 1915 by architect Waddy Butler Wood, the same architect behind the Masonic

Temple, in the Georgian Revival style. The home was originally the residence of Henry Parker Fairbanks, an executive of the Bigelow Carpet Company.

Over the years, the building has undergone some interior changes with a billiard room, stacks for a library and elevator added, but it is relatively unchanged since Wilson lived there. After the death of Wilson, his wife continued to live in the property for nearly forty years before it was donated to the National Trust for Historic Preservation. Now, it serves as a house museum with original furnishings and items owned by Wilson.

## MARY McLEOD BETHUNE COUNCIL HOUSE NATIONAL HISTORIC SITE

1318 Vermont Avenue NW
Approximate distance to Metro: 1 mile

This Victorian town home, known as the Council House, was the first national headquarters for the National Council of Negro Women, as well as the residence of the council's founder, Mary McLeod Bethune, from 1943 until her death in 1955. Bethune is known as an educator, civil rights leader, international consultant on human rights and adviser to four presidents. She also served in President Franklin D. Roosevelt's "Black Cabinet" as director of the National Youth Administration's division of Negro affairs.

In an interview with the *Washington Post* in May 1982, California representative Philip Burton described her as "one of the giants of political history."

When Bethune lived in this home, it was a meeting place for other legendary figures in black history, including Dr. Charles Drew, Ralph Bunche and Mary Church Terrell. Eleanor Roosevelt was also a guest in this home.

In 1981, the property became a museum, celebrating the legacy of Bethune and notable African American women. One year later, the building officially became a national historic site with approximately $150,000 going to the restoration of the property. The National Park Service purchased the Council House in 1994.

# THE PHILLIPS COLLECTION
# (DUNCAN PHILLIPS HOUSE)

1600 21st Street NW
Approximate distance to Metro: 0.2 miles

When this museum first opened in 1921, it was fairly small, only encompassing two exhibition rooms, but it took the nation by storm. As America's first museum of modern art, the venue was headed by Duncan Phillips, a published art critic and heir to the co-founder of the Jones and Laughlin Steel Company. During this time, Phillips was described as "one of the foremost collectors in this country" by the *Sun*.

The Georgian Revival property that the museum is located in was formerly Phillips's home, at least until 1930. The home was first constructed in 1897, designed by D.C.-based architectural firm Hornblower & Marshall, the same firm behind the National Museum of Natural History. Over the following decades, the structure would undergo many changes with a library

wing and skylight added, a mansard top story constructed by D.C.-based architect Frederick H. Brooke and renovations done to a 1960-built addition, known as the Goh Annex. In 2006, the Sant Building opened.

Here, visitors can find the works of artists like Auguste Renoir, Mark Rothko, Georgia O'Keeffe, Vincent van Gogh and Claude Monet.

# EMBASSY ROW

Massachusetts Avenue NW between Scott Circle and the north side of
the United States Naval Observatory
Approximate distance to Metro: 0.5 miles

As can be surmised from the informal name of this section of Massachusetts Avenue NW, this is an area of Dupont Circle that is well populated with embassies, diplomatic missions and other government organizations. Stately mansions also occupy much of this strip. It's worth knowing that not every embassy in Washington, D.C., is located on Embassy Row, and not every building in Embassy Row is an embassy or chancery.

While there were embassies that popped up in this area in the 1920s and 1930s, such as the Embassy of Britain, the greatest number of embassies and chanceries that relocated or were built anew here was in the 1940s and 1950s. Architectural styles vary from Georgian to Colonial Revival to Beaux Arts and beyond with notable local architects having built in the neighborhood, such as Appleton P. Clark Jr. and Waddy Butler Wood.

By 1901, there were only 4 countries that had built embassies in the nation's capital. Today, there are over 160.

If searching for a few prominent embassies in this row, here are a few to consider:

Located at 2020 Massachusetts Avenue NW, the Embassy of Indonesia is in a building also known as the Walsh-McLean House. This fifty-room mansion was constructed in 1902, designed by architect Henry Andersen. The first owner was gold miner Thomas F. Walsh. His daughter, Evalyn, took residence at the site and later went on to marry Edward McLean, whose family owned the *Washington Post*. Evalyn is known as the last private owner of the famous jewel known as the Hope Diamond. Evalyn lived in the home until 1932.

The residence often held lavish affairs with guests that included Queen Elizabeth, Chief Justice Edward Douglas White, Senator and co-author of the Thirteenth Amendment John B. Henderson and Attorney General of the United States Wayne MacVeagh. Eventually, the building was used by the U.S. Suburban Resettlement Administration, U.S. Rural Electrification Commission and the American Red Cross. In 1951, the Republic of Indonesia purchased the building, and it has been used as an embassy ever since.

Another embassy worth seeking is the three-story, modern-style chancery of the Embassy of Brazil, located at 3006 Massachusetts Avenue NW. Designed by Brazilian architect Olavo Redig de Campos, there is Brazilian rosewood and Brazilian granite used throughout the gray glass-covered building. When the building opened in 1971, the *Washington Post* wrote that it "gives the impression...of a dynamic, self-confident country on its way to becoming a world power...but still aware of its ties with the past."

Next door, at 3000 Massachusetts Avenue NW, is the residence for the Brazilian ambassador, known as the McCormick House. This Italian

Renaissance–style residence was designed by John Russell Pope in 1908 and completed in 1931. Pope is the same architect behind the Thomas Jefferson Memorial and the West Building of the National Gallery of Art.

One final suggestion is the Embassy of Finland, located at 3301 Massachusetts Avenue NW. At first, from the outside, it might look fairly boxy and bleak, but in 2010, it became the first eco-friendly embassy in the nation, receiving a LEED Gold certification. The building was designed by Heikkinen-Komonen Architects in 1994.

Finally, for those who care for worthwhile statues, there is a statue of Mahatma Gandhi in mid-step, cane in hand, welcoming visitors in front of the Embassy of India, at 2107 Massachusetts Avenue NW. The eight-foot-eight-inch-tall bronze statue was unveiled in September 2000.

## HEURICH HOUSE MUSEUM (BREWMASTER'S CASTLE)

1307 New Hampshire Avenue NW
Approximate distance to Metro: 0.2 miles

On a trapezoidal lot near Dupont Circle, this late Victorian brownstone town home stands, once the residence of one of D.C.'s wealthiest and most distinguished citizens and philanthropists. The home was first owned by German immigrant Christian Heurich, a brewmaster and owner of the Christian Heurich Lager Beer Brewery, later known as the Christian Heurich Brewing Company. Heurich was the District's second-largest landowner and largest non-governmental employer. At the time of his death, at the age of 102, he was the world's oldest brewer.

Over time, the John Granville Meyers–designed building had additions by Appleton P. Clark Jr. Still, much of the interior of the house is preserved, including the family furniture. When it was constructed in 1892, it had the most modern technology at the time, with indoor plumbing, an elevator shaft and gas and electric lighting fixtures. It is said that none of the fifteen fireplaces, with their individually carved mantels, has been used.

After Heurich's death, the building served as the headquarters of the Columbia Historical Society, now known as the Historical Society of Washington, D.C. Now, the home is managed by nonprofit Heurich House Foundation, which continues to operate the house museum today.

## CAIRO CONDOMINIUMS

1615 Q Street NW
Approximate distance to Metro: 0.5 miles

This one building totally changed the course of architectural history for the nation's capital. Constructed in 1894, this was the city's first "residential skyscraper," towering at 165 feet tall. It is the city's tallest residential building, tallest privately owned and built structure and the first apartment building in the District constructed with a steel frame. It is because of this building that the Height of Buildings Act of 1899 was approved, causing every building thereafter to be no higher than 110 feet.

Designed by architect Thomas Franklin Schneider, this residential building was originally dubbed by locals as "Schneider's Folly" before being renamed Cairo Hotel circa 1900. The structure expanded over time with a one-story glass and iron conservatory added in 1897 and another one-story addition erected in 1904.

By 1957, the building was sold with plans for a $100,000 refurbishing project. A fire a year later resulted in $25,000 worth of damage but no structural problems. By the 1960s, the building was known for being inhabited by squatters, prostitutes, drug addicts and other criminals. In 1966, the D.C. Department of Health considered leasing the building for use as a rehabilitation center for alcoholics, but the structure instead closed down by 1972.

D.C.-based architect Arthur Cotton Moore was able to successfully restore the building in 1976 and convert it into apartments with sixty-six studios, forty-four one-bedrooms and sixty-six two-bedrooms. Three years later, the residences were converted once again, this time to condos.

Over the years, some of the most famous guests to grace this building's halls were F. Scott Fitzgerald and Thomas Edison.

## NATIONAL MUSEUM OF AMERICAN JEWISH MILITARY HISTORY

1811 R Street NW
Approximate distance to Metro: 0.3 miles

This museum offers two floors of exhibitions, a chapel and a study center for those interested in studying the history of Jews who have served in the U.S. Armed Forces. This museum was chartered by an act of Congress in September 1958 and is the only museum solely dedicated to Jews in the U.S. military. Throughout the year, this organization offers lectures and other special programs.

This organization operates under the auspices of the Jewish War Veterans, USA, National Memorial, Inc.

## THE MANSION ON O STREET

2020 O Street NW
Approximate distance to Metro: 0.3 miles

On a tree-lined street, four row houses have been joined to create one maze-like hotel, museum and private club. Known as the Mansion on O Street, this four-story venue offers seventy secret doors to discover, as well as more than one hundred rooms to meander through. Many of these rooms are themed with such examples being the log cabin room and the French Renaissance room. Inside each are curiosities and knickknacks, Beatles and John Lennon memorabilia, a signed Bob Dylan guitar, artworks, furnishings, thousands of books—nearly everything for sale, though some objects are pretty much priceless. A self-guided tour can take hours. Thankfully, there are treasure hunts to help make the journey even more fun.

H.H. Leonards-Spero founded the Mansion on O Street on February 14, 1980.

# JAMES G. BLAINE MANSION

2000 Massachusetts Avenue NW
Approximate distance to Metro: 0.2 miles

Even though James G. Blaine lived in this 1881-constructed mansion for fewer than two years, he remains one of the most famous owners. Blaine was a Pennsylvania-born Republican politician who served as the Speaker of the U.S. House of Representatives, then as a U.S. senator, then secretary of state.

After architect John Fraser designed the Queen Anne/Second Empire–style property for Blaine, rumors spread that Blaine may have financed the construction by a railroad bribe—rumors that may have cost him the presidency. Soon after, Blaine sold the home to George Westinghouse, the inventor of the railway air brake. Ownership continued to change hands over the years with the use of the property shifting to being a government document repository after the Civil War, later a headquarters for the United Service Club, then a headquarters for the Japanese Embassy and eventually a high-end apartment house.

# KRAMERBOOKS & AFTERWORDS CAFÉ

1517 Connecticut Avenue NW
Approximate distance to Metro: 0.1 miles

This cultural institution has been a staple to Washington, D.C. life since it was founded in 1976 by Bill Kramer, Henry Posner and David Tenney. Part restaurant, bar and bookstore, some of the most famous clientele to have visited this site include Barack Obama, Andy Warhol, Maya Angelou, Toni Morrison and Monica Lewinsky. It has even been featured in the HBO series *Veep*.

In 2016, Kramer's was sold to Steve Salis, co-founder of local chain &Pizza. At this time, the bookstore also experienced an expansion, creating a children's book annex.

# WASHINGTON HILTON

1919 Connecticut Avenue NW
Approximate distance to Metro: 0.5 miles

While not listed in the National Register of Historic Places, this 1965-built hotel is still noteworthy for the many famous clients who have walked through its doors. Some of these celebrities have included Jimi Hendrix and The Doors. The venue has also hosted the White House Correspondents Association dinner.

One of the most famous incidents to occur at the hotel is that it was the site of an assassination attempt on President Ronald Reagan by John Hinckley Jr. on March 30, 1981.

The architect behind the structure is William B. Tabler. When the hotel made its debut near Dupont Circle, the *New York Times* described the structure as "a huge seagull in arrested flight or a pair of giant, welcoming arms." When it opened, it had the city's largest pillar-less hotel ballroom with a capacity of 3,000 people for dinner or 4,300 for meetings.

In 2007, basketball star Magic Johnson, along with Canyon-Johnson Urban Fund and Lowe Enterprises Investors, purchased the hotel for $290 million. Shortly thereafter, the property had an estimated $100 million renovation.

# SPANISH STEPS

22nd Street NW, south of S Street NW
Approximate distance to Metro: 0.5 miles

This slope was so steep that urban planners knew it would be too impractical to create a street for automobiles, carriages or pedestrians on it. If a street passing through this space had been developed, then adjacent buildings would also have been forced to be razed. Thankfully, a new plan was formed to create two flights of stairs, lined with flowers and separated by a lion-head fountain with an oval-shaped basin. This is the only D.C. public park that occupies a street.

Behind the design of the Spanish Steps is architect Robert E. Cook. The Spanish Steps were constructed in 1911 following Beaux-Arts precepts with the aesthetic preferences of D.C.'s City Beautiful movement. In 1999, the steps were restored and rehabilitated. While not listed in the National Register of Historic Places, the Spanish Steps have been listed as a contributing feature in the Sheridan-Kalorama Historic District since 1989.

# DUPONT UNDERGROUND

19 Dupont Circle NW
Approximate distance to Metro: 0.2 miles

Originally, the purpose of this seventy-five-thousand-square-foot subterranean space was as a trolley station. From 1949 to 1962, the city's trolley service rolled through the newly built tunnels until it officially shut down. For some time, it remained vacant and unused, though it did temporarily serve as a fallout shelter before vandals broke in and stole the emergency food supplies.

In 1975, the D.C. government selected architect Arthur Cotton Moore to design an underground shopping mall in the space, but he was unable to obtain financing. It wasn't until 1993 that a lease was signed for a food court, known as Dupont Down Under. It wouldn't open for another two years, and it closed within a year. Part of what caused Dupont Down Under to go under was the developer behind the project, Geary Simon, who was known for having three convictions for larceny, mail fraud and insurance fraud.

After Dupont Down Under opened several months behind schedule, the mall tenants and visitors quickly understood the lack of care that had been taken to redevelop it. A lawsuit from many of the tenants alleged that the developer did not develop the space as promised in the renderings; it had an insufficient air-conditioning system and was "crudely built," according to an article published by the *Washington Post* in May 1996.

In 2014, Arts Coalition for the Dupont Underground, now simply known as Dupont Underground, successfully obtained a five-and-a-half-year lease to control the underground tunnels. Since then, the Dupont Underground space has thrived with several visual arts, theater and film events. Behind this new venue are architects Julian Hunt and Lucrecia Laudi of architecture firm Hunt Laudi Studio.

At one point, there were plans to create a micro-hotel, winery, artist studios or restaurant in Dupont Underground, but these were all long-term, conceptual ideas.

## THE WHITTEMORE HOUSE

1526 New Hampshire Avenue NW
Approximate distance to Metro: 0.2 miles

While this residence's exterior is rather simple in form, it is listed in the National Register of Historic Places as an example of a building of the 1890s, similar to those in the English Arts and Crafts movement with American Shingle–style architecture. While the building is lacking in applied decoration, the National Register of Historic Places nomination prefers to describe this residence as having a "restrained dignity."

Since 1927, it has been the home of the Woman's National Democratic Club, an organization that has been focused on educating women in political philosophy since it was incorporated in 1922. The home was constructed in 1892, designed by Harvey L. Page and built by Charles Albion Langley. In 1967, a two-story wing was added, designed by Nicholas Satterlee and dedicated by Lady Bird Johnson.

This one site has been the home of many notable occupants, including Walter D. Wilcox, a photographer who went on scientific explorations in Canada, Cuba and Hawaii. He also was a representative of the War Trade Board in Cuba. Other prominent residents were Senator and co-founder of Prudential Insurance Company in America John F. Dryden and Senator and later Secretary of War John C. Weeks. One previous owner was Sarah Adams Whittemore, a descendent of President John Adams.

Currently, the Whittemore House is available for weddings and other private events.

# PATTERSON MANSION

15 Dupont Circle NW
Approximate distance to Metro: 0.3 miles

What is now an apartment building was once a single mansion, built in 1903 for Robert Wilson Patterson, the editor and publisher of the *Chicago Tribune* newspaper. Patterson hired architect Stanford White of the New York–based firm McKim, Mead and White to design the Neoclassical home. The property later passed down to publisher of the *Times Herald* Elinor Patterson and, by 1948, the American Red Cross. For a brief time, President Calvin Coolidge also lived here.

From 1951 to 2014, the Patterson Mansion remained in the ownership of the Washington Club, a women's club that mostly consisted of wives of prominent government employees or businessmen. Finally, it was sold in June 2014 for $20 million to Bethesda-based developer SB-Urban, which converted the mansion into ninety-two fully furnished luxury apartments, each measuring fewer than four hundred square feet. With rents starting at $2,800 per month, the units are targeted for highly transient urban professionals. This apartment building is known as Ampeer.

The entire structure spans nearly 36,500 square feet across four levels. The major façade is made of brick with a marble and stone facing. In 1955, the residence was renovated, and a small two-story addition was built. The Patterson Mansion was added to the National Register of Historic Places in 1972.

# 14

# Farragut North

## SEE FARRAGUT WEST

...on page 157.

# 15

# Metro Center

## FORD'S THEATRE

### 511 10th Street NW
### Approximate distance to Metro: 0.2 miles

This historic theater is most famously known for being the site of the assassination of President Abraham Lincoln on April 14, 1865. When this building was first constructed, though, it was a house of God. Designed by James J. Gifford in 1833, this building was known as the First Baptist Church of Washington.

By 1859, the congregation had relocated to a newly built structure, eventually leaving their first home in the hands of Baltimore-based theater owner and producer John T. Ford, who rented the structure in 1861 and later purchased it and renovated it into a theater. The theater was first known as Ford's Athenaeum. Trouble first came in 1862 when the structure was destroyed by a fire; it was later rebuilt. It reopened in 1863 with a new name, Ford's New Theatre, and a new design based on Ford's Holliday

Street Theatre in Baltimore, Maryland. By 1865, everything came to a close.

After Lincoln's assassination, the U.S. government appropriated the theater, prohibiting its use as a place of public amusement. It then served as a facility for the War Department until 1893. At this point, a portion of the former theater collapsed, resulting in twenty-two deaths and sixty-eight injuries. After some time as a government warehouse, Ford's Theatre languished, vacant, until 1932, when a Lincoln museum opened on the first floor. A year later, the building was transferred to the National Park Service.

No entertainment was performed on the Ford Theatre's stage until 1968, four years after a restoration began. At that point, it once again reopened as a theater during a dedication ceremony with Vice President Hubert Humphrey in attendance. Another renovation occurred after 2009 with a reconfigured basement museum that told the story of Lincoln's life rather than solely his death.

## PETERSEN HOUSE

516 10th Street NW
Approximate distance to Metro: 0.1 miles

Directly across the street from Ford's Theatre, one can find the Petersen House, a site well known for having been the location where President Abraham Lincoln passed away after he was shot on April 14, 1865. This three-story brick building was constructed in 1849 and was owned by a German tailor known as William A. Petersen.

Congress later purchased the house in 1896 before the National Park Service acquired the property in 1933. Ever since, the National Park Service has maintained the Petersen House as a house museum that re-creates the scene of Lincoln's death.

## FREEDOM PLAZA

Approximate distance to Metro: 0.2 miles

Set on a raised terrace platform, this plaza offers a look at a map of Pierre Charles L'Enfant's 1791 plan for the Federal City. Incised in the platform are historic quotations, while the western end of the plaza features a fountain. On the eastern end is an equestrian statue of Polish patriot and U.S.

colonial army officer Kazimierz Pułaski. If the architect behind this plaza had his way, though, this site would have looked different.

Originally, the architect planned for this site was M. Paul Friedberg, but a design competition held by the Pennsylvania Avenue Development Corporation ended up selecting architect Robert Venturi of Venturi, Rausch and Scott Brown with landscape architect George Patton to plan the project. Venturi's design called for large marquettes of the White House and Capitol buildings, two tall sculptural pylons and a sculpture by Richard Serra. After pushback from the D.C. government and the American Society of Landscape Architects, these elements were abandoned.

The plaza opened in 1980 as Western Plaza. It was renamed Freedom Plaza in 1988 in honor of Martin Luther King Jr., who is said to have finished writing his famous "I Have a Dream" speech at the nearby Willard Hotel.

## PERSHING PARK

### Approximate distance to Metro: 0.3 miles

After M. Paul Friedberg's design for Freedom Plaza was passed over for the design by architect Robert Venturi of Venturi, Rausch and Scott Brown, Friedberg was chosen for the design for the adjacent site, known as Pershing Park.

This plaza is named in honor of General John J. Pershing. In comparison to Freedom Plaza, Pershing Park is a more traditional urban open space with a central sunken plaza, pool basin, waterfall and amphitheater-style seating. There is also a monument to Pershing.

Since 2016, there have been efforts to redevelop the site into a new World War I memorial, designed by Joseph Weishaar, Sabin Howard, Phoebe Lickwar and GWWO Architects.

Other projects completed by Friedberg have included New York's Battery Park City and Minneapolis's Peavey Plaza.

## WARNER THEATRE

513 13th Street NW
Approximate distance to Metro: 500 feet

Originally known as the Earle Theatre, this venue dates all the way back to 1924, when it was constructed by Detroit-based theater architect C. Howard Crane and his New York–based partner Kenneth Franzheim. The exterior was built in the Renaissance Revival style with terra-cotta ornamentation, while the interior reflects a French Renaissance style with barrel vaults. In 1927, an eleven-story addition was constructed by John J. Zink before it was demolished in 1992 and a new addition constructed in its place.

The venue was built for vaudeville and silent movies before it eventually expanded to concerts with performers like Frank Sinatra and The Rolling Stones. By the 1970s, the theater had fallen into disrepair and disrepute. In 1989, it closed for three years for an extensive renovation.

The current name of the theater comes from its original owner, Harry Warner, who was one of Hollywood's Warner Brothers.

## INTERCONTINENTAL THE WILLARD HOTEL

1401 Pennsylvania Avenue NW
Approximate distance to Metro: 0.3 miles

With the White House only steps away, this luxury Beaux-Arts hotel has been the gathering place for many notable politicians and cultural figures.

One such figure was Martin Luther King Jr., who is said to have written his "I Have a Dream" speech in one of the rooms. Other figures have included Mark Twain, Ulysses S. Grant, Charles Dickens and Nathaniel Hawthorne. The term "lobbyist" was also allegedly coined at this site, meant to describe those who frequented the lobby to speak with politicians.

The original Willard Hotel was constructed here in 1850 with 100 guest rooms, but it was demolished in order to make way for the current building on the site, constructed in 1901 with 389 guest rooms, designed by Henry Janeway Hardenbergh. By 1968, the building had closed down due to lack of business, facing threats of demolition before the Pennsylvania Avenue Development Corporation intervened. After a $73 million restoration and refurbishing project, the hotel reopened in 1986 with 394 guest rooms.

Inside, there is a block-long promenade known as Peacock Alley and the Round Robin Bar, which is supposedly where the mint julep was made famous.

This hotel was added to the National Register of Historic Places in 1974.

## MASONIC TEMPLE
## (NATIONAL MUSEUM OF WOMEN IN THE ARTS)

1250 New York Avenue NW
Approximate distance to Metro: 0.2 miles

Constructed in 1908, this six-story limestone-covered building contains large auditoriums, a library and a banquet hall. The architect behind the project was Waddy Butler Wood, who is also known for the Woodrow Wilson House, located at 2340 S Street NW.

Two months after opening, the first-floor auditorium showcased motion picture shorts. It later was used as a commercial movie theater, known as the Pix Theatre in the 1940s. By the 1950s, the Pix was replaced by the Art Cinema before being replaced once again in 1959 by the Town Theatre.

In 1987, the structure underwent an $8 million renovation, converting into a museum, known as the National Museum of Women in the Arts. This museum remains the only major museum in the world dedicated to the achievements of women in the arts, highlighting the works of artists like Frida Kahlo and Mary Cassatt.

# 16

# Gallery Place–Chinatown

## FRIENDSHIP ARCHWAY

H and 7th Streets NW
Approximate distance to Metro: 25 feet

In the heart of Chinatown, visitors will discover the nation's largest Chinese archway, designed by architect Alfred Liu. The decorative project encompasses over seven thousand glazed tiles, more than thirty-five thousand separate wooden pieces decorated with twenty-four-karat gold and more than 280 dragons with a mixture of Ming and Qing dynasty styles incorporated. The entire forty-eight-foot-tall archway spans a total

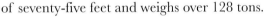

of seventy-five feet and weighs over 128 tons.

Created as a symbol of friendship between D.C. and its "sister city" Beijing, this archway was completed in November 1986. It was later restored in August 1993 and again in 2009. The cost of building and repairing the archway was split between the two cities.

## SMITHSONIAN AMERICAN ART MUSEUM AND NATIONAL PORTRAIT GALLERY (OLD PATENT OFFICE)

F and 8th Streets NW
Approximate distance to Metro: 250 feet

In this one Greek Revival National Historic Landmark, there are two Smithsonian museums that amass more than one million visitors per year.

This building was described by Walt Whitman as "that noblest of Washington buildings," while historian Charles J. Robertson's words were that it is "an expression of America's creative genius and technical superiority."

Before this marble and sandstone building was constructed, the site had other plans. Pierre Charles L'Enfant originally envisioned a nondenominational shrine to American military and civic heroes, but these plans ended up falling through. Instead, in the 1830s, it was chosen to be a patent office, with the first wing built in 1840.

To choose who would design this building, there was a design competition won by a consortium of A.J. Davis, Ithiel Town and William P. Elliot. President Andrew Jackson made Robert Mills the supervising architect; he was later replaced by Thomas U. Walter. By 1867, after a thirty-year period of construction that involved building each wing as needs and resources dictated, the Old Patent Office became the largest office building in the nation's capital at the time.

The patent office issued 500,000 patents to well-known individuals like Alexander Graham Bell, Cyrus McCormick and Thomas Edison. During the Civil War, the property was used as a hospital with nurses like American Red Cross founder Clara Barton and Walt Whitman, who based his poem "The Wound Dresser" on his experiences here. President Abraham Lincoln's second inaugural ball was also held in the building's Great Hall.

During the 1950s, this building was on the chopping block. For several years, it remained vacant, while demolition seemed inevitable. Thanks to President Dwight D. Eisenhower, the property was offered to the Smithsonian, which later opened two separate museums in the space in 1968.

The façades of this rectangular building are composed of giant Doric porticoes with pilasters, while each wing's interior differs in its spatial configuration, structural principles and architectural articulation. Inside, there is also a courtyard with a glass undulating ceiling, completed in 2004. This indoor-outdoor space is known as the Robert and Arlene Kogod Courtyard and was designed by London-based architects Foster + Partners.

Over the years, this building has experienced numerous renovations. In the 1880s, German-born architect Adolph Cluss, who is most known for having designed D.C.'s Eastern Market and Arts and Industries Building, completed a renovation. In 2017, a $300 million, thirteen-year restoration and renovation was completed by Hartman-Cox Architects.

A HISTORY & GUIDE

# SIXTH AND I HISTORIC SYNAGOGUE

600 I Street NW
Approximate distance to Metro: 0.2 miles

Constructed in 1908, this is one of Washington, D.C.'s oldest synagogues. It was built for the purpose of housing the Adas Israel Congregation, a Conservative Jewish congregation that was founded in 1869 by thirty-eight members. At the time, this was the congregation's second home. By 1951, Adas's congregation had grown too big for the space, so it relocated to its current location in Washington, D.C.'s Cleveland Park neighborhood. The building was sold to a Christian congregation, known as Turner Memorial African Methodist Episcopal Church.

After large-scale renovations in the 1980s, the Turner congregation placed the building on the market, offered for sale as a possible nightclub or restaurant. The Turner congregation relocated to Prince George's County, Maryland. In order to save the building from being converted into anything other than a house of worship, Jewish Historical Society of Greater Washington executive director Laura Cohen Apelbaum, whose father's bar mitzvah took place in the building, appealed to members of the Jewish community to save the structure.

Thankfully, in 2003, the building was sold to three local Jewish businessmen—former Washington Wizards owner Abe Pollin and two local developers, Shelton Zuckerman and Douglas Jemal—who intended to renovate and restore the building into a nondenominational Jewish synagogue. After the restoration by D.C.-based architects Shalom Baranes Associates was completed in 2004, it was rededicated as Sixth and I Historic Synagogue, with Mayor Anthony Williams, D.C. delegate to Congress Eleanor Holmes Norton and Ambassador of the State of Israel Daniel Ayalon in attendance. One year later, President George W. Bush toured the synagogue.

Still to this day, the synagogue offers a place of worship for those in the Jewish community and also often features events that can appeal to those of any faith, such as authors' talks and concerts.

THE RED LINE | 69

## CAPITAL ONE ARENA (VERIZON CENTER, MCI CENTER)

601 F Street NW
Approximate distance to Metro: 230 feet

When this twenty-thousand-seat, privately owned venue opened in December 1997, the general public perception of Washington, D.C.'s Downtown area was that it was known for being infested with crime. When former Washington Wizards owner Abe Pollin decided to invest $200 million into a world-class sports arena on this site, there was indecision from some as to whether this was a good investment.

At the time, the *Washington Post* described what was originally known as MCI Center as "perhaps the biggest bet yet on downtown," with comparisons made to developer James Rouse's Inner Harbor project, which revived downtown Baltimore, Maryland. This was the first major sports facility to be built in the city since Robert F. Kennedy Memorial Stadium opened in 1961. The hope was to transform the Downtown area of D.C. into a regional entertainment center where people could live, work, shop and have fun, and this hope has become a triumph. Since the MCI Center opened, Chinatown has undergone a massive renaissance with new shops, hotels, restaurants and office buildings.

In January 2006, MCI Center was renamed Verizon Center before being renamed once more in August 2017 Capital One Arena. The site is home of the Washington Wizards, Capitals and Mystics.

## MARTIN LUTHER KING JR. MEMORIAL LIBRARY

901 G Street NW
Approximate distance to Metro: 200 feet

On the outside, this might seem like another simple glass box, but it is actually the only public library ever designed by German-born architect Ludwig Mies van der Rohe, who is argued to be one of the most influential modernist architects. It is also his last building and the only building he ever constructed in the District.

After Mies presented his design in 1966, D.C. Public Library Director Harry Peterson said it was "the most functional, the most beautiful and most dramatic library building in the United States, if not in the world." Despite this high praise, architect Louis Justement described the decision to hire Mies as a "great mistake," arguing that a local architect should be the designer for the city's central library. Despite this, the *Washington Post* described the design as "a work of art" and "undoubtedly, the best example of the art of modern architecture…we shall have in Washington."

Before the building was named a historic landmark by the D.C. Historic Preservation Review Board in 2007, former mayor Anthony Williams considered selling the building to finance a $207 million mixed-use complex on the site of the old convention center.

Until 2020, the 400,000-square-foot building will remain closed as it undergoes a more than $200 million renovation by Dutch firm Mecanoo Architecten and D.C.'s Martinez+Johnson. Once open, the new library will offer 3D printers in maker spaces, public art, a larger and more interactive children's area and a new auditorium and conference center. There will also be the addition of a fifth floor and a rooftop event space with a terrace.

## TERRELL PLACE (HECHT COMPANY WAREHOUSE)

575 7th Street NW
Approximate distance to Metro: 300 feet

This mixed-use project is named after segregation protester, women's suffrage advocate and teacher Mary Church Terrell. Originally, this site was the flagship store of Hecht's, a chain of department stores founded in 1857 in Baltimore, Maryland. In the 1950s, Terrell was refused service at Hecht's lunch counter for being black. Because of this, she worked toward integrating the lunch counter. Terrell is also known for being appointed to the D.C. Board of Education and being one of the founders of the National Association for the Advancement of Colored People.

In 2003, Bethesda-based Clark Construction Group renovated and reopened this nearly 480,000-square-foot building and gave it its current name. This mixed-use project consists of three connected buildings with office and retail space. On the exterior and interior of the building, there are informative panels installed with information on Terrell and her impact.

17

# Judiciary Square

## NATIONAL BUILDING MUSEUM (PENSION BUILDING)

401 F Street NW
Approximate distance to Metro: 25 feet

For some time after this building was constructed in 1887, it was ridiculed for not fitting in. Designed by army quartermaster general Montgomery C. Meigs, this property, originally known as the Pension Building, was often called "Meigs's old red barn" due to it having red bricks as opposed to D.C.'s typical medium of white stones. When designing the Pension Building, Meigs used the Palazzo Farnese and the Cancelleria in Rome as his models and used a style representing an early revival of the Italian Renaissance style. Neoclassical is the style typically adopted for most federal buildings in the city.

Despite this, the building has found respect after the American Institute of Architects described its courtyard as "the most astonishing room in

Washington" in a 1957 exhibit of buildings worthy of preservation. It was also added to the National Register of Historic Places in 1969 and was designated a National Historic Landmark in 1985. Despite this, there was a point in time when the government considered demolishing the building. During the 1960s, the building was in dire need of repair.

Thanks to the works of preservationists, the government instead opted to commission architect Chloethiel Woodard Smith to explore other possibilities. Her proposal was to convert the building into a museum, a proposal that came true in 1980 when Congress mandated the creation of the National Building Museum as a private nonprofit educational institution.

Originally, the Pension Building housed the U.S. Pension Bureau, which awarded pensions to Civil War Union veterans and was the first federal veterans' agency to operate on a national scale. The building itself also served as a memorial to the soldiers, sailors and marines of the Civil War. This can be seen with the exterior terra-cotta detailing, consisting of a continuous running frieze between the first and second levels with images of a procession of Civil War forces parading around the building. This frieze was designed by Bohemian-born sculptor Casper Buberl. Other notable architectural features are the building's central atrium courtyard, eight seventy-eight-foot-tall columns and a two-story arcaded gallery.

U.S. presidents continue to host celebrations in this building. For many years, it was used for presidential inaugural balls. The presidents who have done so include Grover Cleveland, Benjamin Harrison, William McKinley, Theodore Roosevelt, William Howard Taft, Richard Nixon, Jimmy Carter and Ronald Reagan.

## NATIONAL LAW ENFORCEMENT OFFICERS MEMORIAL

450 F Street NW
Approximate distance to Metro: 15 feet

Since this memorial was dedicated by President George H.W. Bush in October 1991, it has had hundreds of names inscribed in its marble walls every year as part of National Police Week. The names are those of federal, state and local law enforcement officers who were killed in the line of duty. So far, there are over twenty thousand names displayed.

The three-acre park features a reflecting pool surrounded by walkways, as well as four bronze lions, two male and two female, each supervising a pair of lion cubs.

The architect behind this memorial is Davis Buckley.

## ADAS ISRAEL SYNAGOGUE
## (LILLIAN AND ALBERT SMALL JEWISH MUSEUM)

575 3rd Street NW
Approximate distance to Metro: 0.1 miles

This wandering former synagogue has been in the news various times for many different reasons. When it was constructed on the corner of 6th and G Streets NW, it was dedicated by President Ulysses S. Grant in June 1876, making him the first U.S. president to attend a Jewish service. By dating back so far, this is the oldest surviving and first synagogue in Washington, D.C., and is one of the oldest synagogue buildings in the country.

After the Adas congregation relocated to a grander location at 6th and I Streets NW in 1907, the building was used for myriad purposes, including a bicycle shop, barbershop, real estate agency, grocery and dentist's office. There were also three separate Christian congregations that used the building. During the 1960s, when Washington Metropolitan Area Transit Authority (WMATA) owned the property and threatened to demolish it to make a new headquarters, preservationists saved it by having it added to the National Register of Historic Places. With this, the structure was relocated for the first time in 1969, saved from the wrecking ball.

In 1975, the Jewish Historical Society of Greater Washington successfully converted the property into the Lillian and Albert Small Jewish Museum, which it continues to be to this day. In 2016, Property Group Partners with Wolfe House and Building Movers began the relocation process, moving the red brick, two-story building once more to 575 3rd Street NW in order to make room for the 2.2-million-square-foot mixed-use project known as Capitol Crossing.

## NEWSEUM

555 Pennsylvania Avenue NW
Approximate distance to Metro: 0.5 miles

Originally, the Newseum was located in Arlington, Virginia, and opened in 1997 with the purpose to promote free expression and the First Amendment.

By 2001, that building closed with big plans in store to cross the Potomac River and head to the nation's capital. It wasn't until April 2008 that the brand-new seven-level museum opened in Downtown, with many critics eager to criticize both the museum's appearance and purpose.

At the time, the *New York Times* wrote, "How many mediocre buildings can one city absorb?" Meanwhile, *Slate* advised readers to "avoid the gilded disaster that is the Newseum." Even in 2017, as the Newseum announced that it could no longer afford to subsidize the building, *POLITICO* wrote, "If the Newseum goes down, it will have deserved its death. Truth be told, it never deserved birth."

Despite this, the interactive museum is still worth visiting, if only to view the largest display of sections of the Berlin Wall outside Germany, the thousands of Pulitzer Prize–winning photos displayed or even the first-person accounts from journalists who covered the terrorist attacks of September 11, 2001. If nothing else, the Today's Front Pages Gallery offers a quick look at the front pages of more than eighty international newspapers.

The building, too, is a sight to behold. Costing $450 million, it was one of the world's most expensive museums under construction at the time. On its façade, there is a seventy-four-foot-high Tennessee marble tablet etched with the words of the First Amendment.

The exterior was designed by Polshek Partnership Architects, while the interior was designed by the acclaimed firm Ralph Appelbaum Associates, which also designed the Holocaust Memorial Museum.

In January 2019, the *Washington Post* reported that the Newseum will close within a year in order to make way for the opening of a university center for graduate studies for Johns Hopkins University.

# 18

# Union Station

## UNION STATION

50 Massachusetts Avenue NE
Approximate distance to Metro: 0 miles

Opened in October 1907 and completed in April 1908, this is one of the first great union terminals created in the nation. This monumental white granite structure was designed by Chicago-based architect and member of the U.S. Senate Park Commission Daniel Burnham. When designing Union Station, he was inspired by the nearby U.S. Capitol and its Neoclassical architecture.

Perhaps one of the most visually stunning sections of this building is its façade. The central pavilion is composed of three arches, each nearly fifty feet high, with six massive Ionic columns. Atop these columns are six eighteen-foot-high draped allegorical figures, created by Louis Saint-Gaudens, against a high frieze course. From west to east, these figures represent fire, electricity, freedom, imagination, agriculture and mechanics.

Since it opened, it has gotten much attention, even in the media, having been seen in films like *Mr. Smith Goes to Washington* and TV shows like *The West Wing.* It hasn't always been so splendid to look at, though.

By the mid- to late 1940s, Union Station was deteriorating. By the mid-1960s, the possibility of demolishing the structure became very real until it was listed in the National Register of Historic Places in 1964. Starting in 1976, Congress converted the station into the National Visitor Center, which failed fairly quickly, leading to its closing in 1978. Thanks to a $160 million restoration, completed in 1988, Union Station reopened with three levels of retail space. The Main Hall was further restored in May 2016 after a restoration repainted, re-gilded and reapplied gold leafing to the structure.

Starting in 2019, Union Station will undergo a $10 billion redevelopment, which has been described as the region's most important development initiative since the construction of Metro's subway system.

## U.S. CAPITOL

East Capitol NE and 1st Street SE
Approximate distance to Metro: 0.8 miles

This lavish, more than two-hundred-year-old structure is one of the most historic and important buildings in the nation's capital. This building houses the meeting chambers of the Senate and the House of Representatives as well as a museum of American art and history. The site is also used for ceremonies, such as presidential inaugurations. While not in the geographic center of the District, the Capitol is the origin point for the city's street-numbering and quadrant system.

Behind this structure were four distinct architectural minds: William Thornton, the original designer; Benjamin Henry Latrobe, who erected the major portion of the first building; Charles Bulfinch, who redesigned and carried out the central section, including the rotunda; and Thomas U. Walter, who managed the building's extensions and created the present dome. So far, there have been eleven architects who have made contributions to the Capitol.

With construction that began in 1793, this is the first major building in the nation to be influenced by the eighteenth-century English Neoclassical

style. Some of the major architectural accomplishments over the years started in 1803 when Latrobe created the building's corn-cob and tobacco-leafed capitals, found in a first-floor vestibule and in the small Senate rotunda. The first dome of the Capitol was completed in 1827, modeled after the Massachusetts State House. By 1850, the dome was replaced with a larger one. Inside the 180-foot-high rotunda, the top was filled with Constantino Brumidi's fresco *The Apotheosis of Washington*, showcasing classical gods and goddesses socializing with the Founding Fathers.

In 1960, the East Front was extended outward 32.5 feet, thereby adding 102 rooms. The old sandstone columns were removed and placed in the National Arboretum. The latest and perhaps greatest addition made to the Capitol is its Visitor Center. Located beneath the East Front plaza, it was completed in 2008, spanning nearly 580,000 square feet, making it the largest project in the building's history, measuring approximately three-quarters the size of the Capitol itself.

## BELMONT-PAUL WOMEN'S EQUALITY NATIONAL MONUMENT (SEWALL HOUSE, SEWALL-BELMONT HOUSE, ALVA BELMONT HOUSE)

144 Constitution Avenue NE
Approximate distance to Metro: 0.6 miles

After this former residence was constructed in 1800 by Robert Sewall, it played a small role in the War of 1812 when the house was a site of resistance to the British invasion before being set on fire. By 1820, Sewall rebuilt it. During the Jefferson administration, Secretary of the Treasury Albert Gallatin used the house. Eventually, it was sold to Vermont senator Porter H. Dale in 1922 before he then sold the property to the National Woman's Party (NWP) in 1929.

When the NWP opened its new headquarters, it named the structure the Alva Belmont House in honor of the woman who financially contributed toward the organization's previous headquarters, which is now demolished. Here, NWP's advocacy advanced, thanks to women's suffrage and equal rights leader Alice Paul, who is known for amending the Equal Rights Amendment with language that became known as the "Alice Paul Amendment."

Over the years, this former residence has gained higher ground as a historic site, becoming listed in the National Register of Historic Places in 1972, designated a National Historic Landmark in 1974 and finally designated a National Monument by President Barack Obama in 2016.

## SMITHSONIAN NATIONAL POSTAL MUSEUM

2 Massachusetts Avenue NE
Approximate distance to Metro: 0.4 miles

From the time it was constructed in 1914 through 1986, this building was Washington, D.C.'s main post office building. By 1990, the Smithsonian Institution had made an agreement with the U.S. Postal Service to open a museum dedicated to postal history. This museum officially opened in July 1993.

The museum only occupies 100,000 square feet of the building, 35,000 square feet of which is exhibition space, while 6,000 square feet is devoted to a research library, stamp store and museum shop. This museum features over forty thousand volumes and manuscript holdings, making it one of the largest and most significant postal history collections in the world and one of the world's most comprehensive library resources on postal history. It also hosts the largest stamp gallery in the world, known as the William H. Gross Stamp Gallery. Other artifacts found here include three vintage airmail planes, a reconstructed railway mail car and an 1851 stagecoach.

The museum's public spaces were designed by D.C.-based Florance Eichbaum Esocoff King Architects.

# JAPANESE AMERICAN MEMORIAL TO PATRIOTISM DURING WORLD WAR II

Louisiana Avenue NW and D Street NW
Approximate distance to Metro: 0.3 miles

Located six hundred yards north from the U.S. Capitol, this memorial commemorates the Japanese Americans who served in World War II despite unjust treatment. Construction of the memorial was authorized and signed into law by President George H.W. Bush in October 1992. The organization behind this project was the National Japanese American Memorial Foundation, originally known as the Go for Broke National Veterans Association Foundation.

At this memorial, visitors will find a semicircular granite wall, known as "Honor Wall," listing the names of more than eight hundred Japanese Americans in the U.S. Armed Forces who were killed in action during World War II, the names of the nation's internment camps and the number of internees held there.

The central bronze sculpture, known as *Golden Cranes*, was designed by sculptor Nina Akamu, former vice president of the National Sculpture Society. These two metal cranes are seen caught in barbed wire, standing on a pedestal incised with grooves meant to suggest drill cores that are used to extract stone from quarries.

There are also three panels inscribed with writings by Japanese Americans and quotes by Presidents Harry Truman and Ronald Reagan.

# ATLAS PERFORMING ARTS CENTER

1333 H Street NE
Approximate distance to Metro: 1.5 miles

Located on H Street NE, this performing arts facility can be found in a renovated Art Deco movie theater. First opened in 1938, this structure was designed by architect John Jacob Zink, the same architect behind the city's Uptown Theater. As many of the District's theaters have done, this theater eventually closed. In 1976, it ceased operation after struggling to stay in business after the 1968 riots that followed the assassination of Martin Luther King Jr.

In 2001, nonprofit Atlas Performing Arts Center purchased the structure with hopes to complete a multiphase renovation that totaled more than $20 million. The Arts Center officially opened in 2005 and was completed in 2006. It now hosts a variety of performances, from films to dances to theater productions. The structure is also listed in the National Register of Historic Places.

# 19

# NoMa–Gallaudet U

## GALLAUDET UNIVERSITY

800 Florida Avenue NE
Approximate distance to Metro: 1 mile

From when it opened its doors in 1864 to today, this is the only freestanding institution of higher education in the world designed to meet the specific needs of deaf students, not only in its studies but in its architecture too.

It all started in 1856 when P.H. Skinner asked former postmaster general Amos Kendall for assistance in founding a school for deaf and blind children. Kendall proceeded to donate two acres of his estate to establish the school. Soon after, in 1857, President Franklin Pierce signed a federal law, allowing what was known as the Columbia Institution for Instruction of the Deaf and the Dumb and the Blind to be created. President Abraham Lincoln signed the school's charter in 1864, allowing the Columbia Institution to grant collegiate degrees. The buildings and grounds plan for the campus was later designed by father of American landscape architecture Frederick Law Olmsted, who is also known for having designed the Smithsonian National Zoological Park.

By 1894, the board of directors changed the name to Gallaudet College in honor of Thomas Hopkins Gallaudet, the founder of deaf education in America, though the legal corporate name did not change until 1954. Gallaudet was officially granted university status in October 1986.

In order to better serve students, architect Hansel Bauman established the DeafSpace Project in 2005 to catalogue architectural design elements that address how to accommodate those who are deaf.

Gallaudet University offers more than forty majors with over one thousand in undergraduate enrollment.

## UNION MARKET

1309 5th Street NE
Approximate distance to Metro: 1 mile

Before Union Market, there was Center Market, a market hall designed by German-born architect Adolph Cluss. When it was constructed in 1871, it ranked as the largest market hall in the country. By 1931, it had closed, with the National Archives taking its place. In order to replace this market, the Union Terminal Market opened that same year, offering a space to sell meats, fish, produce and dairy. The indoor market wasn't built until 1967, five years after the city banned the outdoor sale of meats and eggs. After the building showed deterioration in 1989, the market closed its doors before reopening decades later in 2012, revitalized by developer EDENS.

Over the years, the space and its surroundings have grown exponentially, creating a food destination worth searching for. In 2013, *Bon Appétit* named Union Market one of the five best food halls in the nation. By 2017, there were approximately fifty vendors in the market, selling everything from kitchen knives to tableware to food and desserts. There is also an outdoor space, known as Dock5, that hosts large-scale events and festivals.

## METROPOLITAN BRANCH TRAIL

Approximate distance to Metro: 2 miles

This eight-mile trail is popular among commuters and those searching for murals along their bike ride or run. One of the most notable sites on the trail is *28 Blocks*, a four-story mural painted by New York–based artist Garin Bake that honors the African American men who quarried the white Georgia marble used to build Abraham Lincoln's statue at the Lincoln Memorial.

Currently, the trail runs from Silver Spring, Maryland, to Union Station in Washington, D.C. It was originally conceived by D.C. resident Patrick

Hare in 1988 as a "grand avenue…without cars, a 'trail and transit' avenue for people aboard trains and bikes and on foot." In the early 1990s, the trail entered the D.C. Comprehensive Plan before Congress allocated $8.5 million in 1998 to fund the project. The first formal ribbon-cutting ceremony for the Metropolitan Branch Trail was held in 1999. Since then, there have been several trail extensions with more expected to come before the trail is complete in 2019.

The name of the trail comes from the Metropolitan Subdivision of the Baltimore and Ohio Railroad.

## NPR HEADQUARTERS

1111 North Capitol Street NE
Approximate distance to Metro: 0.6 miles

Inside this glassy, LED-decorated workplace are flexible, open spaces, perfect for some of the radio industry's best minds to be able to collaborate. This two-story newsroom and studio was completed in April 2013 after NPR divisions and employees worked in three separate buildings in Downtown D.C. for many years. NPR has had its headquarters in the District since it was founded in 1970.

This new headquarters was designed by D.C.-based Hickok Cole Architects and built by Balfour Beatty Construction. Originally a 1926-built warehouse known as the C&P Telephone Company building, this structure spans 440,000 square feet and is combined with a seven-story office tower. It is divided into three segments: public, news and office. The LEED

Gold–certified building's design has won numerous awards from the *Washington Business Journal* and *Interior Design Magazine*, as well as the IIDA Mid-Atlantic Silver Award for interior architecture.

Every day, NPR hosts tours in its headquarters. Be sure to utilize this opportunity to get a glimpse of daily life in the newsroom.

# WOODWARD & LOTHROP SERVICE WAREHOUSE

131 M Street NE
Approximate distance to Metro: 0.3 miles

This six-story, industrial modern–style building is considered to be the most ambitious warehouse built in the D.C. area before World War II and is one of the city's largest warehouses. Its façade is composed of buff-colored brick, formed limestone and reinforced concrete. When it was constructed in 1939 by New York–based department store architects Abbot, Merkt & Company, it was meant to serve as a warehouse for the Woodward & Lothrop Company. This company was one of the D.C. area's largest and oldest mercantile retail operations, founded in 1880 by Samuel Walter Woodward and Alvin Mason Lothrop.

By 1946, the warehouse was enlarged after being connected with the adjacent Palais Royal warehouse. Approximately twenty years later, the east side of the building was excavated to expose the basement. Federated Department Stores Inc., the owner of Macy's, eventually purchased the Woodward & Lothrop Company in 1995. After the company disbanded, the space was taken over by San Francisco–based The Bristol Group and converted into office space. It is now leased by the government agencies represented by the U.S. General Services Administration (GSA).

Before being added to the National Register of Historic Places, the building underwent an extensive rehabilitation project from 2000 to 2003, which led to cleaning the exterior, replacing windows, refurbishing the water tower and reconfiguring the interior spaces.

Still, a sign indicating the warehouse's original title is installed on the southeastern corner of the façade, three stories high.

# ULINE ARENA (WASHINGTON COLISEUM)

201 M Street NE
Approximate distance to Metro: 0.4 miles

Directly adjacent to the NoMa–Gallaudet U Metro station, history seekers will be able to find the venue for the first American concert by The Beatles in 1964. Uline Arena dates all the way back to 1941 when it was constructed by Miguel "Mike" Uline. Before it closed in 1986, it offered a space for President Dwight D. Eisenhower's first inaugural ball in 1953, professional hockey and basketball games, a speech by Malcolm X and the pro-wrestling debut of boxer Joe Louis.

The property also houses a 1931-built Ice House building, the city's original ice manufacturing facility, which provided ice for the skating rink within the Arena building.

By the mid-1990s, it was used as a trash transfer station before being used as a parking garage. In 2004, D.C.-based developer Douglas Development acquired the site and finished a full redevelopment of it in 2016, opening REI's fifth flagship store and the first REI in the nation's capital. The entire property spans 244,000 square feet, 70,000 of which is retail and 174,000 of which is office.

Uline Arena was added to the National Register of Historic Places in 2007.

## ST. ALOYSIUS CHURCH

19 I Street NW
Approximate distance to Metro: 1 mile

This is one of Washington, D.C.'s most prominent, historic Jesuit institutions, joining the likes of Georgetown University, Holy Trinity Catholic Church and Gonzaga College High School. This church is named after St. Aloysius Gonzaga, an Italian Jesuit, who cared for victims of the plague in Rome in 1581, leading to his death at the age of twenty-three.  The St. Aloysius Church was constructed in 1858, designed by Father Benedict Sestini, a Jesuit priest who was a well-known mathematician, astronomer and physicist. The bells in the tower were later dedicated in September 1866.

In 1973, this building was added to the National Register of Historic Places. Exactly ten years later, the Father McKenna Center was established in the building, and it continues to serve the community to this day. This organization serves those who struggle with homelessness or low incomes. The name memorializes Father Horace McKenna, a Jesuit priest who devoted his life to the service of those who are poor or homeless.

By 2012, St. Aloysius Church's parish had closed with the congregation merging with the nearby Holy Redeemer Catholic Church.

# 20

# Rhode Island Avenue

## ENGINE COMPANY 26
## (TRUCK COMPANY 15, THE FARM)

1340 Rhode Island Avenue NE
Approximate distance to Metro: 1 mile

This historic firehouse was designed by American architect Nathan Wyeth, who is best known for having designed the West Wing of the White House and the Francis Scott Key Bridge. When this structure was built in 1937, it was part of a Depression-era construction campaign to bolster the fire service to the suburbanizing Northeast quadrant of the city. This was the last truck house built in the city, designed in the Colonial Revival style. It is still used for the city's professional firefighting force.

Engine Company 26 was added to the National Register of Historic Places in 2011.

## THE HECHT WAREHOUSE

1401 New York Avenue NE
Approximate distance to Metro: 2 miles

In Washington, D.C.'s Ivy City neighborhood, this Art Deco– and Streamline Modern–style mixed-use complex was originally a warehouse for Baltimore, Maryland–based Hecht's. Founded in 1857, Hecht's was a chain of department stores. Not to be confused with Terrell Place (formerly the Hecht Company Warehouse), this more than 460,000-square-foot building was constructed in 1937 with additions later added in 1937, 1948, 1961 and 1986.

When this building was still under construction, the *Washington Post* wrote in 1936 that the building was "the biggest [warehouse] south of New York City and...the most modern warehouse in the United States." It was also one of the earliest and most significant examples of glass block construction in Washington, D.C. An additional notable feature of this building is its twelve-point, star-shaped cupola, which is illuminated at night.

In 2011, D.C.-based developer Douglas Development purchased the property before redeveloping it into a retail and residential complex with three hundred apartments, more than 125,000 square feet of retail, a grocery store and a parking garage.

## ALEXANDER CRUMMELL SCHOOL

1900 Gallaudet Street NE
Approximate distance to Metro: 2 miles

This vacant, neglected school was named after clergyman, teacher, missionary and orator Alexander Crummell, who worked with Frederick Douglass to abolish slavery. Throughout his life, Crummell devoted himself to uplifting African Americans and was one of the founders of the American Negro Academy, the first organization in the nation to support African American academic scholarship.

This school was designed by municipal architect Snowden Ashford and built by Allan T. Howlson in 1911. A second story at the rear of the building was constructed in 1932. After years of overcrowded classrooms, the Crummell School closed and was transferred to the D.C. Department of General Services in 1977. Since then, it has remained vacant and neglected, but there are plans to redevelop the site. In 2016, a development team, known as Ivy City Partners—consisting of the Jarvis Company, Stonebridge Carras and ProFish—was selected to revitalize it with thirty-five thousand square feet of industrial space, twenty-two thousand square feet of retail space and 320 apartments, 60 of which will be designated for affordable housing. Additionally, thirty-five thousand square feet will be occupied by seafood company ProFish.

This school was added to the National Register of Historic Places in 2002. Ten years later, community organization D.C. Preservation League deemed the property one of the most endangered historic sites in the city.

# NATIONAL ARBORETUM

3501 New York Avenue NE
Approximate distance to Metro: 2 miles

A little over two miles from the U.S. Capitol, visitors can still find traces of the building in the National Arboretum. Atop a tranquil hill stand twenty-two of the original Benjamin Henry Latrobe–designed sandstone Corinthian columns from the east front of the U.S. Capitol. After the columns were removed from the original building during an expansion in 1958, they remained in storage for many decades. It wasn't until English landscape architect Russell Page designed a setting perfect for them with a nearby fountain in the mid-1980s that they found a new home at the National Arboretum.

The impressive features of this tranquil area don't end there as the entire site spans over 440 acres of land contiguous to the Anacostia River. Here, visitors can find a 12-acre classical Chinese garden, designed by a joint team from China and the United States; the National Grove of State Trees, which offers specimens of most of the U.S. state trees; and the National Bonsai and Penjing Museum. There is also a nearly four-hundred-year-old bonsai tree that survived an atomic bomb, donated to the arboretum in 1976 by bonsai master Masaru Yamaki.

This is the only federally supported arboretum and is one of the largest arboretums in the country. Its origin dates as far back as 1901 when lobbying began for a national arboretum that could allow for research and education concerning tree and plant life. In 1927, Congress approved legislation to create the National Arboretum, but progress remained slow. A 1930 preliminary plan was created by Arthur A. Shurtleff with the assistance of Frederick Law Olmsted Jr. and others, but it was never executed. Thanks to a master plan created in 1948 by the Public Buildings Administration, a set vision was in place for the construction of an administration building, greenhouses and service areas as well as a road system that would fit with the hilly topography. Still, by the end of World War II, the arboretum remained to a large extent unimproved. Construction of the permanent road system would not be complete until 1958, and five greenhouses were not finished until 1962. Two years later, the administration-laboratory building, designed by Deigert & Yerkes, was dedicated. Afterward, Deigert & Yerkes received an award from the American Institute of Architects and a positive nod in the *Washington Post* from Wolf Von Eckardt, who described the building as "a graceful almost delicate garden pavilion."

The National Arboretum was listed in the National Register of Historic Places in 1973.

# 21

# Brookland-CUA

## CATHOLIC UNIVERSITY OF AMERICA

620 Michigan Avenue NE
Approximate distance to Metro: 0.4 miles

In a tree-lined street in the quiet, suburban neighborhood of Brookland, this is one of the best undergraduate schools in the country, ranking in the top 15 percent, according to the Princeton Review. This school is one of only three universities in the country to have hosted the pope and the only one to have had three separate popes visit its campus: Pope John Paul II in 1979, Pope Benedict XVI in 2008 and Pope Francis in 2015. With this and its long history, the Catholic University of America deems itself the flagship Catholic educational institution in the United States and the bishops' university.

The name of the university wasn't chosen until 1885 by a committee appointed by the Third Plenary Council of Baltimore. At the time, New York and Philadelphia were considered as possible sites for the school, but in the end the nation's capital was the final choice. Two years later, the Catholic University of America was incorporated in D.C. on sixty-six acres of land adjacent to the grounds of Lincoln's Cottage. It didn't open as an institution of higher education until November 1889, with its undergraduate programs initiated in 1904. Now, nearly seven thousand students attend this university.

# FRANCISCAN MONASTERY
# OF THE HOLY LAND IN AMERICA

1400 Quincy Street NE
Approximate distance to Metro: 0.7 miles

This forty-four-acre complex is the perfect respite from the city life. Not only do the landscaped gardens offer a calm, contemplative space for relaxing, but the highly elaborate interior of the monastery is enough to wow any who care for architectural masterpieces. It is also a first-rate site for those searching for structures emblematic of typical ecclesiastical styles.

Dedicated in September 1899, this monastery is the headquarters of the Commissariat of the Holy Land for the United States, an 1880-founded organization dedicated to the preservation and maintenance of the shrines of the Holy Land. It was later chartered as a college where American friars could be educated for work in the Holy Land and where visitors could be imbued with the spirit of the Holy Land as well.

From the outside, the monastery is imposing yet simple with a structure composed of tightly massed elements, including outdoor shrines and small chapels, dating back to the 1910s. The complex is in the form of a five-fold Cross of Jerusalem with a large square cloister. The centerpiece is a Byzantine-style, buff-colored brick church. On the nearby grounds, there is also a cemetery laid out in 1901 and a replica of the catacombs in Rome. Other notable structures include the 1926-constructed Rosary Portico, which is based on the arcaded cloister walls of Romanesque monastic architecture and commemorates the fifteen mysteries of the Rosary. It was designed by architectural sculptor John J. Earley with architectural firm Murphy and Olmsted.

# BASILICA OF THE NATIONAL SHRINE
# OF THE IMMACULATE CONCEPTION

400 Michigan Avenue NE
Approximate distance to Metro: 0.8 miles

If searching for Brookland, the easiest landmark to watch out for is this national shrine, rising up 329 feet. At this height, it is one of the ten largest churches in

the world, the largest Roman Catholic church in the United States, the second-largest in North America and the tallest habitable building in the nation's capital. It's a big deal in more ways than just one. Several well-known figures have celebrated Mass here, including President Harry Truman, Robert F. Kennedy and two popes, Pope John Paul II and Pope Benedict XVI.

The cornerstone was laid in 1920 with the final architectural element of the church completed nearly one hundred years later in 2017 when the "Trinity Dome" glass mosaic was finalized. In style, this church is Romanesque on the outside and Byzantine on the inside. Construction is made of stone, brick, tile and mortar. No steel structural beams, framework or columns were used during construction.

## ST. ANSELM'S ABBEY

4501 South Dakota Avenue NE
Approximate distance to Metro: 1 mile

The very first church and monastery building constructed for this community of Benedictine monks was completed in 1930, but it wasn't until approximately thirty years later that a big figure in architecture made his mark here. Over the years, the number of monks at St. Anselm's Abbey grew, in part thanks to them opening the secondary day school for boys, Priory School, in 1942. Eventually, a major addition was needed, and thanks to the help of Pritzker Prize–winning architect Philip Johnson, that addition was completed in 1960. This was Johnson's first development in D.C., before he went on to design the city's Kreeger Gallery. One year later, Pope John XXIII elevated the priory to the rank of abbey, and the name of the Priory School was changed to St. Anselm's Abbey School.

Visitors at this abbey are described by the *Washington Post* as often being "hypertensive stockbrokers, burned-out journalists, depressed lawyers… [people] wanting to check in for a few days of serious contemplation." If interested in some serious rumination—or a casual glance at an addition designed by one of the country's foremost architects—head to this historic religious site.

St. Anselm's Abbey is named after the eleventh-century archbishop and theologian St. Anselm of Canterbury, who is known for his ontological argument for the existence of God.

## GLENWOOD CEMETERY

2219 Lincoln Road NE
Approximate distance to Metro: 1.7 miles

This more than fifty-acre secular cemetery offers burial sites for well-known figures like former D.C. mayor William A. Bradley, Pulitzer Prize–winning cartoonist Clifford Kennedy Berryman and George Atzerodt, who was a conspirator with John Wilkes Booth in the assassination of President Abraham Lincoln. The cemetery was listed in the National Register of Historic Places in 2017.

Also located in the cemetery is a one-story brick building known as the Mortuary Chapel, which was completed in 1892 and listed in the National Register of Historic Places in 1988. The D.C.-based architect behind this structure was Glenn Brown, who went on to be secretary of the American Institute of Architects from 1899 to 1913. The building is small and simple, rectangular and with a large saddleback roof with eaves.

There are more than forty-eight thousand burials and re-interments at this site, which was established in 1852.

## BROOKS MANSION (BELLAIR)

901 Newton Street NE
Approximate distance to Metro: 100 feet

This Greek Revival mansion might not look like much from the outside. It's not as gargantuan as some estates in the D.C. area or as intricate, but it is one of the oldest residences in the nation's capital. Dating back to the late 1830s or early 1840s, this country estate was constructed for Colonel Jehiel Brooks, a lawyer and War of 1812 veteran, and his wife, Ann. At the time, they dubbed their residence Bellair.

In 1887, after the two passed away, the house and its land were sold to Ida U. Marshall and then immediately resold to Benjamin F. Leighton and Richard E. Pairo. It wasn't until 1891 that it switched hands to the Marist Society, an order of missionary priests. A year later, the Marist Society established an administrative center and house of studies on the property. Over time, the society outgrew the mansion. In order to accommodate its needs, an eastern addition was constructed in 1894, effectively doubling the space of the mansion.

From 1903 to 1905, after the Marist Society moved out, the property became vacant until the site once again became a space for a religious organization. This time, in 1905, the Order of Benedictine Sisters, a community-oriented teaching order of nuns, purchased the mansion and founded St. Benedict's Academy there that same year. It later served as the order's house of studies before becoming a convent.

By 1970, the fate of the estate was in the hands of the Washington Metropolitan Area Transit Authority, which hoped to demolish the home to construct a parking lot for the nearby Brookland Metro station. Thanks to neighborhood opposition, Brooks Mansion was saved and then listed in the National Register of Historic Places in 1975.

Since 1979, when the D.C. government purchased the site, it has been the headquarters for DCTV, the city's public access TV station.

# 22

# Fort Totten

## FORT TOTTEN PARK

Approximate distance to Metro: 1 mile

During the Civil War, Washington, D.C., had several forts surrounding the nation's capital. From 1861 through 1865, there was a 272-yard fort with twenty guns and mortars found in this park. The garrison had a total of 180 artillerists with 350 officers and other men. The fort is still relatively intact with a Civil War Centennial Plaque located in the park to remember the efforts fought there.

Fort Totten Park is named after Brigadier General Joseph Totten, who worked as chief of engineers at the U.S. Army, regent of the Smithsonian Institution and co-founder of the National Academy of Sciences.

## ROCK CREEK CEMETERY

Webster Street NW and Rock Creek Church Road NW
Approximate distance to Metro: 1.5 miles

When it was founded in 1719, this burial place opened as both a cemetery and a park, and it continues to be the city's oldest public burial place. It didn't become a public burial place until 1840. Spanning eighty-six acres, this site is host to myriad memorials, monuments, mausoleums and sculptures. There are over seventy-five thousand graves at this cemetery.

A few worth knowing include William Ordway Partridge's Kauffman Memorial (also known as Seven Ages and Memory), finished in 1897 as a tribute to former owner of the *Washington Star* Samuel Kauffmann. There is also Louis Amateis's Heurich Mausoleum, built circa 1895, and Gutzon Borglum's Rabboni-Ffoulke Memorial, which was completed in 1909 as a tribute to D.C. banker and tapestry collector Charles Matthews Ffoulke.

When it comes to which burial places are worth searching for in this cemetery, it is difficult to narrow it down to a final few, as those who are located here vary from Revolutionary War heroes to inventors to politicians and judges to entrepreneurs to journalists. Original landowners and developers of Washington, D.C., are also buried here, including David Burnes and Anthony Holmead, while two early mayors of the nation's capital, Peter Force and Matthew G. Emery, can be found at this cemetery.

Other worthwhile politicos located at Rock Creek Cemetery include D.C. governor Alexander Shepherd, statesman and signer of the Constitution Abraham Baldwin and Chief Justice and U.S. Attorney General Harlan Fiske Stone.

There are several members of the media who have been buried at Rock Creek Cemetery. They include Pulitzer Prize–winning author Upton Sinclair, *Washington Star* newspaper co-owner and publisher Samuel H. Kauffman, *National Geographic Magazine* editor and Alexander Graham Bell's son-in-law Gilbert Grosvenor and the *Washington Post* founder and publisher Stilson Hutchins. Other final noteworthy burials worth mentioning are television inventor Charles Francis Jenkins, Wonder Bread inventor Charles Corby and Timothy John "Tim" Russert, who was NBC's longest-serving moderator of *Meet the Press* and also senior vice president of NBC News.

In 1977, Rock Creek Cemetery was added to the National Register of Historic Places.

## ST. PAUL'S EPISCOPAL CHURCH (ROCK CREEK PARISH)

Webster Street NW and Rock Creek Church Road NW
Approximate distance to Metro: 2 miles

Opposite the entrance gate toward the center of Rock Creek Cemetery is St. Paul's Episcopal Church, the oldest church in the nation's capital. Church services first initiated on the site in 1712 with the first church built in 1719. This building was later replaced in 1775 with a brick structure whose walls still remain. By 1868, the north wall was torn down, while the entire structure was remodeled. By 1922, it had to be rebuilt after damage from a fire a year earlier. It was further restored in 2004.

This structure was added to the National Register of Historic Places in March 1972.

## ADAMS MEMORIAL (*GRIEF, THE PEACE OF GOD*)

Webster Street NW and Rock Creek Church Road NW,
east of St. Paul's Episcopal Church
Approximate distance to Metro: 1 mile

This contemplative bronze figure is known as one of American sculptor Augustus Saint-Gaudens's greatest works, if not his greatest work. On a hexagonal plot, approximately twenty feet in diameter, this sculpture was completed in 1891 with a setting designed by architect Stanford White of McKim, Mead and White.

The heavily draped figure's right arm is raised to the chin, while the left arm is concealed in the folds of the drapery. Meanwhile, the legs are parted and the face expressionless, while the figure is framed by two smooth monoliths of polished granite with classical molding.

This sculpture was erected by historian Henry Adams, a descendant of John Quincy Adams, as a memorial to his wife, Marian "Clover" Hooper Adams, who suffered from depression and committed suicide in 1885. He hoped for it to convey "the acceptance of intellectuality, of the inevitable," according to the application for the National Register of Historic Places.

This sculpture is often referred to as *Grief*, but this is a misnomer, a result of Mark Twain's comment that it symbolized all of human grief. In fact, it has multiple names: *The Peace of God*, *Kwannon* and even *The Mystery of the Hereafter*.

The Adams Memorial was listed in the National Register of Historic Places in March 1972.

# 23

# Takoma

## TAKOMA THEATRE

6833 4th Street NW
Approximate distance to Metro: 300 feet

John Jacob Zink, the architect behind this Classic Revival building, was the same one behind D.C.'s Atlas Performing Arts Center and Uptown Theater. In 1923, the Takoma Theatre first opened before closing down in 1980. Three years later, aspiring playwright Milton McGinty reopened the venue for live performances. Since 2005, the building has been vacant ever since nonprofit Takoma Theatre Arts Project's lease ended.

In 2017, the proposal for repurposing the building into a satellite clinic space for Children's National Medical Center was finalized. During the conversion, a second story was added, bringing the total size of the building to more than 23,000 square feet. The ground floor was also planned for more than 860 square feet of ground-floor retail.

## *FROM A MODEL TO A RAINBOW*

327 Cedar Street NW
Approximate distance to Metro: 450 feet

This may be the most modern landmark currently in Takoma. Dating back to 2011, this ceramic and glass tile mosaic on aluminum was created by

D.C.-based Sam Gilliam. Gilliam was chosen from a design competition that had over 130 submissions.

The artwork is sponsored by the D.C. Commission on the Arts and Humanities in cooperation with the Metro Art in Transit program. It is located directly outside the Takoma Metro station.

## TAKOMA PARK LIBRARY

416 Cedar Street NW
Approximate distance to Metro: 0.1 mile

Opened in 1911, this was the first neighborhood library constructed in Washington, D.C. It is also one of the four library buildings in the city funded by Andrew Carnegie, who donated $40,000 to the project. This building has undergone several renovations and restorations over the years, one in 1940 and one in 2009. Still, it remains a community gathering place and a contributing building to the Takoma Park Historic District.

The one-story Renaissance Revival building was designed by architectural firm Marsh & Peter with a hipped roof, a main reading room at the front and a combined children's room and lecture hall at the rear.

## TAKOMA PARK ADVENTIST CHURCH

7700 Carroll Avenue
Approximate distance to Metro: 1.5 miles

This is a "headquarters church," serving as the international headquarters for the Seventh Day Adventist Church. The Adventists are unique in that they observe Saturday as the Sabbath and believe in the second coming. Their Takoma Park congregation was organized in 1904.

This American Gothic building offers high vaulted ceilings, large rose windows and a 110-foot-high spire. When it was built in October 1953 and dedicated a year later, President Dwight D. Eisenhower called the church "a splendid addition to the religious life of the Capital city." At the time it was built, the cost totaled $640,000.

# THE CADY LEE MANSION (LUCINDA CADY HOUSE)

7064 Eastern Avenue NW
Approximate distance to Metro: 0.5 mile

This is one of the most lavish single-family homes in Takoma Park. It was designed by D.C.-based architect Leon Dessez, the same architect behind the Admiral's House at the Naval Observatory. When it was constructed in 1887, it was one of the largest structures built in Takoma Park, which had only recently been developed by Benjamin F. Gilbert in November 1883.

Inside, there are twelve-foot-high ceilings, ornate mantels, carved woodwork and a Tiffany-style stained-glass window. To save this structure from demolition, this three-story Queen Anne residence was listed in the National Register of Historic Places in 1975 and later purchased by nonprofit Forum for Youth Investment in 2002.

The current name, the Cady Lee Mansion, reflects the building's ownership by Lucinda Cady and her daughter, Mary Lee.

# ROSCOE THE ROOSTER MEMORIAL STATUE

6927 Laurel Avenue
Approximate distance to Metro: 0.5 mile

For ten years, one rooster ruled the roost in Takoma Park, Maryland. Starting in 1989, Roscoe the rooster became somewhat of a town mascot, roaming the streets freely, not owned by anyone. He was also a bit of an outlaw, constantly avoiding the clutches of animal control officials.

There is no certainty as to where exactly Roscoe came from, but there are theories; perhaps he was an escapee from a cockfighting ring or maybe an illegal henhouse in a resident's yard. Still, it's up in the air.

This bird's final year of life was 1999 when he fell victim to a hit and run. Thereafter, the community came together to commission artist Normon Greene to create a life-sized bronze statue in the animal's likeness. That statue was installed a year later. If a statue wasn't enough, there was also a memorial service for the bird with thirty or so mourners. A eulogy published at the time by *Takoma Voice* reads, "With each crow, he reconnected us, however briefly, to a world more sane and simple."

# BOUNDARY STONE

6980 Maple Avenue
Approximate distance to Metro: 0.5 mile

Near the intersection of Maple and Carroll Avenues, there sits a stone so historic that it has its own cage to protect it from theft or damage. This boundary stone dates all the way back to 1792, making it one of the oldest monuments in the country. The history behind this stone is that Major Andrew Ellicott received a letter from Secretary of State Thomas Jefferson to establish the boundary lines of the nation's capital. He did so by surveying ten-mile stretches and placing granite boulders to mark each mile along the route. In total, there were forty boundary stones placed. Over the years, two have been replaced and two are missing.

When visiting this monument, be sure to place one foot on either side of its path; those who do will be able to have both legs in two states at once.

# 24

# Silver Spring

## SILVER SPRING BALTIMORE AND OHIO RAILROAD STATION

### 8100 Georgia Avenue
### Approximate distance to Metro: 0.5 miles

Since this station was constructed in 1945, it has experienced very few alterations. The complex includes a main station, smaller waiting station and underground pedestrian tunnel. Until 1997, it was used as a passenger ticketing facility for long distance and/or commuter railroad travel. Operations ceased when an automobile damaged the front façade.

According to the application to the National Register of Historic Places, "The station…represents the evolution of Silver Spring from a small, country town centered around the railroad depot to a major suburban transportation, retail and residential center." The station has also been used for footage in minor films and commercials.

The station is owned and operated by nonprofit preservation organization Montgomery Preservation, Inc.

# AFI SILVER THEATRE AND CULTURAL CENTER

8633 Colesville Road
Approximate distance to Metro: 0.3 miles

When this theater reopened in 2003, the *Washington Post* believed that this was the start of Silver Spring eventually becoming one of the area's most significant cultural centers. To save this historic space, the American Film Institute (AFI) and Montgomery County invested $20 million on the building's renovation, led by architecture firm Gensler.

The three-screen movie theater complex originally opened in 1938 as the Silver Theatre. The architect behind the art moderne cinema house was John Eberson. By 1985, the failing theater was boarded up and it remained vacant until its reopening in 2003. Thanks to preservationists, led by the Art Deco Society of Washington, the building was saved from demolition and continues to be an arts destination in the D.C. area.

One of the most famous visitors to this site is actor and director Clint Eastwood.

# SLIGO CREEK TRAIL

Approximate distance to Metro: 1.5 miles

If in search of a space in Montgomery County for getting active and staying fit, this roughly ten-mile trail is perfect for just that. Named after the adjacent Sligo Creek, this hard-surface trail is one of the oldest in the country. Designated a National Recreation Trail in 2006, this is also the heaviest-used facility in the steam valley park. Alongside this trail are nine parks.

# 25

# Forest Glen

## NATIONAL MUSEUM OF HEALTH AND MEDICINE

2500 Linden Lane
Approximate distance to Metro: 1.5 miles

The nation's military medical heritage is documented in this museum with artifacts like the bullet that killed President Abraham Lincoln, Paul Revere's dental tools and the amputated right leg of Union major general Daniel Sickles.

This museum was originally founded in 1862 as the Army Medical Museum by U.S. Army surgeon general William A. Hammond. At the time, the *New York Times* reported that the museum was for "whatever is suitable to illustrate military medicine and surgery," including a series to illustrate the diseases, injuries and surgical afflictions of soldiers.

The museum got its current name in 1869. Its original location was demolished in 1969, to be replaced by the construction of the Hirshhorn

Museum. The museum relocated to the Walter Reed Army Medical Center before relocating once again in 2011 to its present site at the army's Forest Glen Annex.

Significant contributions to this museum were made by Dr. Daniel S. Lamb, who contributed over 1,500 specimens to the museum and later went on to develop Howard University's anatomy program.

# NATIONAL PARK SEMINARY

9615 Dewitt Drive
Approximate distance to Metro: 1.2 miles

With over 120 years of history, this development has undergone many name changes and new uses with a flurry of varying architectural styles dotted throughout the site. This weird and wonderful location offers a Japanese pagoda, Dutch windmill, Italian villa, English castle with a drawbridge and Swiss chalet. There are also sorority houses, each in a different architectural style.

Originally, the land was a wooden glen and tobacco plantation, but in 1887, a fancy summer vacation retreat was formed, called Ye Forest Inne. This hotel was designed by architect Thomas Franklin Schneider, the same architect behind the Cairo Condominiums. Unfortunately, the hotel did not succeed financially and ended up closing in 1892. Two years later, the site became a private girls' school, open until 1942. In the later years, it was known as National Park College.

Thanks to the War Powers Act, the school was sold to the Walter Reed Army Hospital, which used the seminary as a rehabilitation and convalescent center and living quarters for soldiers. The U.S. Army officially stopped using the property in 1977 but owned it until 2004.

At that point, a development team led by the Wisconsin-based Alexander Company created a plan to save the vandalized, neglected site, which was listed as a national historic district in 1972. The seminary was redeveloped into a residential neighborhood with condominiums, apartments and single-family homes.

# 26

# Wheaton

## WHEATON REGIONAL PARK

2000 Shorefield Road
Approximate distance to Metro: 1.5 miles

Named after Union General Frank Wheaton, this 536-acre park is perfect for those looking for places to get active. There are eleven miles of paved and natural-surface trails, a lake for fishing, picnicking areas and a playground with slides, swings and a sand castle. As an added bonus, there are also six outdoor tennis courts, an ice arena, a carousel dating back to 1915 and a replica of an 1863 C.P. Huntington engine train.

# 27

# Glenmont

## OAKLEY CABIN AFRICAN AMERICAN MUSEUM AND PARK

3610 Brookeville Road
Approximate distance to Metro: 10 miles

Learn about the African American experience at this house museum. This log cabin dates back to the 1820s when more than a dozen slaves once lived in the house at a time. When this was used as slave quarters, it was located on Oakley Farm, part of Revolutionary War colonel Richard Brooke's large land tract. The cabin remained a residence until 1976. In 1988, an arson fire terrorized the property before it was later restored by Hank Handler of Oak Grove Restoration, Inc.

The house museum now showcases nineteenth-century tools and artifacts excavated from the park's grounds.

## NATIONAL CAPITAL TROLLEY MUSEUM

1313 Bonifant Road
Approximate distance to Metro: 4 miles

Here, the public is able to learn about streetcars through rotating exhibits as well as interactive displays and a mile-long demonstration railway. The National Capital Trolley Museum (NCTM) features a total of eighteen streetcars from both D.C. and from other international cities, including Berlin, Dusseldorf, Toronto and Philadelphia. There is also a model layout of the D.C. streetscape available from the 1930s.

Three years before Washington, D.C., ceased streetcar operations in 1962, the museum was founded in Robert E. Lee Park at Lake Roland in Baltimore, Maryland. The NCTM officially opened in 1969 after relocating to its present site on Montgomery County parkland in Colesville, Maryland, in 1966.

Eight historic streetcars in the museum's collection were damaged in a fire in September 2003. The cost of the fire damage is estimated around $10 million, though staff members have described the lost streetcars as priceless.

The museum eventually reopened in three new buildings in January 2010 due to the construction of the Intercounty Connector (ICC), otherwise known as Maryland Route 200, which connects Gaithersburg and Laurel in Maryland.

## BROOKSIDE GARDENS

1800 Glenallan Avenue
Approximate distance to Metro: 1.2 miles

Smell the roses (and many other flowers and plants) at this fifty-acre landscape. There are more than ten distinct gardens here with spaces for herbs, shrubs, perennials, ponds, butterflies and a Japanese teahouse. In 2005, a space called Reflection Terrace opened, established to remember the ten individuals who passed away due to a series of shootings in Washington, D.C., by John Allen Muhammad and Lee Boyd Malvo in 2002.

There are also two conservatories and a horticultural reference library. To further cultivate a love of plants in Montgomery County, this venue offers classes on gardening and horticulture.

Brookside Gardens first opened in 1969, developed under the direction of horticulturist Carl Han and landscape architect Hans E. Hanses.

# Part II

# The Blue Line

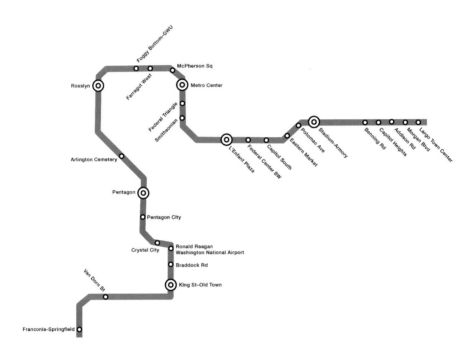

## HIGHLIGHTS ON THE BLUE LINE:

> The White House at Farragut West
> The Lincoln Memorial at Smithsonian
> The Washington Monument at Smithsonian
> The Jefferson Memorial at Smithsonian
> The Library of Congress at Capitol South
> Eastern Market at Eastern Market
> RFK Stadium at Stadium-Armory

# 1

# Franconia-Springfield

## FRANCONIA MUSEUM

6121 Franconia Road
Approximate distance to Metro: 2.5 miles

At one point, Franconia Road was a rural location, the birthplace of the first Virginia governor from Northern Virginia. Purchased in 1859 by Alexandria merchant and businessman William Fowle, 191 acres of the area were formerly known as Frankhonia Farm. This history and more are celebrated with the Franconia Museum.

The goals of this museum include promoting the heritage of the Franconia area and providing educational opportunities for students. Throughout the year, the museum does exhibits at local libraries.

## LAUREL GROVE COLORED SCHOOL MUSEUM

6840 Beulah Street
Approximate distance to Metro: 1.5 miles

In the early 1880s, freed slaves constructed this one-room schoolhouse in order for it to serve the African American community, which it did until 1932. At the time, it was known as the Laurel Grove Colored School. By

1999, plans were solidified to restore the schoolhouse in order to celebrate the school's history and reopen the property as a "living museum" and teaching center.

Still, the school survives as the only remaining African American schoolhouse in Northern Virginia.

## 2

# Van Dorn Street

## ARMISTEAD BOOTHE PARK

520 Cameron Station Boulevard
Approximate distance to Metro: 1.2 miles

Armistead Booth is known for being a Virginia Democratic legislator who represented Alexandria and was later a state senator from 1955 through 1964. During his time in office, he promoted integration of Virginia's public schools. He also served as a special assistant in the United States Office of the Attorney General from 1934 to 1936 and as city attorney of Alexandria from 1938 to 1943.

In June 2000, the Alexandria City Council approved the naming of the park at the former U.S. Army base at Cameron Station. In honor of Booth, this approximately eleven-acre park offers walking and biking trails, a picnic pavilion and a playground. There are also athletic fields, a basketball court, tennis courts and restrooms.

# 3

# King Street–Old Town

## STABLER-LEADBEATER APOTHECARY MUSEUM

105–107 South Fairfax Street
Approximate distance to Metro: 1 mile

This museum, opened in 1939, still stands with remnants of the site's original contents and archives intact. Originally, the building housed a family business that was founded in 1792 and operated at this location from 1805 to 1933. It was Alexandria, Virginia's oldest continuously run business that combined retailing, wholesaling and manufacturing. Some of its customers have been very well known, such as Martha Washington and Robert E. Lee.

When in operation, the business sold medical equipment, hand-blown glass and herbal botanicals. The business was founded by Quaker and businessman Edward Stabler, who apprenticed in the apothecary business in Leesburg, Virginia. After his death in 1831, he left the business to his son, William. His brother-in-law, John Leadbeater, eventually acquired the business in 1852. In its heyday, during the mid-1860s, the business supplied nearly five hundred pharmacies throughout the region. The museum still houses many of the original journals, letters, diaries, prescriptions, ledgers, orders and invoices that were formed here.

In an auction on July 1933, Baltimore-based ice cream merchant L. Manuel Hendler purchased the majority of the business's contents and archives. The Landmarks Society of Alexandria acquired the site a year later, and Hendler donated the contents and archives to the society thereafter. The building was restored to its original eighteenth-century appearance by architect Thomas Tileston Waterman.

In November 2006, the Landmarks Society of Alexandria donated the museum and its items to the City of Alexandria.

# ATHENAEUM

201 Prince Street
Approximate distance to Metro: 1 mile

What was once a facility for wounded Union soldiers during the Civil War is now an art gallery. This Greek Revival–style building was built circa 1851, originally used as the home of the Bank of the Old Dominion. Once the Civil War began, Federal troops commandeered the building and used it as the chief commissary office of the U.S. commissary quartermaster. It was later reused as the First Virginia Bank before Leadbeater and Sons purchased the building in 1907 for its wholesale pharmacy business. In 1925, it was used as a house of worship by the Free Methodist Church of North America.

It wasn't until 1964 that the Northern Virginia Fine Arts Association purchased the building and then repaired and restored it. Still, it is used as an arts space, exhibiting local artists in solo, group and theme-based shows. The building is part of the Virginia Trust and in the National Register of Historic Places.

# TORPEDO FACTORY ART CENTER

105 North Union Street
Approximate distance to Metro: 1.3 miles

This arts center was originally a naval munitions factory whose construction began in November 1918, the day after Armistice Day, the end of World War I. Before becoming munitions storage, the factory constructed torpedoes for five years and was known as the U.S. Naval Torpedo Station. By 1945, the space was used as storage for things such as congressional documents, Nazi trial records and dinosaur bones and other artifacts from the Smithsonian Institution. The City of Alexandria officially purchased the building in 1969.

It wasn't until 1974 that renovations began to convert the building into art studios, galleries and classrooms. It formally reopened as the Torpedo Factory Art Center in 1983. The building now houses over 165 artists who work, exhibit and sell their artworks here with over half a million visitors per year.

## GADSBY'S TAVERN MUSEUM

134 North Royal Street
Approximate distance to Metro: 1 mile

Take a glance into Alexandria, Virginia's past with this eighteenth-century museum. This site consists of two buildings, a circa 1785–built tavern and a 1792-constructed hotel, both named after Englishman John Gadsby. Gadsby operated at the site from 1796 to 1808. When it was in use as a tavern and hotel, it served as a center of political, business and social life in early Alexandria. Prominent patrons have included John Adams, Thomas Jefferson, James Madison, James Monroe and the Marquis de Lafayette. Even George Washington walked these halls, having twice attended the annual Birthnight Ball held in his honor at the tavern.

With period furnishings, tours and informational programs, Gadsby's Tavern Museum offers a space for the public to learn about the history, decorative arts, food, clothing and customs of eighteenth-century America.

## GEORGE WASHINGTON MASONIC NATIONAL MEMORIAL

101 Callahan Drive
Approximate distance to Metro: 0.3 miles

Standing atop Shooter's Hill (also known as Shuter's Hill) at an elevation just over 100 feet, this 333-foot-tall memorial can be seen from the far reaches of the D.C. region. This concrete and granite Masonic building and memorial is dedicated to George Washington and is known as one of the most architecturally significant projects to honor Washington and one of the boldest efforts by a private entity to memorialize him. It is designated a National Historic Landmark and is listed in the National Register of Historic Places.

To create the building, the Freemasons established the George Washington Masonic National Memorial Association, whose first official meeting was in 1911. Construction didn't begin until 1922. While the building was dedicated in 1932, it was not fully complete until 1973, according to the development's National Register of Historic Places nomination form. Financing issues were one reason why construction went on for so long.

This site was the final choice for the George Washington Masonic National Memorial due to it being home to a Masonic lodge that Washington helped to charter. Alexandria, Virginia, was also the town where Washington attended church and maintained a business office. There are also some who believe that the site was once selected by Thomas Jefferson as a possible location for the planned U.S. Capitol, but this might be a local myth. Despite this, the ties to Jefferson were not refuted during the memorial's fundraising and construction.

The architecture firm behind the project was New York–based Helmle & Corbett, with Harvey Wiley Corbett as the principal architect.

## ALEXANDRIA AFRICAN AMERICAN HERITAGE PARK

309 Holland Lane
Approximate distance to Metro: 0.3 miles

With the intention to acknowledge that Alexandria, Virginia, has a strong African American presence and history, this approximately eight-acre park opened in 1995. The bronze sculptures found here, titled *Truths that Rise from the Roots Remembered*, were designed by African American artist Jerome Meadows. As a focal point to the park, there are three stylized bronze trees that list the names of African American civic leaders, doctors, lawyers, printers, schools and churches, as well as those who participated in the Alexandria library sit-in of 1939.

Inside the park, there is also a one-acre, nineteenth-century African American cemetery with more than twenty burials, only six of which have identified headstones in their original locations.

The landscape architecture firm EDAW was behind the design of the park.

# CONTRABANDS AND FREEDMEN CEMETERY MEMORIAL

1001 South Washington Street
Approximate distance to Metro: 1.5 miles

From 1864 through 1869, this cemetery was the burial place for approximately 1,800 freed African American slaves, or "contrabands," and black Union soldiers who fled to Alexandria, Virginia, to escape bondage during the Civil War. By 1865, the cemetery's black veterans were moved to the Alexandria National Cemetery. The last burial at this burial ground was in January 1869.

For approximately fifty years, starting in 1948, this cemetery was unmarked on city maps of Alexandria. It wasn't until 1996 when a remote sensing survey was conducted on the land that it was revealed that the site was formerly a Civil War–era African American burial ground. One year later, the nonprofit Friends of Freedmen's Cemetery was formed in order to preserve the history of the site. After a design competition in 2008, the city awarded local architect C.J. Howard the task of creating the memorial that has stood here since it was dedicated in 2014. Stones throughout the site indicate the locations of approximately 540 graves that archaeologists have identified.

Since 2015, the cemetery has been included in the National Underground Railroad Network to Freedom.

# FREEDOM HOUSE MUSEUM (FRANKLIN AND ARMFIELD OFFICE)

1315 Duke Street
Approximate distance to Metro: 0.4 miles

This historic building is a National Historic Landmark, once housing one of the largest, most infamous slave trading companies in the pre–Civil War United States, known as Franklin and Armfield. Located in the basement level of the building is the Freedom House Museum, which hopes to serve as a reminder of slavery by displaying original artifacts and first-person narratives told through video and exhibits. The museum was founded by the Northern Virginia Urban League, which purchased the property in 1996.

## FRIENDSHIP FIREHOUSE MUSEUM

107 South Alfred Street
Approximate distance to Metro: 0.7 miles

This museum preserves the history of the Friendship Fire Company, the first volunteer fire company in Alexandria, Virginia. The fire company was established in 1774 with this building constructed in 1855. By 1992, the City of Alexandria had restored the structure. Today, it houses historic firefighting equipment and exhibits.

## LLOYD HOUSE

220 North Washington Street
Approximate distance to Metro: 1 mile

This two-story, rectangular brick building serves as one of only five buildings of the Georgian style remaining in the city. It was constructed circa 1796, built by Alexandria resident John Wise, and only portions of the original interior remain. Currently, the building serves as the administrative headquarters for the Office of Historic Alexandria, a department of the City of Alexandria government.

In order to prevent the demolition of the building, the City of Alexandria purchased the Lloyd House in 1968. It was later added to the National Register of Historic Places in 1976.

## MURRAY-DICK-FAWCETT HOUSE

517 Prince Street
Approximate distance to Metro: 1 mile

This residence is one of Alexandria, Virginia's earliest homes and possibly the least altered eighteenth-century home in Northern Virginia. The timber frame and brick dwelling was constructed in three separate building campaigns, dating to circa 1772, circa 1784 and circa 1797, with two more additions sometime around 1807 and 1823. It comes with a small garden.

The name of the historic property is a reference to three past owners: Patrick Murray, Dr. Elisha Cullen Dick and Mary Goulding Hooff Fawcett.

In 2017, the City of Alexandria purchased the Murray-Dick-Fawcett House with plans to use it as an educational center, focused on life in the eighteenth and nineteenth centuries.

## THE SPITE HOUSE (HOLLENSBURY HOUSE)

523 Queen Street
Approximate distance to Metro: 1 mile

Homeowners can be pretty finicky people, and this property proves that. In 1830, the original owner, John Hollensbury, built this 7-foot-wide, 25-foot-deep property in order to ensure that people and horse-drawn carriages wouldn't use the alleyway adjacent to his home. The teeny property spans a total of 325 square feet.

While small, it has certainly drawn a lot of attention, not just from locals but the entire nation. The Spite House has been featured in the *New York Times* and on *The Oprah Winfrey Show*.

## THE LYCEUM

201 South Washington Street
Approximate distance to Metro: 0.8 miles

Originally when this Greek Revival two-story brick structure was constructed between 1837 and 1839, it was to be used as a grand hall for lectures, scientific experiments and reading. Benjamin Hallowell founded the Lyceum in 1834 as a society for scholarly activity. Originally, meetings were in Hallowell's school, but they were relocated to this building, which also became the first home for the Alexandria Library Company, founded in 1749 as the city's first organization for the advancement of learning.

Once the Civil War began, all Lyceum activities were disrupted as the building became a hospital facility for the Union army. The Lyceum dissolved after the war ended, and the building was eventually used as a private residence and later as a commercial office. In 1974, the structure was restored and converted to the nation's first bicentennial center. It didn't open as the city's history museum until 1985. Still to this day, the Lyceum offers a focus on the culture of Alexandria, Virginia, and the surrounding Northern Virginia area with exhibitions, public programs and facility rentals.

The building was listed in the National Register of Historic Places in 1969.

## ALEXANDRIA NATIONAL CEMETERY (SOLDIERS' CEMETERY)

1450 Wilkes Street
Approximate distance to Metro: 0.7 miles

In 1862, this five-and-a-half-acre burial ground was established for Union soldiers. Here, visitors can find over four thousand graves, all marked and with rectangular white marble stone markers. Four who are buried here were Quartermaster Corps employees who drowned in the Rappahannock River on April 24, 1865, while in pursuit of Abraham Lincoln's assassin, John Wilkes Booth. The cemetery did not officially close until May 1967.

Originally, this site was known as the Soldiers' Cemetery, but it was renamed the Alexandria National Cemetery in 1936. The superintendent's lodge found here was built in 1887, designed by U.S. Army quartermaster general Montgomery C. Meigs, the same designer of the National Building Museum, otherwise known as the Pension Building. This structure was built over the former walls of a similar lodge destroyed by a fire approximately ten years earlier. Still, all of the original windows and door moldings of this building are in place, though the floors were replaced and fireplaces removed in 1952. In 1887, a 522-square-foot brick Italianate building was constructed nearby and later connected to the lodge by a wing for the dining room in 1927.

One additional historic element of this area is that it houses the Alexandria Bicentennial Tree, one of Alexandria's oldest trees. It dates back approximately two hundred years and is located centrally in the cemetery.

The Alexandria National Cemetery was officially added to the National Register of Historic Places in 1995.

# CHRIST CHURCH

118 North Washington Street
Approximate distance to Metro: 1 mile

This little-altered church has been visited by numerous U.S. presidents and foreign dignitaries, including George Washington, Franklin D. Roosevelt, Winston Churchill, Ronald Reagan, Gerald Ford, Harry Truman and George W. Bush. Robert E. Lee is also said to have visited.

Designed by Colonel James Wren, this house of worship was completed in 1773. It has experienced multiple additions and restorations, including the construction of a tower at the west end. The rectangular, two-story brick church still comes with its original and unaltered walls, windows, doors and exterior woodwork.

In 1970, Christ Church was declared a National Historic Landmark and added to the National Register of Historic Places.

# WOODLAWN AND POPE-LEIGHEY HOUSE

9000 Richmond Highway
Approximate distance to Metro: 10 miles

It might take a hop, skip and a jump to get to this historic home, but it's worth it for those who have a passion for all things related to Frank Lloyd Wright. This home, dating back to 1939, is the only Wright-designed property open to visitors in the D.C. area. Originally, the home was located in Falls Church, Virginia, but it was relocated in the 1960s to avoid demolition when Interstate 66 expanded. The first owner was Loren Pope, the copy editor of D.C.'s *Evening Star* newspaper.

The two-bedroom home is fairly small, measuring 1,200 square feet, which was an intentional choice in order to keep the building costs low. Despite this, it feels large when walking inside, thanks to the high ceilings, open floor plan and walls of windows. The wooden property used locally sourced materials and custom-built furniture. It was dedicated a National Trust Historic Site in 1965.

Currently, the home is managed by the National Trust for Historic Preservation. It underwent a $13,000 restoration that was completed by the summer of 2015.

Wright is an American architect who is most known for the iconic Fallingwater building in Pennsylvania, but he designed hundreds of buildings across the nation. This one in particular is an example of one of Wright's Usonian homes, which were inexpensive buildings for middle-income homeowners.

# 4

# Braddock Road

## ALEXANDRIA BLACK HISTORY MUSEUM
## (ROBERT ROBINSON LIBRARY)

902 Wythe Street
Approximate distance to Metro: 0.4 miles

In 1939, five young African American men staged a sit-in at the whites-only Alexandria Library. This event successfully led to the formation of the Robert Robinson Library. After desegregation in the early 1960s, the building was used for community service programs before later reopening as a museum. With two exhibition galleries as well as artifact storage and offices, the Alexandria Black History Museum is focused on documenting the local and national history of black America.

This museum operates the nearby Alexandria African American Heritage Park. Next door to the museum is the Watson Reading Room, opened in October 1995. This non-circulating reading room has over three thousand holdings on African American life and culture, from books to dissertations and theses to video and audio.

# FORT WARD MUSEUM AND HISTORIC SITE

4301 West Braddock Road
Approximate distance to Metro: 3.1 miles

Alexandria, Virginia, endured the longest military occupation by Union troops of any U.S. town during the Civil War, spanning four years from 1861 to 1865. During this time, Fort Ward was created as the fifth-largest fort in the fort system built to protect Washington, D.C. At the time, it spanned five acres and never came under Confederate attack. It was dismantled in November 1865 and named after James Harmon Ward, the first Union naval officer to die in the war.

To date, approximately 90 percent of the fort's earthwork walls are preserved. The Northwest Bastion has also been restored and reconstructed to its original condition. The museum offers self-guided tours through exhibits on Civil War topics.

# 5

# Ronald Reagan Washington National Airport

## RONALD REAGAN WASHINGTON NATIONAL AIRPORT

2401 South Smith Boulevard
Approximate distance to Metro: 0 miles

The opening of this airport was more than just the signaling of a new mode of transportation in the D.C. area; it was significant as a milestone in American aviation technology and as a symbol of the broad pattern of New Deal government initiatives. The Ronald Reagan Washington National Airport was the first federally constructed commercial airport in the country designed for civilian flights.

Architectural plans for the airport were first approved in 1939 by President Franklin D. Roosevelt, who endorsed the idea of building the world's most modern "aerodrome" in the D.C. area. Once the airport opened in 1941, the *New York Times* wrote positively of the new development, describing it as "a peak of engineering achievement."

The builder behind the project was John McShain, whose company built or was the prime contractor for structures that included the Pentagon, the Thomas Jefferson Memorial and the John F. Kennedy Center for the Performing Arts. He also was behind the renovations of the White House under President Harry Truman's administration.

Originally, the airport was simply known as Washington National Airport or its industry abbreviation, DCA. In February 1998, President Bill Clinton signed legislation renaming the airport Ronald Reagan Washington National Airport. At the time, Air Traffic Controllers Association executive

A HISTORY & GUIDE

vice president Randy Schwitz said that he was "dumbfounded" when he heard there was consideration to rename the airport after Reagan. "Ronald Reagan never did anything for aviation in this country," he said in the *Day*. Despite this and despite neither Reagan nor his family lobbying for the renaming, Nancy Reagan described the legislation as "a wonderful gift."

In early 2018, construction began on a $1 billion revitalization project for a new concourse for short-hop flights and fourteen new security screening areas. With full completion expected around 2021, the project will also feature new security checkpoint structures, ticketing kiosks, concession space and changes to National Hall, the main glass-enclosed walkway on the concourse level. This is the first major construction project at the airport since Concourses B and C opened in July 1997, designed by César Pelli, who once worked for Finnish-American architect Eero Saarinen.

Each year, this airport serves approximately twenty-four million passengers.

## GRAVELLY POINT

Approximate distance to Metro: 1.2 miles

For great views of the Washington, D.C. skyline, head to this grassy knoll. This popular green space is perfect for picnics and feeling like you're on the edge of the nearby airport's runway since airplanes fly by so low.

In an article in the *Washington Post*, one passerby described being here as "a real adrenaline pumper" because of how loud the airplanes can be.

Other activities possible here include fishing, bicycling—almost anything except kite flying.

## LONG BRIDGE PARK

475 Long Bridge Drive
Approximate distance to Metro: 2 miles

Built atop an abandoned brownfield in the fall of 2011, this park offers more than thirty acres of recreation and open space. With views of the

THE BLUE LINE | 129

Washington, D.C. monuments, Long Bridge Park features three full-size, multi-sport athletic fields that Marymount University helped pay for and uses. There are also walkways and a three-quarter-acre rain garden that directs runoff to the park's planted garden. One final additional highlight to this park is *Wave Arbor*, a two-part, kinetic, wind-activated sculpture by artist Doug Hollis.

The design of the park was led by a group that consisted of Hughes Group Architects, Hargreaves Associates with LSG and CH2M HILL.

# 6

# Crystal City

## SIGNATURE THEATER

4200 Campbell Avenue
Approximate distance to Metro: 3 miles

 In the Village at Shirlington community, this Tony Award–winning theater is worth a visit for those who are die-hard arts lovers. Here, the theater focuses on contemporary musicals and plays and has produced fifty world-premiere works, including nineteen new musical commissions. Founded in 1989, the Signature Theatre is home to what the venue claims to be the largest musical theater commissioning project in the nation, known as the American Musical Voices Project. This program consists of musical theater composer grants and musical theater leadership awards.

This $16 million, two-theater venue was completed in January 2007 and reaches more than 100,000 people annually. The founders of this theater are graphic designer and performer Eric Schaeffer and actor Donna Migliaccio.

7

# Pentagon City

## U.S. AIR FORCE MEMORIAL

1 Air Force Memorial Drive
Approximate distance to Metro: 1.1 miles

For those who serve in the U.S. Air Force, this memorial was dedicated on October 2006 with three stainless steel spires, the tallest of which reaches 270 feet high. The three spires are meant to evoke the image of the "bomb burst" maneuver performed by the U.S. Air Force Thunderbird Demonstration Team. Typically, the "bomb burst" maneuver features four contrails, but the absent fourth suggests the missing man formation traditionally used at air force funeral fly-overs. Beneath the spires is

the air force star, which serves as the rank insignia of every member of the air force.

The designer of this memorial is American architect James Ingo Freed, who is also known for having designed the Ronald Reagan Building and International Trade Center as well as the U.S. Holocaust Memorial Museum.

# 8

# Pentagon

## THE PENTAGON

1400 Defense Pentagon
Approximate distance to Metro: 0 miles

During President Franklin D. Roosevelt's term, the first headquarters designed and constructed for the U.S. Department of Defense was deemed too small. It was built in Washington, D.C.'s Foggy Bottom neighborhood, and eventually the department was scattered across seventeen apartment buildings, warehouses, private homes and garages. Foggy Bottom is currently home to the U.S. State Department.

To ease pressure for the growing department, Brigadier General Brehon Burke Somervell, the head of the army's Construction Division, tasked Lieutenant Colonel Hugh J. Casey, the chief of the design section, with creating a headquarters in Arlington, Virginia, large enough for forty thousand workers with parking for ten thousand cars. It also needed to be short because a tall building would obstruct views of Washington, D.C., and use up too much steel, a resource urgently needed for weapons and battleships. The original site chosen caused problems, though. The only way to make a building of that magnitude fit the shape of the land would be to shape it with five sides—a pentagon. This shape was useful, not only to fit the site but also because, similarly to a circle, it would create shorter walking distances within the building. Architects at the time calculated that it would be 30 to 50 percent less than in a rectangle. Roosevelt was also very approving of the shape, quoted as saying, "I like it because nothing like it has ever been done that way before."

The Pentagon project officially launched in July 1941 with Roosevelt approving it later that year. Groundbreaking officially began in September 1941. But there was still one last change that had to happen before any shovels could hit the ground. Roosevelt ended up altering the site to a location known as Hell's Bottom. One of the reasons why he relocated the project was that it had too prominent of a position overlooking the National Mall from the Virginia side of the Potomac River. With hopes to finish construction within a year, there wasn't time to alter the design of the building, so the pentagon shape remained.

The first employees moved into the Pentagon in April 1942 with the building completed by February 1943. At the time, it was the largest office building in the world, and it continues to be one of the largest. The building measures over six million square feet of space with over seventeen miles of corridors and a five-acre central plaza. It is composed of five reinforced concrete concentric buildings with the outermost ring spanning a full mile around. The area covered by the building is twenty-nine acres, large enough to accommodate five U.S. Capitol buildings, while there is enough parking to span sixty-seven acres. By 1992, the structure was proclaimed a National Historic Landmark.

Work was not yet over. In October 1994, Congress approved more than $1 billion for the renovation of the building. Then tragedy hit on September 11, 2001, when a hijacked Boeing 757 struck the building thirty yards wide and ten yards deep, puncturing three outer rings. One month later, a $501 million repair and renovation initiative, dubbed the Phoenix Project, began. It was completed in February 2003 at a cost of approximately $5 billion with sweeping security upgrades.

To memorialize the 184 people who were killed on 9/11, 184 illuminated benches were installed outside the Pentagon on September 11, 2008.

# 9

# Arlington Cemetery

## ARLINGTON HOUSE (THE ROBERT E. LEE MEMORIAL, THE CUSTIS-LEE MANSION)

700 George Washington Memorial Parkway
Approximate distance to Metro: 0.8 miles

This is the most visited historic house museum in the National Park Service system, clocking in over 650,000 visitors per year. It was constructed in 1802 by George Washington Parke Custis, an adopted son of President George Washington, as a memorial to Washington. The estate, designed by architect George Hadfield, overlooks Washington, D.C., and has been cited as one of the earliest examples of Greek Revival architecture in the nation. An addition to the structure was constructed in 1818.

Starting in 1831, Custis's daughter, Mary Randolph Custis, lived in the residence with her husband, Robert E. Lee. Thirty years later, the Union army commandeered the house and its grounds before the U.S. government took possession of the estate under an Executive Order issued by President Abraham Lincoln in 1863. The Lee family was able to take back their property in 1882 after winning a case with the Supreme Court. Later, the property was sold back to the government for the price of $150,000.

In 1863, the government established Freedman's Village at the Arlington House site, which provided housing, education, employment training and medical care to slaves transitioning to freedom. It officially closed in 1900.

In 2014, philanthropist David M. Rubenstein provided a $12.35 million donation to the National Park Service to restore and improve access to the Arlington House. The property now serves as the nation's memorial to Robert E. Lee. It is listed in the National Register of Historic Places.

# ARLINGTON NATIONAL CEMETERY

1 Memorial Avenue
Approximate distance to Metro: 0 miles

The Arlington National Cemetery is one of only two cemeteries classified as Army National Military Cemeteries in the nation. It serves as the final resting place of more than 400,000 military veterans, both well known and unknown. It was first established as a military cemetery in 1864 on the estate of the Custis and Lee family. The design is attributed to army quartermaster general Montgomery C. Meigs, who is buried at this site and also known for having designed the National Building Museum, otherwise known as the Pension Building. One reason for choosing this site was in order to take advantage of the existing roadways and other infrastructure already in place.

The cemetery currently spans approximately 625 acres of land, roughly the size of 472 football fields. Some of the most well-known figures buried here include National Geographic Society founder Adolphus W. Greely, Supreme Court justice Thurgood Marshall and Senator and presidential candidate Robert F. Kennedy. Pierre Charles L'Enfant, the architect and designer of Washington, D.C., is also buried here, along with Presidents William Howard Taft and John F. Kennedy with his wife, Jacqueline Kennedy Onassis.

More than three million visitors come to the Arlington National Cemetery every year. The cemetery was listed in the National Register of Historic Places in April 2014.

# TOMB OF THE UNKNOWN SOLDIER

Approximate distance to Metro: 1 mile

As a memorial to unidentified U.S. soldiers who died while serving in World War I, World War II, the Korean War or the Vietnam War, this tomb was established in 1921 and completed in 1932. It was designed by New York–based architect Lorimer Rich and New York–based sculptor Thomas Hudson Jones. The structure entails a white marble tomb with a flat-faced form and Neoclassical pilasters set into the surface. On the east panel, facing

A HISTORY & GUIDE

Washington, D.C., there are three Greek figures representing Peace, Victory and Valor. On the sides, there are six wreaths, which signify the six major campaigns of World War I.

This site is guarded twenty-four hours a day.

## WOMEN IN MILITARY SERVICE FOR AMERICA MEMORIAL

Approximate distance to Metro: 0.3 miles

The site where this memorial was located was originally known as the Hemicycle, and at one point, it was in serious disrepair, with overgrown landscaping. The thirty-foot-high, Neoclassical, semicircular structure served as the ceremonial entrance of Arlington National Cemetery since it was dedicated in April 1932. Its diameter spans 226 feet, while the structure covers over four acres. Once the 1980s rolled by, the Hemicycle was rarely visited and barely ever maintained. When plans arose in 1985 for a memorial for women who have served in the U.S. Armed Forces, this site was chosen. After a design competition won by New York–based architects Marion Weiss and Michael Manfredi, groundbreaking occurred in June 1995 with a dedication in October 1997.

Part of the reason why there were delays in the design process was that the architects' first design did not "receive a fair hearing," according to Brigadier General Wilma Vaught, as the design was leaked to the *Washington Post* early and received opposition from the National Park Service. The original plan was to build ten thirty-nine-foot-tall, translucent, inner-lit glass pylons on the terrace atop the Hemicycle. The final memorial did not use this design element.

Instead, the final design restored a low water feature to the central niche, removed the grass circle and created a paved plaza and circular reflecting pool. Along with an elevator, 108 horizontal thick glass panels were added, creating an arch in the back of the Hemicycle's terrace, in turn forming the skylights for the memorial. These panels contain quotes from women who have served in the military. Underground, there is an auditorium, offices and an exhibition hall.

When the memorial opened, the *Washington Post* described it as a "resounding success," adding, "aesthetically, the design is a gem."

# NURSES MEMORIAL (SPIRIT OF NURSING MONUMENT)

Approximate distance to Metro: 1 mile

Erected in 1938, this ten-foot-tall marble statue depicts a military nurse overlooking the Arlington National Cemetery's graves of army, navy and air force nurses. Designed by sculptor Frances Rich, the statue originally honored the nurses who served in the U.S. Armed Forces in World War I with an inscription that simply read "Army and Navy Nurses."

In 1971, thanks to the work of U.S. Navy captain Delores Cornelius, the deputy director of the U.S. Navy Nurse Corps, the statue was rededicated in order to expand the original intent to include all military nurses, not just those who served in World War I. A bronze plaque was installed over the existing inscription to indicate this expansion.

This memorial is sometimes called the Spirit of Nursing Monument.

# SPANISH-AMERICAN WAR MEMORIAL

Approximate distance to Metro: 1.1 miles

In 1898, the United States and Spain fought a ten-week-long conflict over Cuban independence, resulting in the deaths of approximately three hundred, not including those who lost their lives on the USS *Maine*. As a memorial to these deaths, President Theodore Roosevelt dedicated this memorial in May 1902. Standing fifty feet tall, this Corinthian column is made of Barre granite, decorated with a bronze eagle and Quincy granite sphere mounted on top. Other decorative elements include black granite spheres measuring eighteen inches in diameter; forty-four bronze stars; and four guns, two of which are Spanish cannons and two of which are U.S. naval guns.

A second bronze plaque was added to the monument when it was rededicated in October 1964.

# LADY BIRD JOHNSON PARK (COLUMBIA ISLAND)

Approximate distance to Metro: 0.8 miles

Lady Bird Johnson earned many awards during her life and during her time as first lady. She is best known for her Beautification Campaign, which sought to positively transform the nation's cities and highways. In 1968, this 121-acre site in Washington, D.C., was given a new name in honor of her, Lady Bird Johnson Park. Originally, the land was built by the U.S. Army Corps of Engineers in 1916 and was named Columbia Island. With this name change came the addition of benches, 1.2 miles of trail for biking and hiking and plantings of 1 million daffodils and 2,700 dogwood trees. The landscape architect behind the project was Edward Durell Stone Jr.

Along with offering a tranquil setting, Lady Bird Johnson Park also features two memorials, the Navy and Merchant Marine Memorial and the Lyndon Baines Johnson Memorial Grove. The Navy and Merchant Marine Memorial was designed by Harvey Wiley Corbett, sculpted by Ernesto Begni del Piatta and dedicated in October 1934. It features seven seagulls above the crest of an aluminum wave overtop a granite base. Appropriately, it is also known as simply "Waves and Gulls." It stands thirty-five feet tall and thirty feet wide and honors the sailors of the U.S. Navy and U.S. Merchant Marine who died at sea during World War I.

The Lyndon Baines Johnson Memorial Grove, of course, honors President Lyndon B. Johnson, with the monument consisting of two parts: a meadow and a Texas granite monolith surrounded by trails. This memorial was dedicated in April 1976 and designed by Meade Palmer. The sculpture was designed by Harold Vogel.

# CONFEDERATE MEMORIAL

Approximate distance to Metro: 1.3 miles

This thirty-two-foot-tall monument commemorates the soldiers of the Confederate army who died during the Civil War. Commissioned by the United Daughters of the Confederacy, the Confederate Memorial was designed by sculptor Moses Jacob Ezekiel and unveiled in June 1914 by

President Woodrow Wilson. Almost every U.S. president since Wilson has sent a wreath to the Confederate Memorial.

At the top of the bronze structure, there is a woman who is crowned with olive leaves who represents the South, her right hand holding the handles of a plow and her left hand holding a wreath, which represents the past. The left hand extends southward in acknowledgement of those who died in the Civil War. Directly below her are four urns, one for each year of the war. Below that are fourteen shields, one for each of the thirteen Confederate states and one for Maryland. The thirty-two life-sized figures near the base are all in full relief.

When the memorial was unveiled, Ezekiel told the *Washington Post*, "The intention is that it is a peace monument. Without forgetting the sacrifices and the heroism of the South, and emphasizing the fact that they were fighting for a constitutional right, and not to uphold slavery. I have attempted to have the dominant idea [be] the future and not the past, to show that the intention of the South is to rest the future on her industry and her agriculture, and let the past go, but not be forgotten."

Since it was erected, there have been criticisms aired about the monument. In August 2017, following the "Unite the Right" rally in Charlottesville, Virginia, *Smithsonian Magazine* described the Confederate Memorial as "perhaps the most egregious loyal slave monument." The *Washington Post* also published a letter from the Ezekiel family that said, "Like most such monuments, this statue intended to rewrite history to justify the Confederacy and the subsequent racist Jim Crow laws. It glorifies the fight to own human beings, and, in its portrayal of African Americans, implies their collusion. As proud as our family may be of Moses's artistic prowess, we—some 20 Ezekiels—say remove that statue. Take it out of its honored spot in Arlington National Cemetery, and put it in a museum that makes clear its oppressive history."

There are currently no official plans to remove the memorial from the Arlington National Cemetery.

# 10

# Rosslyn

## U.S. MARINE CORPS WAR MEMORIAL (IWO JIMA MEMORIAL)

Approximate distance to Metro: 0.6 miles

This seventy-eight-foot-tall memorial was dedicated by President Dwight D. Eisenhower on November 10, 1954, the 179th anniversary of the U.S. Marine Corps. It serves as a memorial to all Marines who have given their lives in defense of the United States since 1775. The image itself is based on one of the most famous incidents of World War II, which was captured in a Pulitzer Prize–winning photograph by Joe Rosenthal of the Associated Press.

The photograph was taken at Iwo Jima, an island located 660 miles south of Tokyo. On February 19, 1945, the Fourth and Fifth Marine Divisions invaded Iwo Jima after an ineffective seventy-two-hour bombardment with the intention to capture Mount Suribachi. On February 23, the troops climbed the mountain's terrain and found a small American flag there, which was later replaced by a second, larger flag in the same location. The men who are featured in the photograph are Sergeant Michael Strank, Corporal Harlon Block, Private First Class Franklin Sousley, Corporal Rene Gagnon, Corporal Ira Hayes and Corporal Harold Schultz.

Created by sculptor Felix de Weldon, the memorial is not a 1:1 reproduction of the photograph. De Weldon intentionally moved the figures closer to one another to make it more compact. To prevent distortion for viewers on the ground, the arms were also elevated, and the hands and helmets were enlarged. The figures stand thirty-two feet tall with a sixty-foot bronze flagpole with a flag that flies every day of the year.

In 2017, a multimillion-dollar project to rehabilitate the memorial began. The project entailed re-gilding the engravings on the sculpture's pedestal, cleaning and waxing the sculpture and granite base and improving lighting, landscaping and infrastructure.

Over 1.5 million visitors come to the memorial every year.

## FORT BENNETT PARK AND PALISADES TRAIL

2220 North Scott Street
Approximate distance to Metro: 1 mile

At this park, there was once a Civil War fort known as Fort Bennett. It was constructed in May 1861 and had a perimeter of 146 feet. It was built to support Fort Corcoran and protect the Virginia end of the Aqueduct Bridge. The name is meant to honor Captain Michael P. Bennett of the Twenty-Eighth New York Infantry, who supervised the fort's construction. There are no visible remains of the fort, though there is a historical marker.

In its place, visitors can find Fort Bennett Park, which offers eleven acres of open space and the Palisades Trail.

## THEODORE ROOSEVELT ISLAND (MASON'S ISLAND, ANACOSTIA ISLAND, ANALOSTAN ISLAND)

Approximate distance to Metro: 0.6 miles

With over eighty-eight acres of land, this island serves as a living monument to President Theodore Roosevelt. Visitors will find an open-air elliptical plaza designed by Eric Gugler with a bronze statue of Roosevelt by sculptor Paul Manship. The plaza includes four granite monoliths, each one inscribed with quotes from Roosevelt, and two large fountains. Over 160,000 people visit the site on an annual basis. There is no entrance fee to enter this site. While only accessible from Virginia, the land is part of Washington, D.C.

The history of this area is long and varied. It was first known as Anacostia Island and sometimes Analostan Island, named after the Algonquin-speaking American Indian tribes who inhabited the land. By 1717, George Mason III purchased the area. His family would continue to own it until 1833, and the island eventually became known as Mason's Island. Later, the land changed hands several times, at one point to former D.C. Mayor William A. Bradley. During the Civil War, Union troops occupied the island. From May 1864 through June 1865, it served as a temporary refugee camp to serve the increasing numbers of African American refugees arriving in Washington, D.C. During the Spanish-American War, the site briefly became an explosives test range. Additionally, in 1907, a New York syndicate planned to create a summer resort here styled like New York's Coney Island with an amusement park with roller coasters and a carousel, but these plans fell through. Famed visitors have included poet Walt Whitman and inventor Alexander Graham Bell.

By the early twentieth century, the island was neglected, overgrown and largely forgotten. That is, until 1932, when Congress authorized the presidential memorial and renamed the area Theodore Roosevelt Island. To develop a general plan for the development of the island as a national memorial, landscape architect Frederick Law Olmsted Jr. and his firm, Olmsted Brothers, along with architect John Russell Pope, were hired. Olmsted is known as the father of American landscape architecture and the designer of the Smithsonian National Zoological Park.

## THE DAWSON-BAILEY HOUSE

### 2133 North Taft Street
Approximate distance to Metro: 0.7 miles

While the actual age of this residence is unknown, it is believed to be the oldest existing example of stone architecture in Arlington County and the second-oldest home in Arlington, Virginia. It is also the only surviving stone structure from either the eighteenth or nineteenth century in the county. There are claims that President Abraham Lincoln and Robert E. Lee may have visited the home. Built in the 1780s by Thomas Owsley as a one-room log cabin, it was enlarged circa 1858. Arlington County acquired the property in 1995.

The name of this home refers to two former families who occupied it, the Dawson and Bailey families.

# NETHERLANDS CARILLON

Approximate distance to Metro: 0.7 miles

Hear that? Those bells aren't from a church but, instead, this approximately 127-foot-tall open steel structure. This carillon is a gift to the United States from the Netherlands in thanks for the nation's aid during and after World War II. Its official dedication was in May 1960, the fifteenth anniversary of the liberation of the Netherlands from the Nazis. Originally, the tower had forty-nine bells, but after a much-needed renovation in May 1995, another bell was added, in part due to it being the fiftieth anniversary of the Netherlands' liberation. The tower was erected in 1960, designed by Dutch architect Joost W.C. Boks.

The fifty bells come in various sizes, each weighing between 35 pounds and 12,654 pounds. Each one offers an emblem, signifying a group within Dutch society and an inscription by Dutch poet Ben van Eysselsteijn. Each bell also has its own meaning, such as the smallest one, which represents the youth of the Netherlands.

# 11

# Foggy Bottom–GWU

## THE WATERGATE HOTEL

2650 Virginia Avenue NW
Approximate distance to Metro: 0.2 miles

The Watergate Hotel is part of the Watergate complex, which consists of six interconnected buildings constructed between 1964 and 1971. The entire complex spans over nine acres. The hotel originally opened in 1967, designed by Italian architect Luigi Moretti. While certainly notable for its modern architecture, the building became famous for a scandal that occurred on June 17, 1972. On this day, five men were arrested for electronically bugging the offices of the Democratic National Committee (DNC). After President Richard Nixon's administration attempted to cover up its involvement, the break-in eventually led to the resignation of Nixon. Since then, "Watergate" and the suffix "-gate" have become synonymous with scandal.

Since the mid-1980s, management and ownership of the hotel has changed several times until 2007, when the property closed for nearly a decade. It did not reopen until 2016 after a $125 million, six-year renovation by developer Euro Capital Properties and architecture firms BBGM and Ron Arad Architects. After the renovation, the room count increased from 251 to 336, with two new restaurants, a rooftop bar, a renovated ballroom, fitness areas and a spa added.

Some of the most famous visitors of this building, which is listed in the National Register of Historic Places, have included Elizabeth Taylor, Ruth Bader Ginsberg and Bob Dole.

# JOHN F. KENNEDY CENTER FOR THE PERFORMING ARTS (JOHN F. KENNEDY MEMORIAL CENTER, NATIONAL CULTURAL CENTER)

2700 F Street NW
Approximate distance to Metro: 0.4 miles

This massive living memorial was designed by architect Edward Durell Stone, who is also known for having designed New York City's Museum of Modern Art (MoMA). During the planning stages, the project was known as the National Cultural Center. In a March 10, 1961 letter to Vice President Lyndon B. Johnson and House Speaker Sam Rayburn, President John F. Kennedy described the project as "the most significant cultural undertaking in the history of this city…[with] enormous importance to the cultural life of the nation as a whole."

Four days after the assassination of Kennedy, Senator J. William Fulbright, a sponsor of the original 1958 bill that started the move toward a National Cultural Center, introduced legislation that proposed to rename the center in honor of Kennedy. At first, the name proposed was the John F. Kennedy Memorial Center, but it was eventually altered to the John F. Kennedy Center for the Performing Arts.

There was much support for this move. Charles Bartlett wrote in the *Washington Post*, "The proposal to construct the National Cultural Center in the name of John F. Kennedy is one answer to the hopes that his death may yield some of the aspirations of his life." Johnson further showed support in a letter, writing, "It seems to me that a center for the performing arts on the beautiful site selected would be one of the most appropriate memorials that a grateful nation could establish to honor a man who had such deep and abiding convictions about the importance of cultural activities in our national life."

Once groundbreaking began in December 1964, Johnson used a gold-bladed spade that was previously used for both the Thomas Jefferson and Abraham Lincoln Memorials. Excavation did not begin until December 1965, with the delivery of the building in September 1971.

Responses to the Kennedy Center were varied with many arguing against the site location. The style of the modern building was also up for debate. When it opened, Ada Louise Huxtable of the *New York Times* described it as a "national tragedy," "big...bland, and...banal," as well as "a cross between a concrete candy box and a marble sarcophagus in which the art of architecture lies buried."

In 2015, construction began on a multimillion-dollar expansion of the building. Designed by Steven Holl Architects, this expansion calls for a 2,500-square-foot performance space, three new rehearsal and multipurpose spaces, a 7,500-square-foot event space and a large outdoor video wall with a complementing terrace with enough seating for over 1,600 people. There are also plans for a grove of thirty-five ginkgo trees that will acknowledge Kennedy's position as the nation's thirty-fifth president.

## HOUSE OF SWEDEN

2900 K Street NW
Approximate distance to Metro: 0.5 miles

Between the Kennedy Center and Washington Harbor, this modern embassy was constructed in 2006. Bold and angular, the sleek style of this building is meant to reflect Sweden and its values. In an interview with the *Washington Post* in 2006, former Swedish ambassador Gunnar Lund said it displays

"transparency and accessibility with a lot of glass, stone and warm wood colors in the interior." He added that it "honors Sweden's respect for the natural environment."

The designers behind the seventy-thosuand-square-foot project were Swedish architects Gert Wingårdh and Tomas Hansen with VOA Associates.

# GEORGE WASHINGTON UNIVERSITY
## (COLUMBIAN UNIVERSITY, COLUMBIAN COLLEGE)

2121 I Street NW
Approximate distance to Metro: 0.3 miles

Known as one of the most prestigious and expensive universities in the nation, George Washington University features more than twenty-six thousand undergraduates and graduate students, stemming from all fifty states, the District and approximately 130 countries. Notable alumni include actor Alec Baldwin, chef Ina Garten, TV personality Tim Gunn, former D.C. Mayor Vincent Gray, former Virginia Governor Mark Warner, former First Lady Jacqueline Kennedy Onassis, former FBI Director J. Edgar Hoover and Prime Minister of Pakistan Shahid Khaqan Abbasi.

The school was established in February 1821 by a congressional charter from President James Monroe. Originally, it was named Columbian College and was located near what is known today as Meridian Hill Park. The school relocated to its current Foggy Bottom location in 1912 and was not renamed George Washington University until 1904.

# MILKEN INSTITUTE SCHOOL OF PUBLIC HEALTH

950 New Hampshire Avenue NW
Approximate distance to Metro: 0.1 miles

This award-winning, LEED Platinum–certified building is owned by George Washington University. Completed in May 2014, the more than 160,000-square-foot Milken Institute houses six academic departments and cost $60 million to construct. The architects behind the project were Boston-based Payette with local firm Ayers Saint Gross. After it was built, the Milken Institute received a top-ten award from the American Institute of Architects Committee on the Environment (COTE).

Inside the building, pod-like learning spaces were designed to accommodate lectures, while multipurpose spaces were added for individual and group fitness pursuits. To keep the structure eco-friendly, low-flow plumbing fixtures and a green roof were installed. Elevators were also screened from view to reduce reliance on them.

The building is named after Michael R. Milken, who established the Milken Family Foundation in 1982 to support innovations in education, public health and medical research. He also founded the Prostate Cancer Foundation, formerly known as CaP Cure, which is known as the world's largest private sponsor of prostate cancer research. From its founding in 1993 through 2003, the foundation raised $210 million. In 2014, Milken also donated $20 million from the Milken Family Foundation to support George Washington University's dean of public health, while offering an additional $40 million from the Milken Institute to support the university's school of public health. With such a philanthropic, public health-driven background, *Fortune* has referred to Milken as "the man who changed medicine."

At one point, Milken was also dubbed the "Junk Bond King." As one of the most influential financiers in U.S. history, Milken is credited for pioneering new uses for the high-risk, high-interest-paying securities that are known as "junk bonds." He was also part of the biggest fraud case in Wall Street's history when he was indicted for racketeering and securities fraud in 1989 in an insider trading investigation. In April 1990, he agreed to plead guilty to six charges of criminal violation of securities laws and paid some $600 million in fines and penalties plus hundreds of millions more in civil settlements.

## WEST END LIBRARY

2301 L Street NW
Approximate distance to Metro: 0.3 miles

This is one of the most recently constructed libraries mentioned in this Metro guide, as the West End Library opened in December 2017. Designed by D.C.-based CORE Architecture + Design, this structure features a green-colored, two-story-high, glassy façade with twenty-one thousand square feet of space and enough seating for two hundred people. Over forty thousand books are housed here, along with e-books, movies and more. The library occupies the ground floor of a mixed-use building known as Westlight.

Westlight was designed by TEN Arquitectos and completed through a partnership of the D.C. government, EastBanc, JBG SMITH and Clark Enterprises. Once West End Library was completed, it became the first library in D.C. to be entirely planned, funded and constructed as a public-private partnership.

The West End Library is separated into sections according to age groups, which include children, teenagers and adults. The children's area is decorated in warm colors and offers communal areas. There is also a courtyard and programming room, which are devoted to community meetings and events. The building also offers two murals, one by Adrienne Gaither, called *Paragons of the West End*, and one by Nekisha Durrett, called *A Garden Party*. The latter mural is colorful and features two young girls reading. Gaither's mural offers a nod to the neighborhood's past with the names of noteworthy West End residents, such as Duke Ellington and Petey Greene.

## C&O CANAL

### Approximate distance to Metro: 1 mile

This 184.5-mile canal stretches from Washington, D.C., to Cumberland, Maryland. When it was in use from 1831 to 1924, its principal cargo was coal from the Allegheny Mountains. Construction spanned from 1828 to 1850. The idea for the canal was originally George Washington's, who envisioned a bustling trade route. The C&O Canal's peak was in the 1870s with nearly 974,000 tons of freight passing through it in 1875.

The canal had some stumbles in its history, thanks to Mother Nature. In 1889, a flood destroyed the canal, causing the C&O Canal Company to go into bankruptcy. The B&O Railroad Company eventually took ownership of the site until another flood destroyed the canal in 1924. Approximately twenty years later, the canal became a tourist attraction with passengers paying for a 1.5-mile ride down its waters. Public, mule-drawn canalboat rides were offered between 1942 and 2010.

The canal's life was threatened at one point by development plans. After the U.S. government acquired the property in 1938, the idea to build a highway overtop the area arose in the 1950s, but there was much opposition from Supreme Court Justice William O. Douglas. In response, Douglas organized a committee to preserve the canal. With these efforts, the *Washington Post* in 1977 deemed him "the man who saved the C&O Canal."

By 1971, the area was declared a national park.

# DUMBARTON OAKS

1703 32nd Street NW
Approximate distance to Metro: 1.5 miles

Behold, one of Georgetown's most famous, elaborately designed mansions. This well-known home-turned-museum spans several acres, many of which are composed of formal gardens, which fuse the best of French, Italian and English styles. By 1990, according to an article published in the *Washington Post*, the museum housed 1,492 artworks and 107,623 books in its Byzantine collection; 685 objects and 17,832 volumes in its pre-Columbian holdings; and 13,000 garden books in the Garden Library. The site is also known as the site of a 1944 conference that would later lead to the creation of the United Nations.

The property was first purchased in 1920 by Mildred and Robert Woods Bliss, avid collectors and patrons of scholarship and the arts. Robert's career was that of an officer and diplomat in the Foreign Service, while Mildred came into fortune because of her family's investment in the patent medicine Fletcher's Castoria. By 1933, the Bliss family had created the estate's name, "Dumbarton Oaks," as a reference to past monikers.

In 1703, this site was owned by Colonel Ninian Beall, an indentured servant who eventually became a member of the Maryland House of Burgesses. At the time, he called the home on the site "The Rock of Dunbarton." In the early 1800s, William Hammond Dorsey purchased a twenty-two-acre portion of the land, building a house on it that would become Dumbarton Oaks' present Main House. Dorsey was a real estate speculator who developed an anchor production company and shipping firm. One later owner was Secretary of War John C. Calhoun, who renamed the estate "Oakly." It was renamed once more to "The Oaks" by a later owner, Edward Magruder Linthicum, a hardware business owner.

After the Bliss family purchased the land, the residence located on it experienced several additions over the coming years. In 1928, a Renaissance-style Music Room was added in order to have a place for musical performances, scholarly gatherings and to have a space for their European furnishings and tapestries. In the early 1920s, architect Frederick H. Brooke stripped off the Victorian fripperies and remodeled several rooms. Brooke is also known for having designed the D.C. War Memorial. The Bliss family then hired architectural firm McKim, Mead and White to further renovate the home. Pritzker Prize–winning architect Philip Johnson, the designer behind the Kreeger Museum, designed Dumbarton Oaks' Philip Johnson Pavilion in 1963 as a museum to pre-Columbian art. A Courtyard Gallery was later constructed in 1987 before Hartman-Cox Architects built a new gallery and basement spaces in the late 1980s.

The gardens of Dumbarton Oaks are also well worth mentioning. The Bliss family hired Beatrix Farrand, the only founding woman member of the American Society of Landscape Architects in 1899, to be in charge of the project. This is perhaps her best-known work. Farrand's basic design has been preserved, but there has been a shift over the years to less plant material. For instance, in the Rose Garden, she lined each bed with English boxwoods, but the high-maintenance shrubs were later removed and replaced with a blue-gray sandstone.

In the mid-1930s, the Bliss family increased their acquisitions of Byzantine and related artworks, creating one of the world's great collections of Byzantine art. In 1940, they opened the Byzantine Gallery to the public and deeded the property, along with their collections and literature, to Harvard University, Robert Bliss's alma mater. Today, the estate serves as a museum and research center.

## DUMBARTON HOUSE
## (CEDAR HILL, BELLEVUE, RITTENHOUSE PLACE)

2715 Q Street NW
Approximate distance to Metro: 1 mile

This site has been known by many names. Not to be confused with Dumbarton Oaks, this property serves as the national headquarters of the National Society of the Colonial Dames of America (NSCDA), founded in Philadelphia in 1891. It also serves as a museum, featuring eighteenth- and nineteenth-century furniture and decorative arts. The exact date that the two-and-a-half-story, five-part Federal mansion was built is uncertain, as is who built the property. Even so, it is believed to have been built in 1799 or 1800.

The land was formerly owned by Peter Casanova, mayor of Georgetown, who sold it to Maryland-born Uriah Forrest, one of the nineteen original proprietors of the District of Columbia, a Revolutionary War leader and a prominent civic leader who served as mayor of Georgetown and later a representative from Maryland. It has also been owned by Gabriel Duval, then controller of the currency and eventually a member of the Supreme Court, as well as Joseph Nourse, who was first registrar of the U.S. Treasury. It was first known as Cedar Hill before being named Bellevue after it was sold to Charles Carroll, cousin of Charles Carroll of Carrollton, a signer of the Declaration of Independence. The name Bellevue was a reference to Carroll's former plantation near Hagerstown, Maryland. When the Rittenhouse family owned the mansion from 1855 to 1896, the residence was known as Rittenhouse Place. It did not become known as Dumbarton House until 1932.

The property has gone through many changes over the years, architecture-wise. It did not have a five-part configuration until around 1900 when west and east wings were erected. It then experienced a renovation that returned it to a "classical" appearance with a widow's walk, roof cornice railing with paneled swags, second-story pilasters and corner quoins. In 1912, the D.C. government decided to complete Q Street NW, requiring the house to move approximately one hundred feet to the north. Once it relocated, the original east and west wings were demolished and later reconstructed on the new site with the original bricks.

The NSCDA finally acquired Dumbarton House in 1928 in order to preserve the mansion and adapt it for use as its headquarters and as a house museum of early American culture. Four years later, a restoration project was completed by designers Horace Peaslee and Fiske Kimball to return it to its original appearance. Peaslee is also known for having designed Meridian Hill Park, while Kimball served as the director of the Philadelphia Museum of Art.

In 1991, Dumbarton House was added to the National Register of Historic Places.

# OLD STONE HOUSE

3051 M Street NW
Approximate distance to Metro: 0.7 miles

Mistaken identity saved this historic structure from being redeveloped. In 1953, when it was a used car dealership, Congress purchased the site in order to restore it to its original appearance when it was constructed circa 1765. At the time, historians mistakenly believed that the building once served as Suter's Tavern (also cited as Suter's Inn and Fountain Inn), which was a common meeting place for George Washington and Pierre Charles L'Enfant. In reality, the tavern was located a few blocks away.

Despite the mistake, few complain about the preservation of this pre–Revolutionary War structure. It stands as the oldest building in Washington, D.C., that still sits on its original foundation as well as one of the oldest surviving buildings on the East Coast. It currently serves as a small museum that opened to the public in 1960. It was later added to the National Register of Historic Places in 1973.

The most recent alterations to the building started in October 2017, when the Old Stone House closed in order to install a new fire-suppression system; stabilize the foundation; fix the exterior stonework; and upgrade the plumbing, electrical and HVAC systems.

# TUDOR PLACE

1644 31st Street NW
Approximate distance to Metro: 1.2 miles

This noteworthy house-turned-museum dates back to circa 1816 when it was constructed by Martha Custis Peter, a granddaughter of Martha Washington, and her husband, Thomas Peter, a son of Robert Peter, a prominent Scottish-born merchant, landowner and Georgetown's first mayor. While the couple was notable for their political and familial ties, the building they created is also well known for its ties to the U.S. Capitol. The original designer behind the U.S. Capitol, William Thornton, was also the architect for this residence. With this history and its largely unchanged principal footprint, it was declared a National Historic Landmark in 1960.

As a museum, Tudor Place offers one of the largest collections of objects that belonged to George and Martha Washington on view outside Mount Vernon. Additionally, there are over fifteen thousand items dating from the mid-eighteenth to the late twentieth centuries, including five thousand books and a manuscript collection that features early land records, maps, photographs, moving pictures, diaries and household receipts.

After it was constructed, Tudor Place remained in the Peter family through six generations and four owners. During this time, it experienced significant interior renovations in 1911 that included installation of steam heat, electricity, updated bathrooms and replastering. Further renovations occurred in 1969 when the garage was enlarged. After the death of the property's fourth owner, Armistead Peter III, in 1983, the estate was deeded to a private foundation created to preserve the site and operate it as a museum. It officially opened to the public as a museum in 1988.

The Neoclassical brick house is covered with stucco and offers a five-part composition made up of a two-story central block flanked by one-and-a-half-story hyphens. Still, the original layout of the five-and-a-half-acre grounds remains intact. The grounds offer a secluded Tennis Court Garden with white pine trees, a brick-edged Lily Pond and a rose-filled English Knot Garden. Historic outbuildings found here also include a Japanese Tea House.

On why the name "Tudor Place" was chosen, that is still a mystery.

## THE EXORCIST STEPS

3600 Prospect Street NW
Approximate distance to Metro: 1.3 miles

This narrow, somewhat eerie stairwell has probably been seen before by many movie buffs, whether they know it or not. It is most famously seen in the 1973 horror classic *The Exorcist*, a film directed by William Friedkin and adapted from William Peter Blatty's novel of the same name. In the movie, a major character plummets to his death down these steps. The rest is history, and *The Exorcist* became the first horror film ever nominated for Best Picture at the Academy Awards.

In October 2015, D.C. Mayor Muriel Bowser commemorated the site with an official city plaque.

While the movie is set in Georgetown, Blatty's novel was inspired by a case in Prince George's County, Maryland, when a fourteen-year-old boy purportedly was possessed by the devil. The exorcism was the subject of a front-page story in the *Washington Post* that was published on August 20, 1949.

## BLUES ALLEY CLUB

1073 Wisconsin Avenue NW
Approximate distance to Metro: 0.9 miles

This jazz and supper club has showcased well-known artists like Dizzy Gillespie, Tony Bennett, Ella Fitzgerald and Wynton Marsalis. In 1965, Blues Alley Club was founded by musician Tommy Gwaltney with an atmosphere that encourages listening and discourages conversation at tables and the bar. Since 2008, the venue has almost exclusively booked jazz artists. The organization also runs a nonprofit that encourages jazz education and performance opportunities for youth.

Blues Alley Club is the nation's oldest continuing jazz and supper club.

# 12

# Farragut West

## FARRAGUT SQUARE

Approximate distance to Metro: 0 miles

Bounded by K, I and 17th Streets NW, this 1.5-acre park is adjacent to both the Farragut North and Farragut West Metro stations, making it well traveled and rather popular as well. The space is often serviced by food trucks, and nearby office workers relaxing on the grass is a common sight. The park is also frequently used for outdoor movies, yoga and other types of exercise, canvassing and political demonstrations.

Originally, in the first half of the nineteenth century, the square was undeveloped. Once the Civil War began, troops were encamped here, while wooden buildings associated with the Freedmen's Bureau were constructed on the site until U.S. Army Corps engineer Nathaniel Michler made the recommendation in 1868 that the plot of land become a public park. Fencing, gravel walkways, shrubbery and trees were added by 1872. At this

point, the area was not rectangular, but two triangular parks, divided by Connecticut Avenue NW. This roadway was later torn up in 1881 when the David Farragut statue was installed in the center.

Farragut was a Union admiral in the Civil War and is credited as "America's first admiral." He is also famous for saying, "Damn the torpedoes, full speed ahead!" on August 5, 1864, when he led the U.S. fleet into Mobile Bay in order to shut down the Confederacy's last great port in the Gulf of Mexico. It's worth noting that mines at the time were known as torpedoes. After the successful shutdown of the port, Farragut became so esteemed that his funeral was attended by President Ulysses S. Grant. This statue, created by Vinnie Ream Hoxie, was dedicated by President James A. Garfield on April 25, 1881.

## THE WHITE HOUSE (PRESIDENT'S PALACE, PRESIDENT'S HOUSE, EXECUTIVE MANSION)

1600 Pennsylvania Avenue NW
Approximate distance to Metro: 0.5 miles

Say hello to the most famous building in the nation's capital. The White House has been known by many names, including the President's Palace, President's House and Executive Mansion. It wasn't until 1901 that President Theodore Roosevelt made its current moniker official. The building features a total of 132 rooms, 35 bathrooms, six levels, twenty-eight fireplaces, eight staircases and three elevators.

While it is known as the residence of the U.S. president, the first president to live in the building was John Adams in 1800. While George Washington chose the site in 1791, construction did not end until 1803. Irish-born architect James Hoban is credited with the design of the White House, having won a design competition held by President George Washington and Secretary of State Thomas Jefferson. The design was inspired by the Leinster House, which was originally the Dublin residence of the Duke of Leinster and today is the parliament house of Ireland. During construction, light brown Aquia, Virginia sandstone was used to create the structure.

The White House has undergone several redesigns and additions since it first opened its doors. In 1807, Benjamin Henry Latrobe redesigned the north and south fronts, adding monumental porticoes. He also redecorated the interiors and landscaped the grounds. After the British set fire to the home in 1814 during the War of 1812, Hoban was in charge of the rebuilding through 1818. The north and south porticoes were finished in 1829 and 1824, respectively. Later, in 1902, President Theodore Roosevelt began a major renovation on the building, planned and carried out by New York–based firm McKim, Mead and White. The Oval Office would not be complete until 1909, designed by American architect Nathan Wyeth. Another major renovation was completed by President Harry Truman, with plans by architect Lorenzo Winslow that gutted the interior to create more space and more structural stability. First Lady Jacqueline Kennedy is also known for having redecorated the ceremonial first-floor rooms in the Federal style in the early 1960s.

Several traditions at the White House continue to this day, including the National Christmas Tree Lighting, the Easter Egg Roll and the ever-changing china and Christmas ornament collections.

## EISENHOWER EXECUTIVE OFFICE BUILDING (OLD EXECUTIVE OFFICE BUILDING, STATE, WAR AND NAVY BUILDING)

1650 Pennsylvania Avenue NW
Approximate distance to Metro: 0.3 miles

Flamboyant and monumental at the same time, this is perhaps the most ostentatious government office building in the city. Since it was constructed, it has certainly received its share of criticism. While deemed Supervising Architect of the Treasury Alfred B. Mullett's masterpiece, it has also been described as "the greatest monstrosity in America" by President Harry Truman and an "architectural orgy" that "we regret most" by President Herbert Hoover.

Several times, there have been attempts to remodel, reshape or demolish the building. In 1929, Hoover hired architect Waddy Butler Wood to renovate the exterior to match the Treasury Building, but the Depression intervened, making the expenditure impossible. It is now designated a National Historic Landmark and listed in the National Register of Historic Places.

The ten-acre, French-inspired building was constructed from 1871 through 1888 in order to bring the State, War and Navy Departments under a single roof. It is known as the most ambitious architectural undertaking of the Grant administration. The gray Virginia granite building features nine hundred projecting and superimposed Doric columns and a synthesis of seven European prototypes. Inside, there are spiraling cantilevered stairways and a pair of libraries that the American Institute of Architects (AIA) describes as "perforated fantasies of cast iron." The floor plan is identical to that of the Treasury Building.

## RENWICK GALLERY OF THE SMITHSONIAN AMERICAN ART MUSEUM (OLD CORCORAN ART GALLERY, U.S. COURT OF CLAIMS)

1661 Pennsylvania Avenue NW
Approximate distance to Metro: 0.2 miles

At one point, the Renwick Gallery was one of the city's most underappreciated art spaces. In 2010, approximately 151,000 people visited the gallery. In 2016, that number grew to approximately 764,000, in part thanks to a visually exciting exhibition and also thanks to a major renovation that closed the building long enough to make people curious about what it would offer afterward. There is more to this gallery than what meets the eye, though. This National Historic Landmark is considered the first building constructed expressly as an art museum in the nation and is one of America's first examples of Second Empire architecture.

The building was constructed by William Wilson Corcoran, co-founder of the Riggs Bank and philanthropist, as a gallery for his private collection of paintings and sculptures in 1861. The designer was American architect James Renwick Jr., the same architect behind the Smithsonian Castle. When designing the gallery, Renwick was inspired by the 1850s additions to the Louvre in Paris, executed by Visconti and Lefuel for Napoleon III. The rectangular building is 107 feet wide and 126 feet long with red brick, sandstone trim and a slate roof. Above the central door was an entablature with the inscription "Dedicated to Art," which was later changed to "Dedicated to the Future of Art" in 2015.

Despite originally being built to house art, it first served as a warehouse. This is because the U.S. Army seized the building in 1861 for the storage of records and uniforms for the Quartermaster General's Corps. It later returned to Corcoran's control in 1869 and was restored for use as an art gallery from 1869 to 1874. On January 19, 1874, it finally opened as an art gallery for private viewing. Additional improvements were made to the building in the 1880s with a bronze plaque with the profile of Corcoran placed on the front façade. A school of art was established in an annex at the rear of the building in January 1890.

Use of the building shifted in the early twentieth century when it was modified by and used for the U.S. Court of Claims. Threats of demolition arose in the 1960s, but help from First Lady Jacqueline Kennedy saved it from the wrecking ball. By 1972, it officially became the home for the Smithsonian's contemporary craft and decorative art program. The most recent changes to the building were from December 2013 through November 2015 when it closed for a $30 million renovation. This renovation improved the building's systems and energy efficiency. Ceiling vaults on the second floor were reopened, and new windows and LED lighting were installed. Moldings were also repaired.

# DECATUR HOUSE

748 Jackson Place NW
Approximate distance to Metro: 0.2 miles

Within walking distance to the White House, this residence is one of the oldest surviving homes in Washington, D.C., the first private residence on Lafayette Square and one of only three remaining houses in the nation designed by Benjamin Henry Latrobe. The first owner of this National Historic Landmark was Commodore Stephen Decatur, who was at the height of his naval career when the three-story brick house was completed in 1819. Decatur often held lavish parties at this home, and it eventually became known as the social center for the city, a reputation it continued to have for many years after Decatur died from a mortal wound in a duel on March 22, 1820.

After his death, his wife leased the residence to a series of foreign diplomats and then Secretary of State Henry Clay. The history of the home became more complex during this ownership as Charlotte Dupuy, a woman enslaved by Clay, sued him for her right to freedom while living in the house. Additional future tenants and owners included Martin Van Buren, English tavernkeeper John Gadsby, Senator Judah P. Benjamin and Vice President George M. Dallas.

During the Civil War, it was used as offices. Frontiersman, diplomat and entrepreneur General Edward Beale purchased the home in 1872 before passing it down to Truxtun Beale, ambassador to Persia, in 1893. It was finally transferred to the National Trust for Historic Preservation in 1956 before opening to the public as a museum in the early 1960s. The residence is currently operated by the White House Historical Association, housing historical documentation, supporting research and providing educational programs related to the White House.

## THE HAY-ADAMS HOTEL

800 16th Street NW
Approximate distance to Metro: 0.3 miles

As one of the city's most iconic luxury hotels, the Hay-Adams Hotel is known well for its long history, impressive architectural embellishments and exceptional location, only a stone's throw away from the White House. It was constructed in 1927 by developer Harry Wardman and architect Mihran Mesrobian with a name referencing residents John Hay and Henry Adams. Hay served as a personal secretary to President Abraham Lincoln, U.S. ambassador to the United Kingdom and secretary of state under both Presidents William McKinley and Theodore Roosevelt. Adams, a descendant of Presidents John Adams and John Quincy Adams, worked as a historian and professor at Harvard University.

Since the Italian Renaissance–style hotel was completed, some of its most famous guests have included Theodore Roosevelt, Mark Twain, Henry James, Ethel Barrymore, Amelia Earhart, Sinclair Lewis and Charles Lindbergh.

The 124-room and 21-suite hotel is well known for its ornamentation. Inside, there are Doric, Ionic and Corinthian columns; wainscoting; the first air-conditioned dining room in the city; and intricate ceiling treatments. The hotel closed from October 2001 to March 2002 for a $20 million renovation by D.C.-based designer Thomas Pheasant. An additional renovatio. happened in June 2010 with the opening of a rooftop terrace in January 2011. Additional amenities at the Hay-Adams include a fitness center, twenty-four-hour business center and two restaurants.

*U.S. News & World Report* ranked the Hay-Adams Hotel the second-best hotel in D.C. and the eleventh-best hotel in the world in 2018.

## THE MAYFLOWER HOTEL

1127 Connecticut Avenue NW
Approximate distance to Metro: 0.3 miles

When it comes to scandalous hotels, the Watergate Hotel is often deemed the most notorious, but the Mayflower Hotel certainly comes close. This ten-story, Beaux Arts–style hotel was once described by President Harry Truman as "Washington's second-best address." The best address was, of course, the White House. Another moniker for this hotel is the "Hotel of Presidents," a name meant to reference the fact that it has hosted a large number of people of national and international importance.

Some of the most famous guests have included Franklin D. Roosevelt, Dwight D. Eisenhower, Richard Nixon, J. Edgar Hoover and John F. Kennedy. It was also here that Harry Truman announced his intention to run for the presidency. Even in its first year, 1925, it hosted the inaugural ball for President Calvin Coolidge. Two years later, Charles Lindbergh was awarded the Hubbard Medal here by the National Geographic Society for the first-ever solo transatlantic flight. Two of the many scandalous instances to have occurred at the Mayflower Hotel include the arrest of Nazi saboteur George Dasch in 1942 and former D.C. mayor Marion Barry Jr.'s conviction on a misdemeanor drug charge in 1989.

The developer behind the 512-room and 69-suite hotel was Allen E. Walker, a businessman credited with developing D.C.'s Northeast Brookland neighborhood, while the designers were New York–based architects Whitney Warren and Charles Wetmore, who are most known for their work on the Grand Central Terminal in New York City. The hotel has undergone several renovations over the years, including in 1983 and a $20 million renovation in 2015.

r Hotel is part of Marriott International's Autograph
d in the National Register of Historic Places and is named
rust's Historic Hotels of America.

# D.C. IMPROV COMEDY CLUB

1140 Connecticut Avenue NW
Approximate distance to Metro: 0.3 miles

The nation's capital is typically described as politically obsessed and rather serious, but this city can certainly have a funny bone if you look hard enough. At the D.C. Improv, this is especially true as it remains the only full-time stand-up club in the city. It first opened in 1992 and has since opened a comedy school in 2003 for both improv and stand-up comedy. The performance space was further expanded in 2006 with a "comedy lounge," which seats approximately sixty people.

Some of the most well-known funny people to have performed here include Robin Williams, Dave Chappelle, Ellen DeGeneres, Chris Rock, Brian Regan, Wanda Sykes and Jim Gaffigan.

# NATIONAL GEOGRAPHIC MUSEUM

1145 17th Street NW
Approximate distance to Metro: 0.3 miles

After the National Geographic Society Headquarters completed construction in 1963, Ada Louise Huxtable of the *New York Times* described the building as having a "notable distinction" that "sets a standard for Washington." It shouldn't be of any surprise that this building was given such high praise as the architect behind this building, Edward Durell Stone, was the same one behind the Kennedy Center in D.C. and the Museum of Modern Art in New York City.

This ten-story office building is constructed with reinforced concrete with an exterior of white marble, black granite and dark glass. The architecture is held up as an example of the New Formalism that emerged within the modern movement during the 1950s and 1960s.

Along with housing the National Geographic Museum, this site also serves as the headquarters for the National Geographic Society, an 1888-founded organization that stands as one of the largest nonprofit scientific and educational organizations in the world. Since it was founded, the National Geographic Society has sponsored more than 9,600 research and exploration projects around the world.

## DAR CONSTITUTION HALL

### 1776 D Street NW
### Approximate distance to Metro: 0.6 miles

The National Society of the Daughters of the American Revolution (DAR) National Headquarters includes three adjoined buildings: the DAR Memorial Continental Hall, DAR Constitution Hall and Administration Building. With the purpose to accommodate DAR's annual Continental Congresses and other activities, the Constitution Hall was constructed in 1929 and has since been a cultural center for the nation's capital for all forms of the performing and literary arts. It continues to boast the largest auditorium in Washington, D.C., with a seating capacity of 3,746 plus an additional 150 chairs on the stage.

Designed by John Russell Pope—the same architect behind the Thomas Jefferson Memorial, National Archives building and the National Gallery of Art's West Building—the cornerstone was laid by First Lady Grace Coolidge in October 1928 with the trowel George Washington used to lay the cornerstone at the U.S. Capitol in 1793. The first event took place one year later, featuring Anna Case, Efrem Zimbalist, Sophie Braslau and Hans Barth. According to the DAR, every president since Calvin Coolidge has attended events at DAR Constitution Hall. During

World War II, the DAR loaned its complex to the American Red Cross to support the war effort.

The Neoclassical, limestone-covered building features an Ionic entrance portico on top of a ninety-foot-wide pediment above the name "Constitution Hall" cut in the stone frieze. To the left and right of a sculpture of an American eagle are the dates "1776" and "1783," representing the Declaration of Independence and the Treaty of Paris, respectively.

This building is considered a National Historic Landmark and is listed in the National Register of Historic Places.

# McPherson Square

## FRANKLIN SQUARE

Approximate distance to Metro: 400 feet

Measuring roughly five acres, this is Downtown D.C.'s largest park. It is partially terraced with a fountain in the center and a statue of Commodore John Barry. Barry was an Irish officer in the Continental navy during the American Revolutionary War and later in the U.S. Navy. Alongside John Paul Jones and John Adams, he is credited as being the "Father of the American Navy."

This park was absent in Pierre Charles L'Enfant's plan for the nation's capital. In 1832, the federal government purchased the land, which offered a spring that supplied fresh water to the White House at the time, in order to create a new park. The statue of Barry wasn't added until 1914. The park was later redesigned by the National Park Service and the Public Works Administration in 1936. The site became notable when scientist Charles H. Townes conceived of the "maser principle," which led to the invention of the laser, on this site on April 26, 1951.

While renovated in the mid-1970s, the park still retains the same look it did in the 1930s. Since the 2010s, the park has been riddled with cracked pathways, eroded trails and few to no events or programming in the public space. In June 2017, D.C. delegate to Congress Eleanor Holmes Norton told the *Washington Post*, "Frankly, it is an embarrassment to the city." Since 2012, there have been plans to rejuvenate Franklin Square with a design by ZGF Architects and the Olin Studio. The renovation, headed by the National Park Service and the Downtown Business Improvement District

(BID), would allow for a small café, better seating, an interactive water feature and a pedestrian mall with space for a farmers' market, musical performances and other events. There are also plans for a playground and new trees.

The name Franklin Square is presumably a nod to Benjamin Franklin.

## FRANKLIN SCHOOL

925 13th Street NW
Approximate distance to Metro: 0.2 miles

Only a few blocks away from the White House, this historic school still stands, dating back to circa 1869. When it was built, it was the flagship building of a group of modern public schools constructed in the city between 1862 and 1875. The architect behind the building was German-born Adolph Cluss, the same designer behind Eastern Market and the Arts and Industries Building. In 1880, inventor Alexander Graham Bell was able to successfully test his photophone machine, which transmitted sound by light waves, from the rooftop of the school. With this long history, the building is in the National Register of Historic Places and is designated a National Historic Landmark.

In 1992, the exterior of the building was restored. By 2002, the building was used as a homeless shelter, which closed only six years later, thereafter remaining vacant for about a decade. The site is expected to be redeveloped into a language arts museum and education space, called Planet Word, in 2019. The project is a partnership of the D.C. Office of the Deputy Mayor for Planning and Economic Development and Franklin School Development LLC, which is a partnership of ABooks LLC philanthropist Ann B. Friedman and developer Dantes Partners. The architecture firm designing the museum is Beyer Blinder Belle.

Once complete, the school-turned-museum will offer a restaurant, classrooms, offices, retail, exhibits and finally a rooftop terrace.

# TREASURY BUILDING

1500 Pennsylvania Avenue NW
Approximate distance to Metro: 0.3 miles

Whether knowing it or not, most Americans have seen images of this building in passing; in fact, the Treasury Building is featured on the back of the ten-dollar bill. Both a National Historic Landmark and listed in the National Register of Historic Places, this is the oldest departmental building in Washington, D.C., and the third-oldest federally occupied building in the District, preceded by the U.S. Capitol and the White House. When it was fully built in the mid-nineteenth century, it was one of the largest office buildings in the world. During the Civil War, it served as a barracks for soldiers. It was also later the site of President Ulysses S. Grant's first inaugural ball in 1869.

It took a total of thirty-three years to fully complete construction on the rectangular, Greek Revival–style building. Erected in four stages, it measures 260 feet wide from east to west and 466 from north to south. The first sections built were the east side and central wing from 1836 to 1842. The architect in charge of the project was Robert Mills, the same architect behind the Washington Monument and Old Patent Office. His most architecturally impressive feature is the ionic colonnade on the 15th Street NW side with thirty 36-foot-tall columns.

Mills was later replaced by Ammi B. Young and Alexander H. Bowman, who were in charge of the construction of the south wing from 1855 to 1861. Isaiah Rogers designed the west wing, which was constructed from 1862 to 1864. The final wing, the north wing, was designed by Alfred B. Mullett, who went on to design the nearby Old Executive Office Building. The north wing was constructed from 1867 to 1869. While the following wings were executed along the lines of the original Mills wings, the interiors reflected changing tastes in technology and aesthetic tastes. Detailing also became more ornate.

Further changes to the building include a rebuilding of the Mills façade in granite in 1908 and the addition of an attic story two years later.

Outside the building, there is a statue of the first secretary of the Treasury, Alexander Hamilton, on the south patio. A statue of the fourth secretary of the Treasury, Albert Gallatin, is on the north patio.

# 14

# Federal Triangle

## FEDERAL BUREAU OF INVESTIGATION HEADQUARTERS (J. EDGAR HOOVER BUILDING)

935 Pennsylvania Avenue NW
Approximate distance to Metro: 0.4 miles

When the Federal Bureau of Investigation (FBI) was formed in 1908, it was housed in the Department of Justice building. Starting in 1962, the Kennedy administration began planning for a new building to house the headquarters of the FBI. After the General Services Administration (GSA) chose a site in 1963, construction officially started six years later. Originally, the estimated cost of the building was around $60 million, but by the time it opened in 1975, it cost more than $125 million. It was dedicated by President Gerald Ford.

In 1972, architecture critic Ada Louise Huxtable described the planned FBI headquarters in the *Washington Post* as the country's largest and most controversial building project. She further described the Brutalist design as reminiscent of Boston City Hall and Le Corbusier's style. The entire building,

designed by Chicago-based firm C.F. Murphy Associates, is eleven stories tall and spans more than 2.5 million square feet of space.

After a decade-long search for a new headquarters, plans to shutter the J. Edgar Hoover Building were abandoned in 2017 due to Congress leaving the project underfunded by approximately $882 million.

## OLD POST OFFICE PAVILION (TRUMP INTERNATIONAL HOTEL, POST OFFICE BUILDING)

1100 Pennsylvania Avenue NW
Approximate distance to Metro: 200 feet

In 1899, this became the first federal building erected on Pennsylvania Avenue NW, and it is currently the second-tallest building in Washington, D.C., measuring 135 feet high. At first, the massive rectangular building served as the headquarters for the Post Office Department, the City Post Office and the postmaster general. By 1914, the City Post Office had moved to a building adjacent to Union Station. The Post Office Department didn't officially move out until 1934.

There were several attempts over the years to tear down the Romanesque Revival–style building, first in the late 1930s and then in the 1970s. Each time, plans were thwarted by limited funds and local preservationist groups. By the 1980s, the structure was renovated, and a food court and retail space were added. These renovations were sorely needed at the time, especially due to water damage. In 1983, Jack Finberg, director of planning for the National Capital Region of the GSA, described the building as "musty, dirty and cold." It's not that way anymore, thankfully.

The GSA, which owns and manages federal properties, invited proposals to redevelop the building in 2011. Work officially began to transform the site into a luxury hotel in 2014, reopening as the Trump International Hotel in 2016. Since its opening, there have been several instances of vandalism and protests to admonish President Donald Trump and his many controversies. The hotel is cited as one of the most expensive in Washington, D.C., with 263 rooms, 35 suites, a spa and a 13,2000-square-foot, 3-room Presidential Ballroom.

In the clock tower, there are bells that are replicas of the ones in Westminster Abbey, created as a present from David Wills, an English tobacco company heir. They were installed in 1983. Public tours to the bell tower were momentarily halted in 2014 before reopening in 2017.

The building was added to the National Register of Historic Places in 1973.

# 15

# Smithsonian

## NATIONAL MALL

Approximate distance to Metro: 0.3 miles

From the beginning, there were high hopes for the National Mall, but it didn't always meet them. In 1791, Pierre Charles L'Enfant imagined it being a grand, tree-lined promenade with gardens, theaters, academies and embassies. Instead, for much of the nineteenth century, it was filled with rubbish, vegetable patches, shacks and the occasional flooding.

The first architect to build on the Mall was Benjamin Henry Latrobe, who created a canal intended to supply markets in the city, starting at the mouth of Tiber Creek and ending at the Anacostia River. The Washington City Canal officially opened in November 1815 and was filled in during the 1870s. In 1816, he also designed a national university on thirty-four acres of land on the Mall with a medical hall, student lodgings and professors' houses, but this ended up falling through.

In 1902, efforts restarted to reimagine the Mall, thanks to the Senate Park Commission Plan, otherwise known as the McMillan Commission Plan. This plan was initiated by Michigan Senator James McMillan, who served as chairman of the Senate Committee on the District of Columbia. With the hope to reinvigorate the avenue as a national symbol worth taking pride in, this plan removed old buildings, railroad tracks and any trees or gardens from the area. Instead, there were plans for museums, each facing one another and arranged around a grassy lawn, flanked by rows of trees. To implement these plans, the Commission of Fine Arts was created in 1910. The first 3,020 of the city's cherry trees were gifted from Japan in 1912 and planted around the Mall. Over the years, the area has continued to evolve with new museums and memorials, most recently the National Museum of African American History and Culture (NMAAHC). To ensure the allure of the area remains constant, Congress declared the Mall a "substantially completed work of civic art" in 2003. It was also added to the National Register of Historic Places in 1966.

Take note that "the Mall" and the "National Mall" can refer to different sections of the area. "The Mall" tends to refer to the green space between the Washington Monument and the U.S. Capitol, while the latter term refers to not only the lawn but also the Abraham Lincoln and Thomas Jefferson Memorials, as well as the Washington Monument. In length, it spans approximately 2 miles between the U.S. Capitol and the Lincoln Memorial, and it stretches roughly 1.2 miles between the U.S. Capitol and the Washington Monument.

## WASHINGTON MONUMENT

2 15th Street NW
Approximate distance to Metro: 0.5 miles

You know it when you see it, and you can spot the Washington Monument from nearly every section of the city. Measuring 555 feet, 5⅛ inches tall, this is the tallest structure in Washington, D.C. Not only that, but when it was built, it was the tallest man-made structure in the world.

The idea for erecting a monument to George Washington first arose in 1783 when the Continental Congress voted to create a statue of the man, who would not become president until 1789. After he was inaugurated, he abandoned these plans due to federal budgetary restraints. It wasn't until after he passed away in 1799 that Congress considered reimagining the monument to him, this time as a pyramid-shaped mausoleum housed in the U.S. Capitol rotunda. Once again, plans for a monument were abandoned, though only temporarily.

It wasn't until 1833 that a group, known as the Washington National Monument Society, was formed with the mission to raise private funds for the project. To decide on the design, a competition was held, which was won by architect Robert Mills, whose works also include the Department of Treasury Building and the Old Patent Office. The winning design differs in many ways from the final product. Rather than a simple, stoic, stone obelisk, Mills instead called for a pantheon with thirty columns and statues of signers of the Declaration of Independence, heroes from the Revolutionary War and Washington driving a horse-drawn chariot. From the center, there would stand an imposing six-hundred-foot-tall obelisk.

Construction on the Washington Monument officially began in 1848, but after rising 156 feet, all progress ceased. Due to a lack of funds, construction stalled from 1854 to 1877. Thankfully, Congress stepped in to complete the remainder of the work with President Ulysses S. Grant authorizing federal funding for the project in 1876, in part motivated by the 100th anniversary of the founding of the United States. Work resumed in 1879, though the quarry stone couldn't be matched, resulting in the multi-toned effect seen today. The monument was finally complete in 1884, dedicated in 1885 and opened to the public in 1888.


## THOMAS JEFFERSON MEMORIAL

701 East Basin Drive SW
Approximate distance to Metro: 1 mile

Thomas Jefferson was many things: president, statesman, architect, author and University of Virginia founder. This Neoclassical-style marble memorial seeks to represent all of these attributes. The idea for a memorial to Jefferson was first proposed in 1926, but Congress didn't establish the Thomas Jefferson Memorial Commission (TJMC) until June 1934. The original location chosen was at the intersection of Constitution and Pennsylvania Avenues NW. One year later, TJMC hired architect John Russell Pope, whose works also include the National Archives and the West Building of the National Gallery of Art.

President Franklin D. Roosevelt declared in 1936 that the original chosen site was too small. One of the following proposals was to create an island in the center of the Tidal Basin in order for the memorial to be in a direct line with the White House. This plan fell through, but having the placement of the memorial be in line with the White House was deemed worth moving forward. Thereafter, the site chosen was on the southeasterly corner of the Tidal Basin with Frederick Law Olmsted Jr. officially appointed as landscape architect.

Construction began in November 1938, but not without controversy. On the day of groundbreaking, a group of fifty women marched to the White House with a petition to stop damage to the cherry trees that were to be uprooted by the construction. In an act known as the "Cherry Tree Rebellion," the women later chained themselves to a tree at the construction site. The memorial's completion was in April 1943 on Jefferson's 200th birthday with President Franklin D. Roosevelt presiding over the ceremony.

The memorial is a circular, open-air structure with Ionic columns, a chamber that measures 165 feet in diameter and a 102-foot-wide portico. Inside, there is a 19-foot-high bronze statue of Jefferson holding the Declaration of Independence in his left hand. The sculpture was created by Rudulph Evans. A sculptured group by Adolph A. Weinman can also be found above the portico, depicting Jefferson standing at a table during the signing of the Declaration of Independence. Figures seated near him include John Adams, Robert Livingston, Benjamin Franklin and Roger Sherman. Another feature of the memorial worth looking for are quotations from Jefferson's writings carved into the walls of the chamber, expressing views on the evolution of law and the Constitution, slavery and religion.

## ABRAHAM LINCOLN MEMORIAL

2 Lincoln Memorial Circle NW
Approximate distance to Metro: 1.5 miles

Congress officially approved this project in 1911, creating the Lincoln Memorial Commission, which was chaired by William Howard Taft. Ground broke in February 1914 with plans to create a sub-foundation made up of 122 poured concrete piers with steel reinforcing rods anchored in bedrock. Foundation work was completed in May 1915. Construction slowed after

World War I began, but the memorial was finally dedicated in May 1922. Since then, this site has been host to several historic events, most notably the "I Have a Dream" speech by Martin Luther King Jr.

Abraham Lincoln's marble and granite memorial was designed by architect Henry Bacon and inspired by the Parthenon in Athens, Greece. It measures 190 feet long, 120 feet wide and 99 feet tall with Doric columns surrounding the structure. The statue inside was designed by sculptor Daniel Chester French and completed in 1920. The original planned size of the statue was approximately half of what it is now, but the plans changed so that it would not be overwhelmed by the gargantuan size of the building. Inside, there are carved inscriptions of Lincoln's Second Inaugural Address and his Gettysburg Address. There are also the names of thirty-six states inscribed on the frieze above the colonnade. These states had all entered the Union by the time of Lincoln's death. The adjacent reflecting pool wasn't complete until a few years after the dedication.

## THE ARTS OF WAR SCULPTURES AND THE ARTS OF PEACE SCULPTURES

### 620 Ohio Drive SW
### Approximate distance to Metro: 1.4 miles

Each day, many drive past these two pairs of sculptures, often missing their beauty and symbolism. First erected in 1951, they flank the eastern end of the Arlington Memorial Bridge and the Rock Creek and Potomac Parkway. The statues were commissioned in the mid- to late 1920s in order to complement the plaza constructed on the east side of the Abraham Lincoln Memorial. In 1939, construction was delayed due to a tight budget, and after being placed in storage, they were not cast until 1951. In the early to mid-1970s, the statues were repaired and re-gilded.

Framing the entrance to the Arlington Memorial Bridge, visitors will find the Arts of War, which depicts Valor and Sacrifice. Designed by sculptor Leo Friedlander, this artwork features a bearded, muscular male, symbolizing the ancient Roman god of war known as Mars. A semi-nude female with a shield is beside him. This statue group represents Valor. The statue group that represents Sacrifice depicts the same figures, but the male holds a small child, while the female is facing backward with her right arm reaching up to touch his right elbow.

Similar to the Arts of War, the Arts of Peace has two statue groups, this time representing Music and Harvest as well as Aspiration and Literature. Each, designed by sculptor James Earle Fraser, faces Rock Creek Parkway. Aspiration and Literature feature a nude male with an open book in his right hand, meant to symbolize literature, and a nude male aiming a bow backward, meant to symbolize aspiration. Wisdom and knowledge are depicted by a serpent behind them. For the depiction of Music and Harvest, there is a nude male holding a sickle and carrying some wheat over his shoulder, and there is also a semi-nude female holding a harp in her left hand, while a turtle trails behind, symbolizing how art persists despite the passing of time. Fraser's statue groups also depict the winged horse, Pegasus.

Both the Arts of War and the Arts of Peace are contributing properties to the East and West Potomac Parks Historic District.

## THE LOCKKEEPER'S HOUSE

17th Street NW and Constitution Avenue NW
Approximate distance to Metro: 1 mile

Dating back to the 1830s, this residence is the oldest structure on the National Mall. It was originally built as the house for the lockkeeper of the Washington City Canal, which was created by Benjamin Henry Latrobe. The duties of the lockkeeper were to collect tolls and keep records of commerce on the canal. After the canal was filled in during the 1870s, the 350-square-foot property was given to the federal government and functioned for some time as the headquarters for the Park Police. It has also been used for park maintenance storage.

In December 2016, work began to restore and relocate the Lockkeeper's House as part of the Constitution Gardens revitalization project. It was moved approximately thirty feet from its previous location. It had been relocated once before in 1915. The house now contains a visitor information plaza and a digital exhibition space that explains the history of the National Mall.

# VIETNAM VETERANS MEMORIAL

5 Henry Bacon Drive NW
Approximate distance to Metro: 1.5 miles

"I imagined taking a knife and cutting into the earth, opening it up, an initial violence and pain that in time would heal. The grass would grow back, but the initial cut would remain a pure flat surface in the earth with a polished, mirrored surface, much like the surface on a geode when you cut it and polish the edge." This was written by Maya Ying Lin on the making of this memorial in an article published in the *New York Review* in November 2000. Her design consisted of two polished black granite walls, located at the west end of Constitution Gardens and beginning at ground level, while gradually descending to a depth of 10 feet. The walls are approximately 246 feet in length, meant to appear as a rift in the earth, while pointing toward the Washington Monument and the Abraham Lincoln Memorial. The most important feature at the wall are the names of more than fifty-eight thousand dead and missing soldiers from the Vietnam War, listed in chronological order. The wall was dedicated in 1982.

While one of the most heavily visited sites on the National Mall, this memorial was also once the most controversial. Despite Lin's design winning a competition that garnered over 1,400 entries, critics disagreed with the abstract shape of the wall, as well as its dark color and lack of patriotic symbols. There were also some who criticized Lin for being of Asian descent, even though she was born in the United States. Despite all of this, the wall has also seen its share of praise. In 2007, it was listed among "America's Favorite Architecture" in a public poll conducted by the American Institute of Architects and Harris Interactive.

Over time, the memorial incorporated additional structures, including *Three Servicemen*, the Vietnam Women's Memorial and a memorial plaque and flagpole. The bronze sculpture, titled *Three Servicemen*, and the flagpole were added in 1984, created by sculptor Frederick E. Hart. Located near the southwest approach to the wall, this artwork depicts three soldiers dressed as if they were in the field. The Vietnam Women's Memorial was designed by sculptor Glenna Goodacre and dedicated in November 1993. It depicts three servicewomen and a wounded male soldier, meant to honor the contributions of women to the war effort. This sculpture is located south of the wall and east of the *Three Servicemen*. The nearby landscaped plaza, designed by George Dickie of the architectural firm HOK, displays eight yellowwood trees, representing the eight women killed during the Vietnam War. The memorial plaque was added in 2004, honoring those who died after the war as a result of injuries suffered in Vietnam. It was reinstalled in 2012 with bronze inlay lettering.

## ALBERT EINSTEIN STATUE

2101 Constitution Avenue NW
Approximate distance to Metro: 1.5 miles

Located near the National Academy of Sciences (NAS), this larger-than-life bronze depiction of Albert Einstein stands twelve feet tall, weighing four tons. It was first unveiled in 1979 to celebrate the genius's 100th birthday. Designed by sculptor Robert Berks, the artwork shows Einstein holding a tablet with sketches of three of his scientific contributions: the photoelectric effect, the theory of general relativity and the equivalence of energy and matter. On the bench where he is seated, there are three engraved quotations by him. Additionally, at the base of the statue is a depiction of the sun, planets, moon and stars with over 2,700 embedded metal studs.

The proximity to the NAS, a private nonprofit filled with scientists, engineers and doctors, was intentional. Einstein was elected to the NAS in 1922 after he won the Nobel Prize in physics. After Einstein became a citizen of the United States in 1940, he was elected a full member to the NAS two years later.

## SMITHSONIAN INSTITUTION (CASTLE)

1000 Jefferson Drive SW
Approximate distance to Metro: 0.2 miles

Since it was constructed in 1855, the Castle has been the Smithsonian's signature building. Construction began in 1847, one year after the Smithsonian Institution was established. The designer was the same as that for the Renwick Gallery of the Smithsonian American Art Museum, American architect James Renwick Jr.

The building has experienced numerous reconstructions over the years. After a fire in January 1865, the upper story of the main segment and the north and south towers needed restoring. The east wing was later fireproofed and enlarged in 1883. The property was also later remodeled in 1969 and further restored in 1987.

Starting in 1849, Secretary of the Smithsonian Joseph Henry lived in the east wing with his family. From 1858 to the 1960s, the building housed an exhibit hall. The Castle has also been home to the city's first children's museum and the Woodrow Wilson International Center for Scholars and is currently used for administrative offices and a visitor information center. There is also a crypt that houses James Smithson, the benefactor of the institution. A statue of Henry stands by the entrance.

The Castle is designated a National Historic Landmark and is listed in the National Register of Historic Places.


# ARTS AND INDUSTRIES BUILDING
## (U.S. NATIONAL MUSEUM)

900 Jefferson Drive SW
Approximate distance to Metro: 0.2 miles

The Arts and Industries Building is the only surviving major structure designed by German-born architect Adolph Cluss. It is also the first building created solely to house the U.S. National Museum. Starting in the 1850s, the museum's collections were housed in the Smithsonian Institution Building, otherwise known as the Castle. Ground was broken in April 1879 directly next to the Castle for this building. Before the museum opened to the public in October 1881, the building was in use by the Smithsonian Institution staff a year earlier, and the inaugural ball of President James Abram Garfield and Vice President Chester A. Arthur was held in March 1881. Once the museum opened, there were exhibits ranging from geology to zoology to architecture to musical instruments and beyond.

The collections outgrew the building by the 1890s. By 1910, a new U.S. National Museum building had been created, currently known as the

National Museum of Natural History. At this point, the former museum was renamed the Arts and Industries Building, continuing to house historic artifacts like the first display of the first ladies' dresses and a small collection of airplanes. Once the National Air and Space Museum and the National Museum of American History were established decades later, the remaining historical collections were relocated. On the east side of the building, the Mary Livingston Ripley Garden was created in 1981 and renovated in 1988.

The Arts and Industries Building was shuttered in 2004 for renovations and reopened in 2016. It is not open to the public, except for private pop-up exhibitions and special events.

## NATIONAL GALLERY OF ART

3rd Street NW and Constitution Avenue NW
Approximate distance to Metro: 0.6 miles

It's all thanks to Andrew W. Mellon that this national art museum was created. Mellon, a financier, art collector and secretary of the Treasury, gained support from President Franklin D. Roosevelt to create the museum, which Mellon would proceed to privately fund and donate his art collection to. Construction began in 1937 with architect John Russell Pope's design for a Neoclassical-style structure, known as the West Building. This building has barrel-vaulted sculpture halls and a main floor plan centered on a rotunda modeled after the ancient Roman Pantheon. Congress set aside an adjacent plot of land once the National Gallery of Art's collections grew to the point where a new building would be necessary.

By 1967, Mellon's children, Paul Mellon and Ailsa Mellon Bruce, had donated funds for the East Building with architect I.M. Pei chosen to design it. This time, the building was in a modern style with an open plaza between the buildings. Construction began in 1971 with the property dedicated by President Jimmy Carter in June 1978. In order for both buildings to match in color, Gallery officials managed to get the quarry that had supplied marble to the West Building reopened.

In May 1999, through an agreement with the National Park Service, the Gallery opened a sculpture garden to the west of the original building. The six-acre garden and outdoor gallery were designed by landscape architect Laurie D. Olin to house large-scale sculptures.

Some of the highlights of this gallery's collection include Edgar Degas's *Little Dancer Aged Fourteen*, a self-portrait by Vincent Van Gogh and Leonardo da Vinci's *Ginevra de' Benci*, which is the only da Vinci painting in public view in the Americas.

## NATIONAL AIR AND SPACE MUSEUM

600 Independence Avenue SW
Approximate distance to Metro: 0.5 miles

In this heavily visited museum, visitors can find the 1903 Wright flyer, Charles Lindbergh's *Spirit of St. Louis*, the Albert Einstein Planetarium and the Lockheed Martin IMAX Theater. The entire building, encompassing four marble-clad monolithic blocks, spans more than 160,000 square feet of exhibition space. The building spans 635 feet in length, 225 feet in width and 82 feet, 9 inches in height. It opened in 1976, designed by architects Hellmuth, Obata + Kassabaum, who later added a glass pavilion at the east end in 1988.

This museum was originally known as the National Air Museum, created by an act of Congress in August 1946. Its collections were first housed in the Arts and Industries Building.

Starting in the summer of 2018, the Smithsonian Institution began a nearly $1 billion overhaul of the building. The renovation is expected to take approximately seven years.

## NATIONAL MUSEUM OF AFRICAN AMERICAN HISTORY AND CULTURE

1400 Constitution Avenue NW
Approximate distance to Metro: 0.5 miles

In the report that was issued to President George W. Bush in 2003 proposing a Smithsonian Institution museum dedicated to African American history and culture, the title was "The Time Has Come." Congress seemed to agree, as it passed the law authorizing the museum later that year. The museum, designed by architects Phil Freelon and David Adjaye, officially opened to the public in September 2016. The museum houses more than thirty-six thousand artifacts with the collection laid out in chronological order, starting from the Middle Passage. Highlights include banners from President Barack Obama's 2008 campaign, posters from the Black Lives Matter movement, Olympic medals of Carl Lewis, statues of Serena and Venus Williams, a Tuskegee Airmen biplane and memorabilia from celebrities like Chuck Berry and Oprah Winfrey.

The building's appearance is also meant to call back to African American culture with the bronze-hued corona stemming from traditional Nigerian designs. The design of the external latticework is also shaped like Yoruban wood carvings, while the shaded porch in the entrance is meant to call back to family gathering spots.

## U.S. HOLOCAUST MEMORIAL MUSEUM

100 Raoul Wallenberg Place SW
Approximate distance to Metro: 0.3 miles

The idea of creating a U.S. Holocaust Memorial Museum began in November 1978 when President Jimmy Carter established the President's Commission on the Holocaust, chaired by author and Holocaust survivor Elie Wiesel. The following year, the commission submitted a report recommending an educational foundation, a Committee on Conscience and a national Holocaust memorial museum. After the U.S. Holocaust Memorial Council was formed by a vote of Congress in 1980, the memorial museum was dedicated in April 1993 with the first visitor being the fourteenth Dalai Lama of Tibet. The architect behind the building was German-born James Ingo Freed.

The U.S. Holocaust Memorial Museum has a permanent exhibition that spans three floors with artifacts, photographs, film footage and other documents that present the full history of the Holocaust. There are more than 12,750 artifacts, 49 million pages of archival documents, 80,000 historical photographs and one thousand hours of archival footage housed here.

## NATIONAL MUSEUM OF NATURAL HISTORY
## (NEW U.S. NATIONAL MUSEUM BUILDING)

10th Street NW and Constitution Avenue NW
Approximate distance to Metro: 0.3 miles

When it opened in March 1910, this building was originally known as the new U.S. National Museum. Designed by local architectural firm Hornblower & Marshall, this museum housed art, geology and natural history collections with over ten million objects. During the construction process, progress temporarily ceased as the Smithsonian Institution found Hornblower & Marshall's French baroque design for the entrance to be too ornate. Charles Follen McKim of the firm McKim, Mead and White was hired to develop a solution that involved a Roman profile for the dome and central pavilion and other simplified elements for the exterior. Eventually, the building ran out of storage, and wings were added to the building in 1965 by Mills, Petticord & Mills. By 1967, the U.S. National Museum was eliminated as an administrative entity, two years later becoming the National Museum of Natural History with the art and history collections relocated.

Some of the biggest focal points in this museum include the Hope Diamond, two Easter Island stone figures and, at the center of the rotunda, a taxidermied male African bush elephant. In total, the National Museum of Natural History houses more than 126 million natural science specimens and cultural artifacts, including insects, plants, fish and photographs.

## NATIONAL MUSEUM OF AMERICAN HISTORY
## (MUSEUM OF HISTORY AND TECHNOLOGY)

1300 Constitution Avenue NW
Approximate distance to Metro: 0.2 miles

When it first opened in January 1964, the National Museum of American History was known as the Museum of History and Technology. New York–based firm McKim, Mead and White designed the building with approximately 750,000 square feet of space. The name wasn't changed until

1980. In 2008, a two-year, $85 million renovation to the building's center core was completed.

Some of the major highlights to the museum's collection of more than 1.8 million objects include the original Star-Spangled Banner, President Abraham Lincoln's top hat, Julia Child's kitchen and Dorothy's ruby slippers from *The Wizard of Oz*.

## HIRSHHORN MUSEUM AND SCULPTURE GARDEN

Independence Avenue SW and 7th Street SW
Approximate distance to Metro: 0.3 miles

Before the Hirshhorn Museum and Sculpture Garden were created on this site, there was the red brick Army Medical Museum and Library, which stood here from the 1880s to 1969. Starting in the late 1930s, Congress began plans for a national museum of contemporary art that was meant to complement the National Gallery of Art. It wasn't until the 1960s that plans gained traction with Smithsonian secretary S. Dillon Ripley reviving the concept alongside modern art collector, financier and philanthropist Joseph H. Hirshhorn. Congress established the Hirshhorn Museum and Sculpture Garden in 1966 with the building opened in 1974. The architect behind this donut-shaped, Brutalist-style building was architect Gordon Bunshaft.

The building is covered with concrete, measuring 231 feet in diameter and 82 feet high. There is a total of 197,000 square feet in indoor and outdoor exhibition space. Not everyone was in agreement with the modern design of the building, but Ripley once said that if the Hirshhorn Museum "were not controversial in almost every way, it would hardly qualify as a place to house contemporary art."

## NATIONAL MUSEUM OF THE AMERICAN INDIAN

Independence Avenue SW and 4th Street SW
Approximate distance to Metro: 0.7 miles

President George H.W. Bush signed legislation in November 1989 to create this museum as part of the Smithsonian Institution. This legislation allowed for a small museum in New York, a storage facility in Maryland and the flagship museum in Washington, D.C. Before this, the Museum of the American Indian was founded in New York City in 1916 by mining engineer and American Indian artifact collector George Gustav Heye. To design the D.C. building, there was collaboration between American Indian communities and architectural consultants, including GBQC and Douglas Cardinal, Ltd. Following this conceptual design work, the project was developed by Jones, House, and Sakiestewa along with the architecture firms Jones & Jones, SmithGroup, Lou Weller, the Native American Design Collaborative and Polshek Partnership Architects.

The National Museum of the American Indian officially opened to the public in September 2004. Its curvilinear form, colors and textures are meant to reflect the American Indian culture. The grouping of trees and other plants on the north side is meant to reflect the dense forests in the Blue Ridge Mountains, while the corn, beans and squash in the museum's croplands incorporate typical irrigation and planting techniques used by American Indians. Across the three facilities in Maryland, New York and D.C., there are over 800,000 artifacts and 300,000 images, the largest collection of American Indian art and artifacts in the world.

## NATIONAL MUSEUM OF AFRICAN ART

950 Independence Avenue SW
Approximate distance to Metro: 0.2 miles

This museum, originally known as the Museum of African Art, was originally located in a Capitol Hill town house that once belonged to African American abolitionist and author Frederick Douglass. The museum began as a private educational institution in 1964 and became part of the Smithsonian Institution in August 1979. Its name changed in 1981, and a new facility opened on the National Mall in 1987. The scope of the museum also expanded from focusing solely on the traditional arts of sub-Saharan Africa to also modern and contemporary artworks.

# THE ARTHUR M. SACKLER GALLERY
# AND THE FREER GALLERY OF ART

1050 Independence Avenue SW
Approximate distance to Metro: 0.2 miles

These two adjacent museums were named after Detroit-based industrialist Charles Lang Freer and New York–based art collector and philanthropist Arthur M. Sackler. Freer donated his collection of Chinese and Japanese art along with a $1 million endowment to the government in 1906 in order to found the Freer Gallery of Art. In 1913, he selected architect Charles Adams Platt to design the building. It wasn't completed until 1923. The Sackler Gallery wouldn't open until 1987, designed by Shepley, Bulfinch, Richardson & Abbott with Jean-Paul Carlhian as the architect in charge. To create the newer building, Sackler donated approximately one thousand objects and $4 million. Both buildings are dedicated to furthering the study of Asian art and culture.

# FRANKLIN D. ROOSEVELT (FDR) MEMORIAL

1850 West Basin Drive SW
Approximate distance to Metro: 1.1 miles

Like many memorials in Washington, D.C., it took many years and redesigns before this one finally came to fruition. Congress first established a memorial commission for President Franklin D. Roosevelt in 1955. Five years later, the first approved design called for eight towering slabs of marble, but it was canceled due to a disapproving article from the *Washington Post* that described it as "Instant Stonehenge." It wasn't until the mid- to late 1970s that San Francisco–based architect Lawrence Halprin created a design that was deemed suitable, though Congress didn't appropriate money for the project until 1990. Still, progress was slow, in part because of a controversy over the depiction of Roosevelt and his disability.

In 1921, Roosevelt was diagnosed with polio and became permanently paralyzed from the waist down. After this, he was careful to be seen in public in his wheelchair, often wearing iron braces or using a cane. In 1995, after the design of the memorial was revealed, the National Organization on Disability and some historians voiced concern that none of the memorial's sculptures or bas-reliefs depicted Roosevelt with a wheelchair, crutches, braces or cane. After these complaints, a statue of the president seated in his wheelchair was incorporated into the memorial. The memorial was officially dedicated in May 1997 by President Bill Clinton.

The 7.5-acre FDR Memorial is the nation's first memorial designed to be wheelchair accessible. It also includes an area with tactile reliefs and braille writing for those with visual impairment. This memorial, which Halprin described as "the apotheosis of all that I have done," involves a sequence of four galleries or garden rooms, which tell a narrative sequence of Roosevelt's four terms. Each are built primarily out of red South Dakota granite with a water feature in the form of pools and waterfalls. There is a total of ten bronze sculptures and twenty-one carved inscriptions from the president's speeches and radio talks. The sculptures were designed by Leonard Baskin, Neil Estern, Robert Graham, Thomas Hardy and George Segal. One notable sculpture, designed by Segal, is a bronze depiction of First Lady Eleanor Roosevelt standing before the United Nations emblem. This is the only presidential memorial to depict a first lady.

## MARTIN LUTHER KING JR. MEMORIAL

1964 Independence Avenue SW
Approximate distance to Metro: 1 mile

This might not be the first memorial to an African American in Washington, D.C., but this is one of the most notable as Martin Luther King Jr. is the first African American honored with a memorial on or near the National Mall. He is also only the fourth non-president to be memorialized in such a way. The design of the memorial involves a 30-foot-tall sculpture of King with a 450-foot curving wall inscribed with fourteen brief quotations from his speeches. The portrait of King is based on a photograph by Bob Fitch. The words engraved in the memorial were done by Nick Benson, while the official sculptor was Chinese artist Lei Yixin. Congress authorized King's fraternity, Alpha Phi Alpha, in 1996 to establish a memorial to him. The design chosen was by San

Francisco–based firm ROMA Design Group, which won a competition in 2000 that garnered over nine hundred entrants.

The entire memorial spans approximately four acres. There are many symbolic elements of this memorial, some more subtle than others. For instance, the location is a reference to the year of the Civil Rights Act of 1964. The site is also about halfway between the Thomas Jefferson and Abraham Lincoln Memorials. The official dedication for the Martin Luther King Jr. Memorial was in August 2011, the forty-eighth anniversary of the March on Washington for Jobs and Freedom.

The theme of the entire memorial is based on a line from King's 1963 "I Have a Dream" speech: "With this faith, we will be able to hew out of the mountain of despair a stone of hope." To reinforce the idea of struggle, there are scrape marks in the memorial's "mountain," which visitors are meant to enter from. King emerges from a "Stone of Hope," facing the horizon.

A major point of controversy in King's memorial was a paraphrased quote that was previously inscribed on the memorial. It was, "I was a drum major for justice, peace and righteousness." Author and poet Maya Angelou spoke against this quote, saying it made him "look like an arrogant twit." His original words were from a February 4, 1968 sermon at Ebenezer Baptist Church in Atlanta where he said, "If you want to say that I was a drum major, say that I was a drum major for justice. Say that I was a drum major for peace. I was a drum major for righteousness. And all of the other shallow things will not matter." In 2013, the quote was removed.

# 16

# L'Enfant Plaza

## L'ENFANT PLAZA

429 L'Enfant Plaza SW
Approximate distance to Metro: 0 miles

This complex features four commercial buildings surrounding a plaza, above a shopping mall, perpendicular to a pedestrian esplanade. The master plan for the site was originally developed by William Zeckendorf of Webb and Knapp and his staff architect I.M. Pei in 1965. Benjamin Banneker Park (also known as the Tenth Street Overlook) was designed by Dan Kiley in 1967. The addition of a hotel and office building in 1973 was completed by Vlastimil Koubek. Edwin F. Schnedl designed the shopping mall and food court. At the time, L'Enfant Plaza was the largest government-aided private urban renewal project in the nation. The name L'Enfant Plaza is a reference to Pierre Charles L'Enfant.

L'Enfant Plaza is part of the colossal Southwest urban renewal project, which was conceived in the early 1960s in order to assert the city's "progress" in the face of "decay." Before the massive concrete structures were built here, there were instead tree-shaded streets lined with Victorian town homes.

The American Institute of Architects has described the complex as having an "air of quiet dignity," though some visitors may find the Brutalist buildings rather imposing. In 1973, the *Washington Post* described the development as both "a superb work of urban design in the best neoclassic tradition" and also with a "widely lamented…damaging flaw," being that it is devoid of liveliness by being a "dead end." This is unfortunately still true, as the area tends to come to a quiet halt after weekday working hours.

## BENJAMIN BANNEKER PARK
## (TENTH STREET OVERLOOK)

429 L'Enfant Plaza SW
Approximate distance to Metro: 0.1 miles

Spanning five acres, this ovoid park, ringed by London Plane trees, serves as the terminus of L'Enfant Plaza. It measures two hundred feet wide with a multi-tiered fountain that projects water more than thirty feet high. Designed by Dan Kiley, this park was constructed in 1967 and named in honor of Benjamin Banneker, an African American mathematician, astronomer, farmer and almanac author.

## ROBERT C. WEAVER FEDERAL BUILDING
## (U.S. DEPARTMENT OF HOUSING AND URBAN
## DEVELOPMENT)

451 7th Street SW
Approximate distance to Metro: 0.1 miles

Serving as the headquarters of the U.S. Department of Housing and Urban Development (HUD), this ten-story, curved building was the first government building to be constructed under the seminal "Guiding Principles for Federal Architecture," written by Senator Daniel Patrick Moynihan and introduced by President John F. Kennedy. Listed in the National Register of Historic Places, it is also recognized as the first federal building in the nation to use precast concrete as the primary structural and exterior finish material. Additionally, it is the first fully modular design for a federal office building.

Completed in 1968, this Brutalist structure was designed by Hungarian-born modern architect Marcel Breuer, who is also known for having designed the Whitney Museum of American Art in New York. A plaza was later designed by landscape architect Martha Schwartz in 1990.

The structure wasn't renamed to honor Dr. Robert C. Weaver, the first secretary of HUD and the first African American cabinet member, until July 11, 2000.

# 17

# Federal Center SW

## U.S. BOTANIC GARDEN

100 Maryland Avenue SW
Approximate distance to Metro: 0.7 miles

With an establishment as far back as 1850, the U.S. Botanic Garden is one of the oldest botanic gardens in North America. Its beginnings arose in 1816 when the Columbian Institute for the Promotion of Arts and Sciences in Washington, D.C., proposed the creation of a botanic garden. This garden was created on the National Mall in 1820, west of the U.S. Capitol grounds, and it functioned until 1837.

After the U.S. Exploring Expedition, otherwise known as the Wilkes Expedition, surveyed the Pacific Ocean and surrounding lands from 1838 to 1842, plans reignited for a national botanic garden. The collection of living plants obtained from the expedition was first held in a greenhouse behind the Old Patent Office Building, now known as the Smithsonian American Art Museum and National Portrait Gallery. In 1850, a botanic garden was constructed by the Columbian Institute to place the plants in. It was relocated once more to the present location in 1934.

Currently, the site hosts three acres of natural spaces, including but not limited to the Rose Garden, Butterfly Garden, an amphitheater for outdoor gatherings and the First Ladies Water Garden, which honors the nation's first ladies. There is also a conservatory, which contains two courtyard gardens, two exhibit galleries and ten garden rooms across nearly thirty thousand square feet of space. In total, there are approximately sixty-five thousand plants at the U.S. Botanic Garden.

# WILBUR J. COHEN FEDERAL BUILDING
# (SOCIAL SECURITY ADMINISTRATION BUILDING)

330 Independence Avenue SW
Approximate distance to Metro: 0.5 miles

This modern, blocky limestone building houses two major tenants, Voice of America and the Broadcasting Board of Governors. When it was constructed in 1940, it was part of a major building campaign to accommodate the rising numbers of federal employees in the District. In 1937, President Franklin D. Roosevelt initiated plans for new government buildings to house workers under New Deal programs as well as the expansion of services of existing agencies. The first occupant of the building was the Social Security Administration (SSA), following the passing of the Social Security Act in August 1935.

The building was designed by Philadelphia-based architect Charles Z. Klauder with centrally located entrance pavilions, monumental pilasters and a continuous cornice line. While the interior is more along the lines of Art Moderne, the façade offers characteristics of the Egyptian Revival style. The building was renamed in 1988 in honor of Wilbur Joseph Cohen, a government official and public affairs educator who was involved in the creation of the New Deal program. He was also the first employee of the Social Security Board and secretary of Health, Education and Welfare (HEW). The building was added to the National Register of Historic Places in July 2007.

# MARY E. SWITZER MEMORIAL BUILDING
# (RAILROAD RETIREMENT BOARD BUILDING)

330 C Street SW
Approximate distance to Metro: 0.3 miles

Along with having designed the aforementioned Wilbur J. Cohen Federal Building, Philadelphia-based architect Charles Z. Klauder also designed the nearby Mary E. Switzer Memorial Building, which was originally known as the Railroad Retirement Board Building. This blocky building was constructed in 1940, made primarily out of Indiana limestone and buff-colored brick. Similarly to the Wilbur J. Cohen Federal Building, this property was designed to accommodate the rising numbers of federal employees in Washington, D.C.

The Railroad Retirement Board (RRB) was established in 1934 in order to provide old-age assistance for retired railroad employees. The RRB is known as the predecessor of the SSA, which was formed a year later. With the imminent World War II, this building ended up being used by the Department of War as opposed to the RRB. After the war, it was turned over to HEW and became known as HEW-South.

The building was renamed in October 1972 in honor of Mary Elizabeth Switzer, who was believed to be the highest-ranking woman in the federal government by the time she retired. With this, this property became the first federal building to be named for a woman. It was later added to the National Register of Historic Places in 2007.

# MUSEUM OF THE BIBLE

400 4th Street SW
Approximate distance to Metro: 0.2 miles

Originally, this 1923-built building acted as a refrigeration warehouse. Since November 2017, it has instead been used as a religiously focused museum, devoted to the impact, narrative and history of the Bible. The 430,000-square-foot building spans eight floors, with a performing arts theater, ballroom, garden and restaurant. Throughout the building, $42 million worth of cutting-edge technology has been used to create interactive tablets, a digital guide for smart phones, a 360-degree projection mapping system for the theater and a 150-foot-long LED screen on the ceiling of the hall where visitors enter.

This museum is unsurprisingly not without controversy. In July 2017, *The Atlantic* reported that Museum of the Bible chairman of the board and CEO of Hobby Lobby Steve Green purchased smuggled ancient artifacts from Iraq in 2010 and 2011, resulting in him having to pay a $3 million fine and forfeit nearly 3,500 cuneiform tablets and clay seals. Additionally, Kipp Davis, a biblical scholar at Trinity Western University in Langley, Canada, claimed that a portion of the museum's fragments of the Dead Sea Scrolls, ancient religious writings found in caves near Qumran, are likely forgeries. Despite this, Steven Bickley, the Museum of the Bible's vice president of marketing, administration and finance, told *The Atlantic*, "We don't have any concerns about our collection. The artifacts that were referred to were never in our collection."

# 18

# Capitol South

## SUPREME COURT OF THE UNITED STATES

1 First Street NE
Approximate distance to Metro: 0.3 miles

At one point, lawyers in the Supreme Court had no room to review their cases, let alone hang their coats. Located in the U.S. Capitol since 1801, the law library overflowed, while many associate justices worked from home. It wasn't until 1921, after President William Howard Taft was appointed chief justice of the United States, that his idea of a new building started getting pushed to members of Congress. A commission with the task to create a building for the Supreme Court was established in December 1928 with architect Cass Gilbert hired in April 1929. The new building, finally with spaces for privacy and quiet, was occupied in October 1935.

## LIBRARY OF CONGRESS

101 Independence Avenue SE
Approximate distance to Metro: 0.3 miles

This library is huge in more ways than one. In size, it is the largest library in the world with more than 167 million items on approximately 838 miles of bookshelves. Its holdings include not only books but also millions of recordings, photographs, maps and manuscripts. Its history is even more lengthy.

The John Adams Building of the Library of Congress.

Established in 1800 in an act of Congress, the library was originally housed in the U.S. Capitol until it was destroyed in a fire by the British in the War of 1812. Afterward, former president Thomas Jefferson sold approximately 6,500 books to restart the library's collection. Unfortunately, in 1851, another fire destroyed a large portion of the holdings. After this, a plan emerged to repair and enlarge the library with fireproof materials. Two years later, the library was restored, but by 1865, the space was deemed too small. A separate library building was necessary.

After an architectural design competition in 1873, the structure known today as the Thomas Jefferson Building was constructed and opened to the public in 1897. After the building opened, the *New York Times* wrote that the building was "more than architecturally respectable," "extremely impressive" and "a just source of national pride."

Still, there was room to grow even further. In 1928, then–Librarian of Congress Herbert Putnam urged Congress to purchase land for an Annex Building, which ended up getting constructed in 1939. It is now known as the John Adams Building, named after the president who approved the establishment of the Library of Congress. The third major Library of Congress building to be completed, the James Madison Memorial Building, opened to the public in 1980.

In 1967, before the James Madison Memorial Building opened, Ada Louise Huxtable of the *New York Times* wrote that the Madison Building was yet "another mammoth mock-classical cookie from the Architect of the Capitol's well-known cookie cutter for gargantuan architectural disasters." She further described the building as "ponderous" and "passé."

## THE COURT OF NEPTUNE FOUNTAIN

68 First Street SE
Approximate distance to Metro: 0.2 miles

In front of the Thomas Jefferson Building of the Library of Congress, this 1898-created fountain depicts Neptune, the god of the sea, and the mermaid-like Tritons, along with frolicking sea nymphs and animals that include turtles and frogs. The entire sculpture with its fifty-foot-wide semicircular granite basin was created by New York–based artist Roland Hinton Perry, while the reliefs of dolphins and stalactites on the retaining wall were designed by sculptor Albert Weinert.

## FOLGER SHAKESPEARE LIBRARY

201 East Capitol Street SE
Approximate distance to Metro: 0.5 miles

Located one block from the U.S. Capitol, visitors can find the world's largest Shakespeare collection at the Folger Shakespeare Library. This library was established in 1932 by Henry Clay Folger and Emily Jordan Folger in order to house their collection of  Shakespeare materials. The Folgers later expanded the building's holdings in order to offer concerts and create a research center with public outreach programs. The architect behind the Neoclassical-style building was Paul P. Cret.

Henry Clay Folger was a president and later chairman of Standard Oil of New York.

19

# Eastern Market

## EASTERN MARKET

225 7<sup>th</sup> Street SE
Approximate distance to Metro: 0.2 miles

From the beginning, Pierre Charles L'Enfant planned three markets for Washington, D.C.: an Eastern, Center and Western Market. In 1931, Center Market was razed to make way for the National Archives Building, while Western Market, located at 21<sup>st</sup> and K Streets NW, closed in 1961. The original Eastern Market opened in 1805, located on 6<sup>th</sup> Street SE between K and L Streets SE, but it was damaged by a fire during the British invasion of 1814. By 1871, it was described as a "disgraceful shed" by a local newspaper. The new Eastern Market was completed in 1873, built under the public works program of the 1870s, and has been in continuous operation since then. The architect behind the building was German-born architect Adolph Cluss, who is most known for designing the Arts and Industries Building. Today, it serves as a kind of "town center" for Capitol Hill.

The building measures approximately 300 feet long and 50 feet wide, containing approximately 16,500 square feet. In 1908, the building experienced two expansions with the North Hall and Center Hall, both designed by Snowdon Ashford, inspector of buildings at D.C.'s Office of Public Works. In 1929, business slowed down to the point where there weren't enough vendors to fill the entire building. Because of this, the North Hall was transferred to the local fire department for storage.

Over the years, the existence of Eastern Market has been threatened several times. In 1943, D.C. bureaucrats proposed redeveloping the site into a supermarket. A decade later, there were plans for a national children's theater. By the early 1960s, only two stands remained in the building, while the D.C. health commissioner declared Eastern Market "a menace to public health." Suggestions arose once more to replace the building with a supermarket, but neighborhood opposition saved the historic property time and time again.

With little knowledge as to what the exact cause was, a massive fire damaged Eastern Market on April 30, 2007, causing it to close down until June 26, 2009. To restore the building, the D.C. government joined the Eastern Market Community Advisory Committee and the Capitol Hill Community Foundation. Immediately after the fire, then-Mayor Adrian Fenty described Eastern Market as "a historic landmark that has been the lifeblood of the Capitol Hill neighborhood and a great source of pride for the entire city for more than a century."

Eastern Market is listed in the National Register of Historic Places and is labeled a National Historic Landmark.


## HILL CENTER (OLD NAVAL HOSPITAL)

921 Pennsylvania Avenue SE
Approximate distance to Metro: 0.2 miles


Formerly known as the Old Naval Hospital, this building took the place of a former hospital that was built on the site in the early 1800s. In March 1864, President Abraham Lincoln appropriated $25,000 for the construction of the new hospital, which ended up costing approximately $115,000. The rectangular building was designed to accommodate 50 beds and provide services for the Navy Department, but by 1885, the number of patients admitted to the hospital each year was 110. In 1906, the hospital moved to a newly constructed facility, known as the New Naval Hospital, located at 23rd and E Streets NW. Afterward, through 1911, the Old Naval Hospital was used for the Hospital Corps Training School where sailors were schooled in nursing, hygiene and anatomy. It ceased operations as a hospital in 1911 and later temporarily was used as a Reserve Force Office.

From the early 1920s to 1963, it was leased for use as the temporary home for Veterans of All Wars with the purpose to aid veterans of the Civil War, Spanish-American War and the two world wars. After the D.C. government took control of the site, it housed several social service organizations before finally becoming vacant in 1998. Despite this, the property's days were not over, thanks to the hard work of several D.C. locals. In 2000, a group of residents founded the Friends of the Old Naval Hospital with the goal to restore the site. They also hired the Urban Land Institute (ULI) to study the historicity of the property and to develop a strategy for its redevelopment and reuse. A plan was finally formed and accepted by the city in August 2007. This plan was to reuse the site as an educational center for both children and adults.

This educational center, otherwise known as Hill Center, was shaped in 2010 by D.C.-based architecture firm BELL Architects with an eighteen-month, $10 million restoration. BELL Architects restored and upgraded with a fully ADA-accessible design and a green footprint. A nearby former carriage house was also repurposed.

The Italianate- and Greek Revival–style building was added to the National Register of Historic Places in 1974.

## BARRACKS ROW

8th Street SE between M Street SE and Pennsylvania Avenue SE
Approximate distance to Metro: 0.3 miles

For many decades since the late 1960s, this commercial strip languished, but it has experienced a rebirth with new, distinctive restaurants that began to arrive in the mid-2000s. The pedestrian-friendly route is known as the oldest commercial district in Washington, D.C., established in 1799. The name is taken from the 1801-established Marine Barracks, which is located along the street.

Part of what helped boost this growth was that the National Trust for Historic Preservation chartered Barracks Row as a "Main Street" in 1999. In 1998, the Shakespeare Theatre Company purchased an abandoned structure on 8th Street SE, known as the Oddfellows Building, restoring and renovating it to establish administrative offices and an acting academy. To further spruce up the area as a vital destination in the city, American elm trees were planted and iron streetlights, known as Washington globes, were installed in 2002. The façades of several dilapidated buildings were also renovated or restored.

This neighborhood is the birthplace of John Philip Sousa, who directed the Marine Band and composed several marches, including his magnum opus, "The Stars and Stripes Forever." This band was established in 1798.

## EBENEZER UNITED METHODIST CHURCH

400 D Street SE
Approximate distance to Metro: 0.3 miles

Twenty-five black and sixty-one Caucasian members founded the original Ebenezer Methodist Church in 1805. Eventually, segregated practices caused the black members to leave in 1827, founding the Little Ebenezer Methodist Church at this site. It is the oldest black church in the city.

In 1870, a larger church took the place of the original along with a brand-new name, Ebenezer Methodist Episcopal Church. Twenty-six years later, a storm destroyed the structure, which was replaced once more in 1897. The architecture firm behind the building was Crump and Wagner.

When it opened, the modest red brick structure became the city's first publicly financed school for black children. According to a historical marker near the church, one of the teachers was Emma V. Brown, who is credited as the first African American public school teacher in Washington, D.C.

# THE MAPLES (MAPLE SQUARE, DUNCANSON HOUSE, FRIENDSHIP HOUSE)

619 D Street SE
Approximate distance to Metro: 0.1 miles

This circa 1795–constructed condo building stands as the oldest building in Capitol Hill. It was designed by builder-architect William Lovering for William Mayne Duncanson, a prosperous Anglo-Indian who came to the United States with Thomas Law and invested in city lots. By circa 1800, Duncanson had experienced financial ruin, and the residence then came into the hands of Francis Scott Key, the lawyer who penned the poem that later became the lyrics for the United States' national anthem, "The Star-Spangled Banner." At this point, in 1814, the house served as a hospital for soldiers wounded in the War of 1812's Battle of Bladensburg.

The Maples didn't change ownership until July 1838, when Quartermaster of the Marines Major Augustus A. Nicholson purchased it. Before he passed away five months later, he added a ballroom and commissioned Constantino Brumidi, the artist of the frescoes at the rotunda in the U.S. Capitol building, to decorate it. Twenty years later, expert oceanographer Count Louis Francois de Pourtales acquired the property and allegedly constructed a wine cellar forty-two feet underground, but its entrance has been lost (or it never existed).

The next owner was Emily Edson Briggs, the first female correspondent for the White House, who bought the house in 1871. She later renamed it Maple Square and passed it down to her daughter-in-law before it was acquired by Friendship House in 1936. The Friendship House organization used the site as a settlement house and community center. That year, architect Horace Peaslee, who is known for having designed Meridian Hill Park, restored the property. The Friendship House organization didn't vacate the property until December 2008.

Throughout the nineteenth and twentieth centuries, several additions were done to the building. The original stables and slave quarters were also extensively remodeled and incorporated into the house. It wasn't converted and reopened as condos until 2015 after developer Altus Realty Partners purchased the site in 2010.

The Maples has been added to the National Register of Historic Places.

# CHRIST CHURCH

620 G Street SE
Approximate distance to Metro: 0.3 miles

This church is both the first Episcopal parish in the nation's capital and also the oldest and probably the first Gothic Revival structure in the city. The first rectory was built in 1824, thought to be designed by Benjamin Henry Latrobe, but was actually designed by Robert Alexander, a member of the vestry, a builder and Latrobe's chief contractor for the Navy Yard. Several early U.S. presidents worshiped here, including James Madison, Thomas Jefferson and James Monroe. Another notable congregant was John Philip Sousa, who directed the Marine Band and composed several marches, including his magnum opus, "The Stars and Stripes Forever."

Over the years, there were several expansions to the building with a bell tower added in 1849, which was later used as an observation post during the Civil War. The present Parish Hall wasn't built until 1874, while Victorian elements were added by architect William H. Hoffman in 1878. Additional changes to the building included raising the central bell tower in 1891 and adding frescoes to the interior, which were later removed by architect Delos Smith in 1921 in an attempt to instead have them resemble Venetian marble blocks. The first rectory was later razed in 1924 with the present one built on the site. Horace Peaslee, who is known for having designed Meridian Hill Park, attempted to return the church to what was considered Latrobe's original intentions by simplifying the interior in the year 1955. Eleven years later, a two-story addition to the Parish Hall was built.

# LINCOLN PARK (LINCOLN SQUARE)

Approximate distance to Metro: 0.6 miles

Lincoln Park is the largest park in Capitol Hill and was part of Pierre Charles L'Enfant's original 1791 plan for the city, a green space intended for public use. Here, visitors can find memorials to President Abraham Lincoln and civil rights activist and educator Mary McLeod Bethune. At first, the space was used as a dumping ground before it became the site of Lincoln Hospital, which was visited by Walt Whitman, during the Civil War.

In 1867, Congress named the area Lincoln Square, making it the city's first monument to Lincoln. The memorial statue wasn't unveiled until 1876. At the unveiling was Frederick Douglass, who delivered the keynote address before President Ulysses S. Grant, his cabinet and members of Congress.

For the Lincoln memorial, the funds were collected solely from freed slaves, while the organization controlling the effort and keeping the funds was a white-run war-relief agency based in St. Louis, the Western Sanitary Commission. The sculpture, known as both the Emancipation Memorial and the Freedman's Memorial, was designed and sculpted by Thomas Ball. Certainly, it is not the most popular sculpture of Lincoln in the city. In 1997, historian Kirk Savage condemned it as "a monument entrenched in and perpetuating racist ideology" due to the subordinate position of the black figure. Frederick Douglass also admonished the artwork for perpetuating racial stereotypes. The statue depicts Lincoln holding the Emancipation Proclamation before a kneeling black man, who is modeled after the last person captured under the Fugitive Slave Act, Archer Alexander. Alexander's arms are extended to show broken shackles. The statue first faced west toward the U.S. Capitol, but it was rotated east in 1974 to face the Bethune memorial.

New York–based artist Robert Berks sculpted the Bethune memorial. He was also behind the large Kennedy bust that is located in the foyer of the Kennedy Center. Bethune is depicted as supporting herself by a cane given to her by President Theodore Roosevelt and also handing a copy of her legacy to two young black children. The memorial was unveiled in 1974, becoming the first monument to honor a black woman in a public D.C. park.

# 20

# Potomac Avenue

## CONGRESSIONAL CEMETERY
## (WASHINGTON CEMETERY,
## THE WASHINGTON PARISH BURIAL GROUND)

1801 E Street SE
Approximate distance to Metro: 0.5 miles

Established in 1807, this more than thirty-acre burial ground was originally founded as a neighborhood cemetery by Capitol Hill residents. It was named Washington Parish Burial Ground in 1812 when the site was turned over to Christ Church, before later shortening to Washington Cemetery. Once it became the official congressional burial ground as well as the first national cemetery, its moniker switched to Congressional Cemetery.

From 1816 through 1877, more than eighty official cenotaphs were added, each designed by Benjamin Henry Latrobe and paid for by Congress. Some of the many notable interments at this cemetery include FBI Director J. Edgar Hoover, photographer Mathew Brady, the first librarian of Congress George Watterson and Philip P. Barbour, who served as Speaker of the House and an associate justice of the Supreme Court. Additional must-know burials are D.C. Mayor and Councilmember Marion Barry Jr. and Elbridge Gerry, signer of the Declaration of Independence, governor of Massachusetts, vice president under President James Madison and creator of the term "gerrymander." A large number of soldiers and sailors from the Revolutionary War and War of 1812 have also been buried here. Three U.S. presidents were originally buried at Congressional Cemetery: W.H. Harrison, Zachary Taylor and John Q. Adams. Their remains were later relocated.

The architects behind Congressional Cemetery were William Thornton, George Hadfield and Robert Mills. The cemetery is both listed in the National Register of Historic Places and designated a National Historic Landmark.

21

# Stadium-Armory

## ROBERT F. KENNEDY (RFK) MEMORIAL STADIUM (DISTRICT OF COLUMBIA STADIUM)

2400 East Capitol Street SE<br/>Approximate distance to Metro: 0.2 miles

Originally known as the District of Columbia Stadium, this multipurpose stadium was built for both football and baseball. It has hosted five NFC Championship games as well as two MLB All-Star games in 1962 and 1969. Here, several U.S. presidents have thrown the ceremonial first pitch, including John F. Kennedy, Richard Nixon and George W. Bush. The building was designed by Dallas-based architect George Leighton Dahl near the banks of the Anacostia River with a campus that spans 190 acres. RFK Stadium was known as the first of eleven "cookie-cutter" stadiums, a national boom of multipurpose stadiums created through the 1970s. RFK Stadium didn't get its new name until after Robert F. Kennedy's assassination in 1968.

Since it opened on October 1, 1961, it has been home to the Washington football team from 1961 to 1996; home to soccer team D.C. United from 1996 to 2017; and home to two Washington baseball teams, the Senators from 1962 to 1971 and the Nationals from 2005 to 2007.

There are plans to raze the stadium and redevelop the campus with several options, including a recreation complex, food hall and pedestrian bridges.

# THE D.C. ARMORY

2001 East Capitol Street SE
Approximate distance to Metro: 0.2 miles

Originally, this domed building opened in 1941 as the headquarters, armory and training facility for the D.C. National Guard. Since then, it has hosted a variety of events, including a performance by Frank Sinatra and acts from the Ringling Bros. and Barnum & Bailey Circus. There have also been several inaugural balls held here by U.S. presidents like Harry Truman, John F. Kennedy and Barack Obama. Its space also served hundreds of New Orleans evacuees during Hurricane Katrina in 2005. The possibility to use the space as a homeless shelter was proposed in the mid-1980s, but plans ended up falling through.

With a ten-thousand-seat, multipurpose arena and seventy thousand square feet of drill floor space, the D.C. Armory is known as one of the most versatile venues in the Mid-Atlantic region. The architect behind this structure is American architect Nathan Wyeth, who is most known for having designed the West Wing of the White House and the Francis Scott Key Bridge.

# THE CAR BARN (EAST CAPITOL STREET CAR BARN)

1400 East Capitol Street NE
Approximate distance to Metro: 0.5 miles

Before this building became what is now known as the Car Barn, a 196-unit condominium building that was completed in 2005, it stood vacant for approximately forty years. The Romanesque Revival–style structure was constructed in 1896 with a red brick façade and an L shape. Structurally, the building is not considered very innovative, but its history granted it enough worth to be listed in the National Register of Historic Places.

Originally known as the East Capitol Street Car Barn, this building was designed by Waddy Butler Wood, the same architect behind the Masonic Temple, to be used as a car barn repair shop and administrative offices for the Metropolitan Railroad Company. In 1864, this was the second streetcar company chartered in D.C., with the first being the Washington and Georgetown Railroad Company, which was chartered two years earlier. When this car barn was built for the Metropolitan Railroad Company, this was during a time when the company was converting all of its streetcar lines to an underground conduit system. After several mergers and bankruptcies of the several streetcar companies that had formed in D.C., the final streetcar to operate in the city was on January 28, 1962. After this, the East Capitol Street Car Barn was used to store buses before finally losing any purpose over the course of several decades.

## ST. COLETTA OF GREATER WASHINGTON

1901 Independence Avenue SE
Approximate distance to Metro: 415 feet

St. Coletta of Greater Washington is known as perhaps the most carefully considered school design in the District. This nonprofit public charter school was specifically designed for those with intellectual disabilities. It consists of five connected two-story school structures, each attached to a double-height central hall with a skylight. This central hall is called "village green." The buildings are designed to be not only playful and whimsical but also practical, with the area inside each house painted like its exterior, allowing students to easily recognize their space. Every building houses a different age group. The school's students range in age from three to twenty-two.

The ninety-nine-thousand-square-foot school was completed in 2006, designed by American architect Michael Graves. When it finished, the final cost was $32 million.

St. Coletta was founded in 1959 by a couple with a child diagnosed with Down syndrome. After struggling to find an educational system that fit well with their child, the couple was determined to establish their own school as a special education charter. Originally, the school began in the basement of St. Charles Borromeo School in Arlington, Virginia, with only five students. It eventually relocated to Alexandria, Virginia, before heading to the D.C. campus.

## LANGSTON TERRACE DWELLINGS

2101 G Street NE
Approximate distance to Metro: 1.1 miles

Situated on approximately thirteen acres of land, this pioneering architectural effort was part of the New Deal relief work initiated by President Franklin D. Roosevelt. It was the first U.S. government–funded public housing project in Washington, D.C., and the second in the United States. Construction completed in 1938, with the entire community designed by Washington, D.C.–born Hilyard R. Robinson, who was described by the *Washington Post*'s Wolf Von Eckardt as "the most successful black architect in Washington." In the *Post*, Eckardt futher described Langston Terrace Dwellings as "a handsome memento of a time when architecture was still a social art." Its prominence is so great that it was listed in the National Register of Historic Places in 1987.

Langston Terrace Dwellings is composed of fourteen housing blocks intermingling two- to four-story row houses with apartments arranged in a U-shape. When it was first built, there were 274 residences, but in 1965, 34 units were added. An additional design element of the community that is worth noting is a terra-cotta frieze by Daniel Olney called *The Progress of the Negro Race*. It lines the central courtyard with images that chronicle African American history from enslavement through World War I.

The complex is named after John Mercer Langston, a U.S. representative from Virginia who was also a member of D.C.'s first board of health, the first dean of the law school at Howard University and briefly the acting president of Howard University.

# 22

# Benning Road

## WOODLAWN CEMETERY

4611 Benning Road SE
Approximate distance to Metro: 0.6 miles

At this racially and culturally diverse cemetery, visitors will be able to find more than twenty acres of land of curving roadways and irregular burial sections. The cemetery is located on a sloping, rectangular-shaped plateau and was established in 1895 by five prominent Caucasian businessmen. The founders were Jesse C. Ergood, Charles C. Van Horn, Seymour Tullock, William Tindall and Odell S. Smith.

When it was established, this cemetery was not designated for any specific race or denomination. Because of this, it became an interracial, intercultural, non-sectarian cemetery. According to the National Register of Historic Places nomination form, this was considered one of the most prestigious burying grounds for African American residents.

After Holmead's Cemetery and Graceland Cemetery were closed, the remains from the burial grounds were reinterred at Woodlawn and Rock Creek Cemeteries. Some of the most notable burials at Woodlawn include Blanche K. Bruce, the first African American to serve a full term in the U.S. Senate, and John Mercer Langston, the first African American to be elected to public office in the nation and the first dean of the law school at Howard University.

Woodlawn Cemetery is listed in the National Register of Historic Places.

# MARVIN GAYE PARK (WATTS BRANCH PARK)

Approximate distance to Metro: 1 mile

This 1.6-mile park was first known as Watts Branch Park. Before it was redeveloped into a park, it was a dump for discarded trash, cars and other types of junk. Lady Bird Johnson dedicated the new park in May 1966. The park was made possible by an $11,000 contribution from Laurance S. Rockefeller. It was designed by landscape architect Katheryn Simmons. In 2006, the park was rededicated with a new name in honor of musician and Washington, D.C. native Marvin Gaye.

With construction begun in October 2014, the park broke ground for a new playground shaped like a grand piano with playground equipment shaped like music notes. In 2015, the project also added a new trail system and a nearby recreation center.

Marvin Gaye Park is the longest municipal park in the city.

# 23
# Capitol Heights

## UH, OH!

You have found a Metro station that is basically in the middle of nowhere. Are there any historical sites nearby worth venturing to? Probably not.

# 24

# Addison Road

## UH, OH!

You have found a Metro station that is basically in the middle of nowhere. Are there any historical sites nearby worth venturing to? Probably not.

# 25

# Morgan Boulevard

## FEDEX FIELD (JACK KENT COOKE STADIUM)

1600 Fedex Way
Approximate distance to Metro: 0.7 miles

Originally, there were plans to construct a new seventy-eight-thousand-seat stadium for the Washington football team next to RFK Stadium, but the National Park Service opposed the plan as it would have filled a portion of the Anacostia River for surface parking. After plans with Washington, D.C., and then Alexandria, Virginia, failed, then owner of the Washington football team Jack Kent Cooke finally reached an agreement to build a new approximately eighty-thousand-seat stadium in Landover, Maryland, in December 1995. At the time, it was the largest stadium in the NFL. The first game at the stadium, originally known as Jack Kent Cooke Stadium, was on September 14, 1997.

After Daniel Snyder purchased the Washington football team in 1999, he renamed it FedEx Field after selling the naming rights to Federal Express. Nearly three thousand new seats were added before the 2000 season before being expanded again to a total of over ninety-one thousand seats before the 2004 season. Further changes included removing over six thousand seats from the end zone areas of both upper decks after the 2010 season and removing an additional four thousand seats after the 2011 season.

# NATIONAL HARMONY MEMORIAL PARK

7101 Sheriff Road
Approximate distance to Metro: 3.5 miles

Located on over 142 acres of land in suburban Prince George's County, this cemetery offers multiple mausoleums, an outdoor garden and many roots to the local African American community. In 1960, more than thirty-seven thousand remains from the cemetery of the Columbian Harmony Society were reinterred in National Harmony. None of the original grave markers or monuments were transferred, and many of the graves are unmarked. Founded in 1829, the Columbian Harmony Society's cemetery was the final resting place for many African Americans of every social and economic status. It relocated three times in the society's history. The remains from the historic African American cemetery known as Payne's Cemetery were also relocated to National Harmony in 1965.

Some of the most notable interments here include Elizabeth Hobbs Keckly, the seamstress to Mary Todd Lincoln who eventually wrote a book on the Lincolns' years in the White House; Alvin Childress, an actor; and Captain Henry Vinton Plummer, who escaped from slavery, joined the U.S. Navy during the Civil War, became a pastor of several D.C. churches and became a U.S. Army chaplain.

At the highest levels of National Harmony Memorial Park, visitors can find views of the U.S. Capitol and the Washington Monument.

# 26

# Largo Town Center

## WATKINS NATURE CENTER

301 Watkins Park Drive
Approximate distance to Metro: 5 miles

More than fifty thousand people visit this nature center every year for events that range from hikes and summer camps to puppet shows to craft events and more. Here, there are live animal displays with insects, amphibians, birds and reptiles. The nature center includes classroom and workshop spaces as well as an auditorium. Final need-to-know details include a butterfly and hummingbird garden, "squirrel gym" and both indoor and outdoor ponds.

Nearby, there are also several trails worth exploring.

# Part III

# The Orange Line

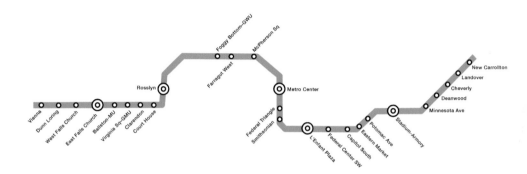

## HIGHLIGHTS ON THE ORANGE LINE:

> Wolf Trap at Vienna
> Mosaic District at Dunn Loring
> Tinner Hill at East Falls Church
> State Theatre at East Falls Church
> Clarendon School at Virginia Square–GMU

# 1

# Vienna

## WOLF TRAP NATIONAL PARK FOR THE PERFORMING ARTS

1551 Trap Road
Approximate distance to Metro: 5.5 miles

Wolf Trap is the nation's only national park for the arts. It has presented performers like Dolly Parton, Diana Ross, Tony Bennett and the National Symphony Orchestra. The entire complex spans over 110 acres and hosts approximately one hundred performances every summer. The Wolf Trap National Park for the Performing Arts is home to the more than seven-thousand-seat outdoor amphitheater known as Filene Center and the Children's Theatre-in-the-Woods. It also features two eighteenth-century barns that house smaller acts and serve as the home of the Wolf Trap Opera. These rustic structures were rebuilt and relocated from upstate New York to Virginia. Together, the barns offer over three hundred seats.

Wolf Trap was founded in 1966 with the first performance on July 1, 1971. The Filene Center was founded by Catherine Filene "Kay" Shouse after she donated her farmland and extra funds to the U.S. government. Shouse had a long background in politics, having worked with every president from Woodrow Wilson to Bill Clinton. Originally, her farmland in Vienna, Virginia, served as a refuge from the city and a gathering place for politicos and other notable people. By donating her land for the purpose of creating a performing arts venue, her goal was to protect the land from becoming a highway, road or suburb.

Before September 2002, the venue was known as Wolf Trap Farm Park for the Performing Arts. Thanks to an act of Congress, its name shifted to the Wolf Trap National Park for the Performing Arts.

In a statement made at the time, Senator John Warner said, "Wolf Trap is a true American treasure," while Representative Jim Moran said in a congressional testimony, "It is a wonderful asset, not just for the Washington metropolitan area, but for the nation."

## MEADOWLARK BOTANICAL GARDEN

9750 Meadowlark Gardens Court
Approximate distance to Metro: 5.5 miles

Spanning ninety-five acres, Meadowlark Botanical Garden is the perfect place for those who appreciate the beauty of life. Stop and smell the flowers at the indoor tropical garden or visit during the winter when the venue hosts its annual holiday light show.

Besides gardens and native plant collections, the most striking feature of this garden is the Bell of Peace and Harmony. This thirty-foot-tall bronze bell signifies a bond of friendship between the United States and South Korea. Other similar Korean bells exist in California, but this is the first one of its kind in the Western Hemisphere. The pagoda structure was built by hand with images of plants, animals and other images symbolic to Virginia. Beside this structure are replicas of ancient Korean monuments and statues.

## FREEMAN STORE AND MUSEUM (LYDECKER STORE)

131 Church Street NE
Approximate distance to Metro: 2.1 miles

Originally named Lydecker Store, this property dates back to 1859 when it was built for Abram Lydecker, an immigrant from New Jersey. During the Civil War, the store/residence also operated as a post office for both the Union and Confederate armies.

One of Abram Lydecker's children, Caroline Lydecker, later passed down the house to her son, Leon Lydecker Freeman. Leon was very active in the town of Vienna, serving on the town council for eight years, including one term as mayor. He established and served as the first president of the Vienna Volunteer Fire Department; was director of Vienna's first bank, the Vienna Trust Company; and was elected as Fairfax County's Republican member of the Virginia House of Delegates in 1929.

After Leon closed the retail operation in 1929, the building served as a residence until 1955. It was sold to the Town of Vienna in 1969 and reopened in 1977 as a general store and museum on the first floor with a museum and administrative office on the second floor.

The building was originally a two-story, frame, seven-bay-wide property. A two-bay section on the northern end was removed and relocated in the late nineteenth century. In 1977, a full renovation was completed with the exterior based on a Civil War–era photograph. The Freeman Store and Museum was added to the National Register of Historic Places in May 2012. It is also the only structure in Vienna to be in the Virginia Landmarks Register.

## ORIGINAL VIENNA LITTLE LIBRARY

Church and Mill Streets
Approximate distance to Metro: 2.5 miles

Dating back to 1897, this one-room clapboard building is one of the oldest museums of its kind in Fairfax County, Virginia. The Vienna Little Library was established thanks to the work of a group of local women known as the Vienna Current Events Club. When it was built, it was located on the corner of Library Lane and Maple Avenue in Vienna. It relocated for the first time in 1912 to the corner of Center Street and Maple Avenue. It relocated once again in 1970 to its current location.

Originally, this library consisted entirely of books donated by locals. In 1935, the library held approximately 1,200 volumes. In 2017, the number escalated to over 5,500 volumes catalogued. Today, the Little Library is operated by nonprofit Historic Vienna. This library is open to visitors, but it is advised that those wishing to tour the inside contact Historic Vienna for the hours of operation

## JAMMIN JAVA

227 Maple Avenue East
Approximate distance to Metro: 2.5 miles

At first, Jammin Java was planned to be a chain of Christian-focused coffeehouses that would also be music venues and retailers for CDs and music lessons. The plan, according to an interview in the *Baltimore Sun* in 1998, was to open these coffeehouses in various locations in the D.C. area. By 2001, any remaining Jammin Java locations were shut down, save for the Vienna, Virginia location. Thanks to an ownership change, a renovation and broader boundaries not confined by one genre, Jammin Java has remained open since then. In 2007, *Paste Magazine* named Jammin Java one of the top forty music venues in the country, further describing it as the "best place to bring the kids to an early show."

The owners who reopened and renovated Jammin Java in 2001 were Daniel, Jonathan and Luke Brindley. After purchasing the venue, they built a new stage and redesigned the lighting. Jammin Java has a capacity of approximately two hundred. Along with comedy shows, the site has also featured musical acts like Nick Jonas, Paramore and Andrew Bird.

# 2

# Dunn Loring

## WASHINGTON AND OLD DOMINION (W&OD) RAILROAD REGIONAL PARK

### Approximate distance to Metro: 2 miles

Virginia's skinniest park spans approximately forty-five miles, running through both urban and countryside areas of the state. For thirty-two of those miles, visitors can ride horses along a gravel trail. Throughout, visitors can run, cycle or skate on an asphalt-surfaced rail trail.

The majority of the trail is located on top of the original rail bed of the former Washington and Old Dominion Railroad, which was originally known as the Alexandria, Loudoun and Hampshire Railroad. Service on this railroad officially ended on August 27, 1968. The Northern Virginia Regional Park Authority purchased the right-of-way from Shirlington to Purcellville in 1978 to reuse it as a trail. The first section of the park opened on September 7, 1974, with the full trail completed in 1988.

There are currently plans to enhance the W&OD Trail with paved trails for walking and biking.

Near the W&OD Trail is Dunn Loring Park, which the *Washington Post* has described as a "very mini version of the National Mall."

# MOSAIC DISTRICT

2910 District Avenue
Approximate distance to Metro: 3 miles

What was once the D.C. area's largest drive-in theater is now a multiplex cinema with a walkable community surrounding it. This neighborhood is now known as the Mosaic District but was previously called Merrifield Town Center. Led by developer **EDENS** and local homebuilders **EYA**,

 the multiphase project has transformed Merrifield into a hip destination with a variety of housing options, restaurants and gourmet drink and food shops. During the summer, there are free yoga sessions in the park, while free movies are broadcasted on a large screen on the side of the movie theater.

# 3

# West Falls Church

## SEE EAST FALLS CHURCH

…on page 228.

# 4

# East Falls Church

## CHERRY HILL FARMHOUSE

312 Park Avenue
Approximate distance to Metro: 1.7 miles

Constructed circa 1845, the Cherry Hill Farmhouse was originally part of a pre–Revolutionary War plantation on a 248-acre tract of land patented to John Trammel in 1729. On this land, the original Falls Church was built in 1746. During the Civil War, there were a few skirmishes on the property, such as the Battle of the Peach Orchard, which was directly behind the house. The two-story Greek Revival–style house was also known as a hiding place for Confederate soldiers.

The Riley family, cousins of the poet James Whitcomb Riley, owned the site from 1870 to 1956. Some of the most notable family members to have lived in this home include Judge Joseph Riley, who is known for helping the town of Falls Church become incorporated in 1875, and his son, J. Harvey Riley, who was an eminent ornithologist connected with the Smithsonian.

The name Cherry Hill was a reference to the many fruit orchards that surrounded the site. The property now serves as a house museum with vintage furnishings meant to reflect what it might have looked like in the 1850s or 1860s. The Cherry Hill Farmhouse was placed in the Virginia Landmarks Register and the National Register of Historic Places in 1973.

# STATE THEATRE

220 North Washington Street
Approximate distance to Metro: 1 mile

This Art Deco theater has had a long history in downtown Falls Church. It opened in 1936 and operated as a movie theater until 1988. At the time, it served as the flagship of the family-owned Neighborhood Theatres chain. In the late 1990s, there was a multimillion-dollar restoration that transformed the property into a music and private event venue. This restoration kept the stage, both lobbies and the two hundred original balcony seats, but the seats on the main floor were removed to allow for the redesign of the auditorium, which now features two bars as well as dining, standing and dancing areas.

When the restoration was still in the planning stages, the new space was touted as the potential "centerpiece" of the revitalization for downtown Falls Church. Now, it features musical acts, comedians and other live performances.

# THE FALLS CHURCH EPISCOPAL

115 East Fairfax Street
Approximate distance to Metro: 1.3 miles

Just south of the existing building on this site was Falls Church, Virginia's first church building. Erected circa 1733, it was built by Richard Blackburn to serve the Truro Parish. By March 1764, George Washington and George W. Fairfax, the appointed church wardens, advertised for people who could construct a new church on the land. By June, the vestry accepted plans by local resident Colonel James Wren with construction completed by December 1769. Past works by Wren also include the Christ Church in Alexandria, Virginia, and Pohick Church in Lorton, Virginia. The Falls Church is one of the oldest remaining church buildings in Virginia.

From the mid-1780s to the early 1800s, the building remained vacant before local community leaders, including Francis Scott Key, helped reopen the church for worship. During the Revolutionary War, The Falls Church served temporarily as a recruiting station as well as a hospital and a stable. Afterward, the federal government awarded the church approximately $1,300 in reparations for repairs.

Over the course of the nineteenth and twentieth centuries, the interior of The Falls Church was renovated or repaired four times. Despite this, the structure retains the original 1769 construction, not including damage from the war and a chancel addition.

The name "The Falls Church" preceded the naming of the community of Falls Church, Virginia, which adopted its name because of the church. The church's name was given due to its closeness to "the falls" of the Potomac River.

## TINNER HILL

### Approximate distance to Metro: 1.5 miles

This area was once the home of Joseph and Elizabeth Tinner, an African American couple who purchased the land in the late 1800s. They fought segregation laws after white Falls Church residents gerrymandered around the Tinners' neighborhood in the late 1880s, shrinking the size of Falls Church by one-third. In 1915, the Falls Church Town Council proposed a law that would further segregate the town by creating a "colored only" zone. The Tinners, along with other citizens in the community, successfully filed a lawsuit against the city, preventing the Falls Church Town Council from enforcing the ordinance. In 1917, the U.S. Supreme Court case of *Buchanan v. Worley* effectively nullified state laws that made residential segregation legal.

It was here in Tinner Hill that the very first rural chapter of the National Association for the Advancement of Colored People (NAACP) was chartered in 1918. Joseph Tinner became the first president of the Falls Church NAACP. Before his death in 1928, Tinner spearheaded civil rights activities, fighting for public utilities, a more modern elementary school, streetlights and more. To commemorate the work of the men and women who formed the first rural branch of the NAACP, the Tinner Hill Heritage Foundation erected a fifteen-foot-tall monument made of pink granite in 1999.

# 5

# Ballston-MU

## MOUNT OLIVET UNITED METHODIST CHURCH

1500 North Glebe Road
Approximate distance to Metro: 1.1 miles

This is the oldest church site in continuous use in Arlington County. It was originally devised on March 12, 1855, when John B. Brown and his wife, Cornelia, deeded approximately nine-tenths of an acre to seven individuals for a Methodist Protestant church and burial ground. The cornerstone wasn't laid until 1855, with the building completed in 1860. A year later, Union soldiers commandeered the property for use as a hospital and later a stable. Despite the soldiers' dismantling the building, a smaller meetinghouse was built on the site in 1870.

This meetinghouse was remodeled and expanded several times over the years before construction began in 1949 for a new sanctuary. Expansions continued several decades later with a renovation in 1997 on the sanctuary and classrooms with the addition of an elevator.

## GLEBE HOUSE (CALEB CUSHING HOUSE)

4527 17th Street N
Approximate distance to Metro: 1 mile

In the beginning, the Glebe was a five-hundred-acre farm provided for the rector of Fairfax Parish. The Glebe House was constructed in 1775, but it burned down in 1808. It was later rebuilt in 1820 as a hunting lodge before a two-story octagonal wing was later added in the 1850s. Since then, the property has been remodeled more than once. Despite this, the Glebe generally appears as it did when it was occupied by one of its notable owners, lawyer and diplomat Caleb Cushing.

Cushing purchased the house in 1870 and continued to live in it until 1878. His greatest contributions included leading the movement for the Treaty of Washington in 1871, which established a Tribunal of Arbitration for settling claims against Great Britain arising out of the latter's participation with the Confederacy in the Civil War. With this tactful solution, he won the United States $15.5 million in reparations. In 1873, he was appointed minister to Spain.

Other distinguished people who have occupied the Glebe House have included former Mayor of Washington, D.C. John Peter Van Ness, State Senator Frank Ball and Reverend Bryan Fairfax, who is known as the Eighth Lord Fairfax.

The National Park Service listed the house in the National Register of Historic Places in 1972.

# 6

# Virginia Square–GMU

## CLARENDON SCHOOL (MATTHEW MAURY ELEMENTARY SCHOOL, ARLINGTON ARTS CENTER)

3550 Wilson Boulevard
Approximate distance to Metro: 465 square feet

This is the second-oldest extant school building in Arlington County. For sixty-three years, this property was also the only elementary school in Clarendon, serving grades one through six. It dates back to 1910 with a rear addition constructed in 1954. The Clarendon School was designed in the Classical Revival style by Virginia-based architect Charles M. Robinson, who designed several buildings at James Madison University, the College of William and Mary, the University of Mary Washington and University of Richmond. According to its nomination form in the National Register of Historic Places, it represents the evolution of public education in Arlington County during the twentieth century.

The three-and-a-half-story brick building sits on a two-acre site that includes Maury Park, which features playground facilities, a picnic area and basketball and tennis courts. The Clarendon School was constructed in two phases. Its main entry is ornamented by a wood frame portico with classical detailing, while the one-bay-wide portico is set upon a poured concrete foundation. This entry is framed with a pair of Tuscan columns and single Tuscan pilasters to support the flat roof.

Originally known as the Clarendon School, it was renamed in honor of Matthew Maury, otherwise known as "Pathfinder of the Seas," in 1944. Maury was born in Fredericksburg, Virginia, on January 14, 1806, beginning his career with the U.S. Navy in 1821. He was later promoted to lieutenant in 1836 before serving as superintendent of the Navy Department's Depot of Charts and Instruments with collateral duty as the head of the Naval Observatory and Hydrographic Office in 1861. His work led him to become commander in the Confederate navy and later secretary of the navy for the Confederacy. After the Civil War, he was a professor of meteorology at the Virginia Military Institute (VMI). Throughout his life, Maury published works on navigation, ocean geography and meteorology.

The building finally ceased to function as a public education facility in 1973, sitting vacant for three or four years before a renovation allowed it to house the Arlington Arts Center (AAC), which continues to operate here. The AAC offers art classes and studio space to local artists and is one of the largest non-federal venues for contemporary art in the D.C. area. The building was renovated once again in 2005.

## BALL FAMILY BURIAL GROUNDS

3427 Washington Boulevard
Approximate distance to Metro: 0.4 miles

As one of Arlington's oldest family burial grounds, this plot of land features the burials of Ensign John Ball, a veteran of the American Revolution, as well as John Wesley Boldin, a Civil War soldier. It also includes members of the Marcey, Stricker, Donaldson and Croson families.

# 7

# Clarendon

## CLARENDON CITIZENS HALL

3211 Wilson Boulevard
Approximate distance to Metro: 1 mile

This building was constructed circa 1921, and the commercial heart of Clarendon developed around it during the 1920s and 1930s. This well-known local landmark has been home to various citizens' organizations, later housing offices of two community newspapers, the *Chronicle* and the *Arlington Press*. Nowadays, it serves as a coffeehouse. It is two and a half stories tall with a hipped roof, tile walls and a stuccoed steel frame.

## ARLINGTON POST OFFICE

3118 North Washington Boulevard
Approximate distance to Metro: 1 mile

This one-story Georgian Revival structure was the first federal building constructed in the county. It represents a milestone in the development of Arlington from a multitude of disparate villages and rural areas to the unified community it is today. Listed in the National Register of Historic Places, this property was constructed in 1937 with a pentagonal plan. At the time it was built, it was the largest consolidation of post offices undertaken by the Post Office Department. When the cornerstone was laid, the *Sun* reported, "Arlington's new post office is a very definitive sign that we're growing up."

In 1967, the original postal windows in the lobby were reworked. Meanwhile, some of the original wood wainscot remain. Inside the lobby, there are murals depicting scenes about Arlington history, painted by Washington, D.C.–based artist Auriel Bessemer in 1939.

According to the nomination form for the National Register of Historic Places, the design of the Arlington Post Office seems to be based on Tudor Place, the historic residence designed by William Thornton in Washington, D.C.'s Georgetown neighborhood.

# 8

# Courthouse

## UH, OH!

You have found a Metro station that is basically in the middle of nowhere. Are there any historical sites nearby worth venturing to? Probably not.

# 9

# Minnesota Avenue

## MAYFAIR MANSIONS APARTMENTS

3819 Jay Street NE
Approximate distance to Metro: 0.5 miles

Before this complex was constructed in 1946, black residents in Washington, D.C., experienced limited amounts of housing and poor conditions for many years. This project was the first and largest privately developed multifamily housing project to be insured by the Federal Housing Administration (FHA) for occupancy by black tenants. Its construction opened the door for blacks across the nation to qualify for FHA financing.

It is also notable for being designed by Albert Irvin Cassell, the third African American architect ever registered in the District. Cassell is also known for having worked with Howard University as a campus planner and architect, notably designing the university's Founders Library. Mayfair Mansions Apartments ended up being the largest of Cassell's work in residential housing. The project was codeveloped with African American radio evangelist Elder Lightfoot Solomon Michaux. Efforts to build this complex were also encouraged by First Lady Eleanor Roosevelt.

On a twenty-eight-acre parcel, Mayfair Mansions Apartments is composed of seventeen Colonial Revival–style garden apartment buildings, organized around a long central common. Each building is

three stories tall, rectangular and made of brick. The property was added to the National Register of Historic Places in November 1989.

Starting in the 1970s, the residential development began to deteriorate. By the late 1980s, the community became notorious for open-air drug markets that led residents to call the Nation of Islam in 1988 in an attempt to restore order. Once the Nation of Islam and officers from the city's Sixth Police District began 'round-the-clock patrolling, drug activity almost completely stopped. That same year, former Mayor Marion Barry Jr. began a major rehabilitation on the buildings.

In 2006, the property was purchased by the Community Preservation and Development Corporation and the Marshall Heights Community Development Organization. One year later, the owners began a redevelopment of Mayfair Mansions Apartments with the plan to maintain the residential units as affordable housing. Renovations were completed in 2009 with improvements to all systems, updated kitchens and bathrooms, new carpeting and flooring as well as new windows and doors. Enhancements were also made to the parking area and to public area lighting.

# 10

# Deanwood

## STRAND THEATER

5129–5131 Nannie Helen Burroughs Avenue NE
Approximate distance to Metro: 1.1 miles

When this theater opened on November 3, 1928, it was the first ever motion picture theater constructed east of the Anacostia River for African American patrons. After over forty years of serving as a center of social life in the neighborhood, it closed in 1959. There are plans to invest $1 million to restore the Renaissance Revival–style property  with funds coming from the Office of the Deputy Mayor for Planning and Economic Development (DMPED).

The owner and builder of the Strand Theater was Abe E. Lichtman, a Caucasian Jewish man who became an advocate for equal economic opportunities for African Americans. In this theater, the white-collar jobs were almost always filled by African Americans. Lichtman also often sponsored recreational opportunities for African American youth.

This theater was added to the National Register of Historic Places in 2008.

# KENILWORTH AQUATIC GARDENS (SHAW GARDENS)

1550 Anacostia Avenue NE
Approximate distance to Metro: 1 mile

Originally, the Kenilworth Aquatic Gardens was a personal project. After the Civil War, veteran W.B. Shaw purchased thirty-seven acres of land, pursuing his hobby of growing water lilies. In 1912, Shaw and his daughter, Helen Shaw Fowler, began to sell their lilies commercially to cities like Chicago, Boston and New York. By 1921, the land was opened to the public on Sunday mornings for visitors to see what was at the time one of the largest lily farms in the world. The National Park Service purchased the land, then known as Shaw Gardens, in 1938. Since then, the gardens have largely remained unchanged.

Situated on the eastern shore of the Anacostia River, the gardens are composed of a series of irregularly sized and shaped ponds. Here, visitors can find approximately seventy-five different varieties of water lilies with day-blooming lilies at their peak in mid-June and night-blooming tropical water lilies open in July and August. There is also a large number of fish, reptiles and amphibians.

# 11

# Cheverly

## MAGRUDER SPRING HISTORIC LANDMARK (CHEVERLY SPRING)

2203 Cheverly Avenue
Approximate distance to Metro: 350 feet

According to a nearby historical marker's inscription, the Magruder Spring was used by British troops on August 24, 1814, before the Battle of Bladensburg. In 1988, this spring and Crawford's Adventure Spring were designated as Prince George's County Historic Sites due to this momentous event. The spring continued to be the primary source of water for town residents even into the early 1920s.

It was later redesignated the Cheverly Spring by Robert Marshall, founder of Cheverly, in December 1918. The name Cheverly comes from Cheverly Gardens, a subdivision founded in 1904 near the Landover Metro station. In 1916, Marshall purchased the remainder of the Cheverly Gardens lots.

## MOUNT HOPE (CRESTLAWN)

1 Cheverly Circle
Approximate distance to Metro: 0.4 miles

This single-family home is the official town symbol, appearing on both the town seal and the town flag. Known as Mount Hope, this former plantation house was constructed by Fielder Magruder circa 1839 with an expansion in the 1860s. The two-story, five-bay frame house was later renovated from 1919 to 1922 as the home and office of Robert Marshall, founder of Cheverly, who lived in the house until 1929. At the time, Marshall dubbed the house Crestlawn. Cheverly's first mayor, Fred W. Gast, later owned Mount Hope from 1941 to 1977.

This property was added to the National Register of Historic Places in November 1978.

# 12

# Landover

## PENNSY COLLECTIONS AND SUPPORT CENTER

3400 Pennsy Drive
Approximate distance to Metro: 0.7 miles

If there is one thing that is true about the Smithsonian Institution, it's that it takes its stewardship of collections very seriously. In December 2008, the Smithsonian Institution opened the Pennsy Collections and Support Center, thereby consolidating and relocating three collections storage and operations support spaces into one facility. The space measures 360,000 square feet with specialized office and training space, exhibit design and fabrication shops, conservation facilities and climate-controlled space to house the organization's collections

This center is not open to the public.

## MUSEUM RESOURCE CENTER

3300 Hubbard Road
Approximate distance to Metro: 2 miles

This central curatorial facility is responsible for the care and preservation of museum objects for park units in the National Park Service's National Capital Region: Maryland, Virginia, West Virginia and Washington, D.C. Some of the archival materials and artifacts found here are from collections like the Arlington House, Ford's Theatre and Vietnam Veterans Memorial.

This center is not open to the public.

# 13

# New Carrollton

## NASA GODDARD VISITOR CENTER

9432 Greenbelt Road
Approximate distance to Metro: 5 miles

The Goddard Space Flight Center was established on May 1, 1959, as NASA's first space flight complex. Perfect for lovers of all things far, far away, this center is home to the nation's largest organization of scientists, engineers and technologists who build spacecraft and technology to study the Earth, our solar system and the universe. It is currently one of NASA's largest research centers with roles that have included studying global precipitation, striving to understand dark energy and managing communications between mission control and orbiting astronauts aboard the International Space Station.

The visitors' center to the Goddard Space Flight Center features informative exhibits about climate change, monthly model rocket launches and artifacts, such as a Gemini capsule model. Those who visit the information desk with a passport will receive a commemorative stamp.

The center is named after Dr. Robert H. Goddard, who is considered the father of modern rocket propulsion.

# Part IV

# The Yellow Line

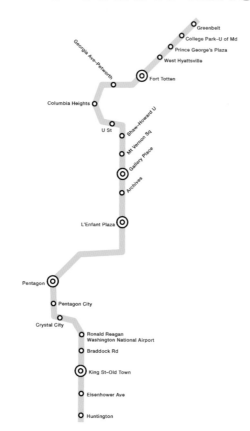

## HIGHLIGHTS ON THE YELLOW LINE:

> Lincoln's Cottage at Georgia Avenue–Petworth
> Tivoli Theatre at Columbia Heights
> Meridian Hill Park at U Street
> Lincoln Theatre at U Street

> Howard Theatre at Shaw–Howard U
> Washington Convention Center at Mount Vernon Square
> Carnegie Library at Mount Vernon Square

# 1

# Huntington

## UH, OH!

You have found a Metro station that is basically in the middle of nowhere. Are there any historical sites nearby worth venturing to? Probably not.

# 2
# Eisenhower Avenue

## HOFFMAN TOWN CENTER

2404 Eisenhower Avenue
Approximate distance to Metro: 0 miles

Adjacent to the Eisenhower Avenue Metro station, visitors will find this mixed-use urban center, ranked as one of Alexandria, Virginia's largest retail and entertainment centers. The entire project spans over seven million square feet across more than fifty-six acres.

The site owner has plans for additional changes to the center with a Wegmans expected to open by around 2020 or 2021 as well as new residential and retail amenities opening around the same time.

## NATIONAL SCIENCE FOUNDATION HEADQUARTERS

2415 Eisenhower Avenue
Approximate distance to Metro: 300 feet

The purpose of the National Science Foundation (NSF) is to promote the progress of science and national health as well as support basic research related to all fields of fundamental science and engineering, not including medical sciences. It's all about "high-risk, high-payoff" ideas when it comes to the NSF. This independent federal agency was created by Congress in 1950 and draws more than sixty thousand visitors every year. The NSF also acts as the funding source for nearly a quarter of all federally supported basic research conducted by the nation's colleges and universities.

Starting in 1993, the NSF was located in Ballston, Virginia, relocated from a location in D.C. proper, near the White House. It remained there until 2017 when it relocated to Alexandria, Virginia, making it one of the largest transfers of federal workers in Northern Virginia ever.

Behind the design of this building is Washington, D.C.–based WDG Architecture, which designed both the base building design and interior design.

# 3

# Mount Vernon Square

## CARNEGIE LIBRARY

801 K Street NW
Approximate distance to Metro: 0.3 miles

Originally known as the city's central public library, this three-story Beaux-Arts building was one of the many libraries funded by Andrew Carnegie in order to promote free library systems. Washington, D.C.'s first public library system was established in 1895, but the first city library wasn't dedicated until January 7, 1903, after Carnegie donated funds in 1899. After a national competition that garnered submissions from twenty-four architects, New York–based firm Ackerman and Ross was selected to design the heavily ornamented building made of pink Milford granite with upper exterior walls composed of white Vermont marble. The exterior marble carvings and other ornaments were designed from models by Philip Martiny.

Before Carnegie Library was constructed, the city's library was based out of a small, three-story row house. Traditionally, libraries were housed in private collections at universities or museums. By the time Carnegie Library opened, its construction ended up costing $350,000, or more than $8 million in 2017 U.S. dollars. It was deemed the "University for the People," as it was the first racially integrated public building in the city. In the District, Carnegie funds were also used for three branches: Takoma Park, Southeastern and Mount Pleasant.

By 1972, the Carnegie Library was severely overcrowded, and the collection had expanded so much that a new library was necessary. This led to the central library system shifting to the Martin Luther King Jr.

Memorial Library. Since then, the building has been used for private events, offices for the city's historical society and as the University of the District of Columbia's graduate library and museum. In the mid-2010s, there were plans to relocate the International Spy Museum to the Carnegie Library building, but these plans were withdrawn.

New plans arose in 2017 when Events D.C., the sports and convention authority that runs the Carnegie Library, approved the lease for an Apple retail store in the building. London-based Foster + Partners and the local office of Beyer Blinder Belle are behind the rehabilitation project.

Carnegie Library was listed in the National Register of Historic Places in 1969.

## WALTER E. WASHINGTON CONVENTION CENTER

801 Mount Vernon Place NW
Approximate distance to Metro: 150 feet

This convention center opened to the public in 2003, only two blocks from the city's original site for a convention center built in 1874. It was designed by a joint venture of Atlanta-based architecture firm Thompson, Ventulett, Stainback & Associates; Washington, D.C.–based architects Devrouax & Purnell Architects; and Mariani and Associates. Named after Walter E. Washington, the District's first home rule mayor, this building spans 2.3 million square feet with 703,000 square feet of exhibit hall floor and seventy-seven breakout and meeting rooms.

In its first year of operation, it was named "Best New Convention Center" by *Meetings East Magazine* and hosted nearly one million visitors. The design also drew much attention over the coming years, receiving awards from the Urban Land Institute (ULI) and the American Institute of Architects (AIA). To further excite visitors' interest in the building, the Walter E. Washington Convention Center launched a public art tour series in 2010, leading to a

$4 million art collection. According to Events D.C., it is the largest in any convention center and one of the largest public art collections in the District outside a museum.

By the building's tenth anniversary, the Convention Center had hosted nearly 1,800 events and welcomed nearly ten million visitors.

## BLAGDEN ALLEY

Blagden Alley NW
Approximate distance to Metro: 0.2 miles

This hip commercial alleyway, filled with street art and popular restaurants, is almost perfectly intact from its original 1865 alignment. This historic district originally housed middle-class residences, churches and small apartment buildings during the 1860s to the 1890s. By the end of the nineteenth century, conditions in the alley system deteriorated with overcrowding, crime and unsanitary conditions. As rents grew and inequality continued, lower-class residents who were often African American crammed into small dwellings in the alleyway. By 1955, a government-funded program known as the Alley Dwelling Authority officially banned the use of alley dwellings in the nation's capital. Conditions in Blagden Alley further worsened after the 1968 riots that followed the assassination of Martin Luther King Jr.

In 1996, the alley was rezoned from residential to commercial, and this helped to ultimately lead to the revitalization of the area.

Blagden Alley was named after Thomas Blagden, who ran a lumberyard and owned property in the area. The alley was designated a National Register Historic District in 1990 and is listed in the D.C. Inventory of Historic Sites.

## SAMUEL GOMPERS MEMORIAL PARK

Massachusetts Avenue NW and 10th and L Streets NW
Approximate distance to Metro: 0.2 miles

In 1933, President Franklin D. Roosevelt dedicated this monument, commemorating London-born Samuel Gompers. Gompers was the founder and president of the American Federation of Labor, which later merged with the Congress of Industrial Organizations to form the AFL-CIO. The sculptor behind the monument is Robert Ingersoll Aitken, who also designed the *Past* and *Future* sculptures at the National Archives.

This bronze artwork features a statue of Gompers sitting in a chair while surrounded by six allegorical figures representing the American labor movement. On the bottom left, the seated female symbolizes the protection of the home. The seated male on the right side signifies the overthrow of industrial exploitation by education. The two standing women represent justice, with one holding a fasces, which is a Roman symbol of power and justice. The two men with clasped hands signify the unity of the labor movement. The image of the 1930s-era steam locomotive engine is meant to symbolize industry. At the granite base, there are also inscriptions of writings by Gompers.

# 4

# Shaw–Howard U

## HOWARD THEATRE

620 T Street NW
Approximate distance to Metro: 2.5 miles

When this theater opened in 1910, it became the first large music venue in the nation for black audiences. It is also one of the oldest theaters in the country, having featured artists like The Supremes, Duke Ellington, James Brown, The Temptations, Miles Davis and Marvin Gaye. According to the *Washington Post*, it is deemed "the nucleus of Washington's Black Broadway." The building was designed by architect J. Edward Storck. The 12,000-square-foot brick building is rectangular in shape, measuring approximately 126 feet by 96 feet. Since it first opened, the interior has been altered greatly, but the original stage remains intact.

At first, the Howard Theatre only served black audiences and was a base for many local black performers. During the 1940s, President Franklin D. Roosevelt attended several Presidential Birthday Balls given here in his honor. After the 1968 riots that followed the assassination of Martin Luther King Jr., the venue became a blighted property, remaining that way for many years to come. In 1986, the D.C. government purchased the site for $100,000 before a major renovation helped to reopen it in 2012. Behind the $29 million renovation were developer Ellis Development Group and architecture firm Marshall Moya Design.

Still, years after the eventful reopening, the venue has encountered many issues. In March 2018, Attorney General Karl A. Racine filed a lawsuit against Howard Theatre Restoration, Inc. (HTR) for allegedly failing to obtain audits, file tax returns and maintain a functioning board. HTR led the revival of the theater in 2012.

## GENERAL OLIVER OTIS HOWARD HOUSE (HOWARD HALL)

607 Howard Place NW
Approximate distance to Metro: 0.7 miles

This sixteen-room mansion was constructed in 1867 for General Oliver Otis Howard. Originally, the residence was one of a group of four early campus buildings at Howard University with this one being the sole survivor. The university officially purchased the house in 1909. Afterward, it temporarily served as the home of Lulu V. Childers and as the Conservatory of Music, which she directed. From the late 1960s to the early 1970s, it housed the African Language Center and African Studies Department. Currently, it is used for conferences and special events.

Howard, the original resident of Howard Hall, accomplished many things during his lifetime. He served as commissioner of the Bureau of Refugees, Freedmen and Abandoned Lands and a member of the Missionary Society of the First Congregational Church of Washington. He was also an officer in the U.S. Army and a Union general in the Civil War. One of his most well-known successes was serving as the founder and third president of Howard University from 1869 to 1874.

The architect of the building is unknown. It is three stories high with an additional story to the southwest corner, forming a tower. It was added to the National Register of Historic Places and designated a National Historic Landmark in 1974.

## SHAW (WATHA T. DANIEL) NEIGHBORHOOD LIBRARY

1630 7th Street NW
Approximate distance to Metro: 280 feet

This glassy, triangular building is one of the city's most recently constructed libraries, opened in August 2010. Designed by architecture firm Davis Brody Bond Aedas, the $12 million Shaw Neighborhood Library has received awards from the Washington, D.C. chapter of the AIA and the ULI and was even deemed one of the best architectural projects of 2010 by the *Wall Street Journal*.

The LEED Gold–certified facility spans three stories and approximately twenty-two thousand square feet with two twelve-person conference rooms, a large program room for up to one hundred people and over thirty public-access computers with free Wi-Fi access. At the east end of the site, the entry plaza features a twenty-two-foot-tall light sculpture with rolled metal tubing created by local artist Craig Kraft, called *Vivace*.

Daniel was a longtime civic activist in Shaw as well as the first chairman of the D.C. Model Cities Commission. When Daniel passed away in December 1973, Mayor Walter E. Washington described him as "one of the city's most remarkable citizens and a splendid public servant for many years."

## CARTER G. WOODSON HOME NATIONAL HISTORIC SITE

1538 9th Street NW
Approximate distance to Metro: 0.2 miles

This three-story Victorian-style building was constructed in the 1870s to 1890s and is most famously known for having housed Carter G. Woodson. During his lifetime, Woodson established the Association for the Study of Negro Life and History (ASNLH), the *Journal of Negro History* and the *Negro History Bulletin*. At this residence, the ASNLH was housed after it was founded on September 9, 1915, and incorporated on October 3 of that year.

Woodson was the son of former slaves, born in December 1875 in New Canton, Virginia, and later educated at Harvard University, becoming the second black American to receive a doctorate from that institution, following W.E.B. Du Bois. His teaching career involved working at Howard University and West Virginia Collegiate Institute. In 1926, he instituted Negro History Week, which eventually gained national support and participation from many schools, colleges and other organizations in the nation.

The row house was added to the National Register of Historic Places and was deemed a National Historic Landmark in 1976. The National Park Service acquired the site in 2005, later restoring it. In 2006, it was authorized as a National Historic Site. The home opened to the public for tours in 2017.

## MARY CHURCH TERRELL HOUSE

326 T Street NW
Approximate distance to Metro: 0.2 miles

Built in 1907, this Victorian-style semi-detached building was the home where Mary Church Terrell lived for the greatest length of time. Terrell was born in Memphis, Tennessee, on September 23, 1863, and later graduated from Oberlin College and Wilberforce University. She was the first black woman to serve on an American school board, and in 1895, she succeeded in receiving one of three appointments to the Board of Education that were designated for women. With this, she became the first black woman in the United States to be in the position, while fighting for quality education, fair hiring employment practices and more adequate appropriations for school. Later in her life, she became president of the National Association of Colored Women and joined the National American Suffrage Association at Susan B. Anthony's request. During World War I, Terrell worked in the War Camp Community Service, organizing recreational facilities for returning black war veterans. One of her most well-known accomplishments was leading the successful fight to integrate eating places in the District.

This National Historic Landmark is in the National Register of Historic Places and is a contributing structure to the LeDroit Park Historic District.

# PHYLLIS WHEATLEY YOUNG WOMEN'S CHRISTIAN ASSOCIATION (YWCA)

901 Rhode Island Avenue NW
Approximate distance to Metro: 2 miles

This is the oldest "Y" in the city and the nation's only independent black YWCA. Washington, D.C.'s YWCA was organized in May 1905 by the Book Lover's Club, a black women's literary group led by Rosetta Lawson, one of the co-founders of Frelinghuysen University. It later relocated to its present location after it was built in December 1920. During World War I, the Wheatley YWCA provided traveler's aid to blacks who came to D.C. During the Second World War, it became a United Service Organizations (USO) center for black servicemen who were denied entrance to segregated USO centers.

The four-story brick building was designed by New York–based firm Shroeder and Parish, which also designed the YWCA building in New York. The Colonial Revival–style building is listed in the National Register of Historic Places. In November 2015, a partnership between the D.C. Housing Authority, the D.C. government and seven other community partners initiated a major face-lift on the building. The $17 million renovation preserved eighty-four supportive and affordable units for low-income women.

The YWCA renamed itself to honor Phillis Wheatley, who is considered the first published female African American poet.

# HOWARD UNIVERSITY (HOWARD THEOLOGICAL SEMINARY)

2400 Sixth Street NW
Approximate distance to Metro: 1 mile

Originally known as Howard Theological Seminary, this private, non-sectarian, historically black university was founded in March 1867 by members of the First Congregational Society of Washington. At first, the society hoped to establish a theological seminary for the education of

African American clergymen. This project later expanded to include the establishment of a university that would end up growing from a single-frame building in the mid-nineteenth century to a campus size of over 255 acres by the early twenty-first century. The name of the school honors university founder, Civil War Union General and U.S. Army officer General Oliver Otis Howard. He was commissioner of the Bureau of Refugees, Freedmen and Abandoned Lands and a member of the Missionary Society of the First Congregational Church of Washington. He also served as the university's third president, from 1869 to 1874.

Howard University is composed of thirteen schools and colleges with a library system that contains more than 1.8 million volumes. The school competes in nineteen varsity sports. Howard's enrollment is approximately 10,300 undergraduate, graduate and professional students with notable alumni that include former U.S. Supreme Court Justice Thurgood Marshall, Pulitzer Prize–winning author Toni Morrison and Emmy Award–winning actress Phylicia Rashad.

A portion of the school's campus is recognized as nationally and architecturally significant. The Founders Library and Frederick Douglass Memorial Hall were both designed by African American architect Albert Irvin Cassell in 1939 and 1935, respectively. Cassell was the third African American architect ever registered in the District. With its Colonial Revival style, Founders Library was designed to resemble Philadelphia, Pennsylvania's Independence Hall. Here, Charles Hamilton Houston, the former dean of Howard University's Law School, served as a part-time professor teaching in the Civil Rights Law course. Frederick Douglass Memorial Hall is a U-shaped, Neoclassical building named in honor of abolitionist and university trustee Frederick Douglass. The Memorial Hall has been used for classrooms and research for NAACP strategy. Additionally, the 1894-built Andrew Rankin Memorial Chapel represents the community support garnered by the university for the NAACP to use desegregation as a tool to obtain civil rights, according to the building's nomination form for the National Register of Historic Places. As a group, these buildings, along with the 1910-built Carnegie Building, were declared a U.S. National Historic Landmark in 2001.

# 5

# U Street

## LINCOLN THEATRE

1215 U Street NW
Approximate distance to Metro: 0 miles

Featuring acts like Chuck Brown, Dave Chappelle and Louis Armstrong, this is one of only a few first-run early movie theaters that remain in the city. Designed by local architect Reginald Geare, this fifty-foot-high building was completed in 1922 and is located in the heart of the city's "Black Broadway," which attracted entertainers like Billie Holiday, Duke Ellington and Nat King Cole.

In 1927, Harry M. Crandall, D.C.'s foremost movie theater operator in the 1920s, sold the building to theater magnate A.E. Lichtman. Approximately sixty years later, in 1984, the Lincoln Theatre closed for a restoration, which ended in 1993. The Lincoln Theatre reopened in 1994 before being threatened with foreclosure in 2011. Two years later, the venue went under new ownership with concert promotions and production company I.M.P., the operator of D.C.'s 9:30 Club and Merriweather Post Pavilion in Columbia, Maryland.

The Lincoln Theatre is listed in the National Register of Historic Places.

# AFRICAN AMERICAN CIVIL WAR MUSEUM AND MEMORIAL

1925 Vermont Avenue NW
Approximate distance to Metro: 0.3 miles

With the goal to have the 209,145 members of the United States Colored Troops remembered, the African American Civil War Museum opened in January 1999. The nearby memorial was completed in 1997 and dedicated in July 1998. The museum offers a wide array of artifacts, documents and technology presented to more than 200,000 visitors each year.

The nine-foot-tall bronze memorial sculpture is known as *The Spirit of Freedom*. Ed Hamilton created the sculpture to depict three infantrymen and a sailor defending freedom on one side and a soldier with his family on the other. A curved wall shows an inscription of the names of the African Americans who served in the Civil War.

# MERIDIAN HILL PARK (MALCOLM X PARK)

Bounded by 16th, Euclid, 15th and W Streets NW
Approximate distance to Metro: 0.7 miles

Before Meridian Hill Park, there was Mount Pleasant, a farm owned by Georgetown merchant Robert Peter. Circa 1815, an elegant mansion was constructed on the site, known as Meridian Hill. It was named this because it was located on the official meridian of the United States on the White House north–south axis, more specifically 16th Street NW. The house offered President John Quincy Adams shelter in 1829. By 1863, the original home had burned down, but another was erected in its place in 1888, designed by architect E.C. Gardner for former Missouri Senator John B. Henderson and his wife, Mary Foote Henderson. The property experienced additions and renovations over the years, but the retaining wall between Florida Avenue NW and Belmont Street NW on the west side of 16th Street NW is all that remains of the original complex. Before the idea of a park was born, John Russell Pope suggested placing the Abraham Lincoln Memorial on this site. Mrs. Henderson was all for this, but the U.S. Commission of Fine Arts

(CFA) selected the western end of the National Mall instead. In 1906, Mrs. Henderson proposed an urban park that would be known as Meridian Hill Park, which the CFA approved in 1914.

Meridian Hill Park was designed and built between 1912 and 1936 and officially opened in 1936. The designers of the park included Ferruccio Vitale of the landscape firm Vitale, Brinckerhoff and Geiffert and Horace Peaslee. The design of the approximately twelve-acre park was inspired by Italian villa landscapes of the sixteenth and seventeenth centuries. It offers symmetrical stairways and a large reflecting pool surrounded by a plaza. The thirteen-basin cascading fountain, modeled after those in Italian and English Baroque gardens, is considered the longest in North America. Some of the statues inside the park that are worth a look include the 1922-built Joan of Arc statue, which is the only equestrian statue of a woman in Washington, D.C., and originally a gift of friendship by the women of France to American women; the 1921-built Dante statue, which depicts poet Dante Alighieri dressed in the robe of a scholar; the 1924-built *Serenity*, a white marble sculpture dedicated to the memory of Lieutenant Commander William Henry Scheutze; and the 1930-built James Buchanan Memorial, the only Buchanan memorial in the city.

Since 1933, the park has been under the jurisdiction of the National Park Service. By the 1950s and 1960s, the park had begun declining in quality and became a popular staging ground for political demonstrations. In the 1970s, activist Angela Davis unofficially renamed it Malcolm X Park. A local organization known as Friends of Meridian Hill worked with the National Park Service in the early 1990s to restore the park as a cultural center.

## BEN'S CHILI BOWL

### 1213 U Street NW
### Approximate distance to Metro: 120 feet

Don't underestimate this shabby hot dog joint. It is one of Washington, D.C.'s most beloved landmarks, open in this location since August 22, 1958. So beloved is this restaurant that it survived the 1968 riots that followed the assassination of Martin Luther King Jr. Ben's Chili Bowl also obtained special permission to stay open after curfew to provide food and shelter to

those working to restore order during the riots. Since then, it has appeared in movies like *State of Play* and TV shows like *Anthony Bourdain: No Reservations* and *Man v. Food*. The founders of Ben's are Trinidad-born Ben Ali and his wife, Virginia.

Originally, in 1910, the building was home to the first black-owned silent movie house in the country, known as Minnehaha. After changing ownership in 1913, it was known as the Dudley Theatre. By 1957, it became vacant and was bought by Ali. On January 19, 1999, D.C. Councilmember Jim Graham named the alley between Ben's and the Lincoln Theatre "Ben Ali Way" in honor of the Ben's Chili Bowl founder. On September 1, 2012, a mural was painted in Ben Ali Way by artist Aniekan Udofia. This mural has taken on many forms since then, each time to much fanfare and celebrity appearances. To see which well-known figures have eaten at this establishment, notice the restaurant's walls, which are lined with autographed photos of everyone from Chris Tucker to Denzel Washington to Dr. Dre.

## MARY ANN SHADD CARY HOUSE

1421 W Street NW
Approximate distance to Metro: 0.3 miles

From 1881 to 1885, this three-story red brick residence was occupied by Mary Ann Shadd Cary. So notable is Cary that her house was declared a National Historic Landmark and is listed in the National Register of Historic Places. It also is a contributing property to the Greater U Street Historic District. Born in Wilmington, Delaware, in October 1823, Cary became the first black newspaperwoman in North America. She founded the *Provincial Freeman* in 1853, a nonsectarian and nonpartisan newspaper focused on the interests of blacks in Canada. During the Civil War, she was appointed to the post of recruiting officer for the Union army. When she moved to Washington, D.C., after the Civil War, she enrolled in Howard University's law program, becoming one of the first black women lawyers in the nation and later fighting for women's suffrage. Another success of hers was being able to speak before the annual convention of the National Suffrage Association in 1878.

## MERIDIAN HOUSE
## (WASHINGTON INTERNATIONAL CENTER)

1630 Crescent Place NW
Approximate distance to Metro: 0.8 miles

Built to resemble an eighteenth-century French-style mansion, this residence was deemed "one of the finest examples of architecture in the French style in America" by *Architectural Record* in 1929. Behind the structure is John Russell Pope, the same architect behind the Thomas Jefferson Memorial and the West Building of the National Gallery of Art. The first owner of the elegant house was Irwin Boyle Laughlin, heir to one of the country's more sizeable steel fortunes. The property stayed in the Laughlin family until it was purchased by nonprofit Meridian International Center in 1960. The building, completed circa 1920, measures seventy-six feet and six inches and is five bays wide.

## PINK PALACE (INTER-AMERICAN DEFENSE BOARD)

2600 16th Street NW
Approximate distance to Metro: 0.8 miles

Not so pink anymore, huh? This "Pink Palace," so named for its original color, is currently known as the headquarters for the Inter-American Defense Board. The organization began leasing the property in 1949 and purchased it a year later for $180,000. When the building was still in the planning stages, Mary Foote Henderson, the wife of former Missouri Senator John B. Henderson, hoped for the grand estate to help transform rural upper 16th Street NW into an avenue of grand diplomatic residences based on European models. This was the first speculative mansion undertaken on Meridian Hill by Henderson and her architect, George Oakley Totten Jr.

At the time, Totten was the city's leading Beaux-Arts architect, later designing Meridian Hall at 2401 15th Street NW, the Embassy of Ecuador at 2535 15th Street NW and the Embassy of Cameroon at 2349 Massachusetts Avenue NW. When this building was constructed in 1906, it was designed for Secretary of the Treasury Franklin MacVeagh and his wife, Nellie.

The Venetian Gothic mansion's structure changed over the years with a two-story ballroom addition on the north end built by Totten in 1912 and interior and exterior renovations undertaken in the 1920s to 1930s. In 1984, eight of nine original balconies were removed. An office addition was also attached to the west wall.

## SCOTTISH RITE TEMPLE

1733 16th Street NW
Approximate distance to Metro: 0.6 miles

The nation's capital may not have any of the Seven Wonders of the Ancient World, but it does have this building, which is modeled after one of them. Dedicated in 1915, this Masonic temple serves as the headquarters of the Scottish Rite of Freemasonry. It was modeled after the Temple at Halicarnassus, in what is now Turkey. The ancient temple was built by Queen Artemisia as a memorial for her husband, King Mausolus, in 350 BC. It was this building that produced the word "mausoleum." The architect for the D.C. temple was John Russell Pope, the same architect behind the Thomas Jefferson Memorial and the West Building of the National Gallery of Art. When the cornerstone of this building was laid on October 18, 1911, builders used the silver trowel that George Washington had used to lay the cornerstone of the U.S. Capitol.

From the inside out, the Scottish Rite Temple is embellished with several symbols, some more obvious than others. The front steps rise in flights of three, five, seven and nine, which reflect numbers sacred to Pythagoras. Flanking these steps are sphinxes. The sphinx on the right side with half-closed eyes represents Wisdom, while the one on the left side with open eyes represents Power. Both sculptures were carved by Adolph

Alexander Weinman. Inside, some of the decorative details are modeled after furnishings in Pompeii. The temple also offers a museum devoted to Albert Pike, who rewrote some Scottish Rite rituals and whose remains are buried in the House of the Temple. The library also contains one of the world's largest collections of materials on and by Scottish poet and Freemason Robert Burns.

# 6

# Columbia Heights

## TIVOLI THEATRE

3301–3325 14th Street NW
Approximate distance to Metro: 0.3 miles

When this historic theater opened in 1923, an article from the *Washington Post* described it as the largest theater in the city and a "temple of the arts." It was originally built as a 2,500-seat movie theater, which later offered shows that included ballet, orchestral and concert numbers. This is the only theater still standing in D.C. by American architect Thomas White Lamb, who was known as one of the foremost designers of theaters and cinemas in the twentieth century. The owner of the Tivoli Theatre was Harry M. Crandall, a local businessman and leading theater owner in D.C.

The Italian Renaissance Revival–style theater closed in 1976 and remained vacant for many years. In 1983, the D.C. government sought to demolish the property for a commercial building to take its place. Two years later, it was added to the National Register of Historic Places. It reopened as the home of the GALA Hispanic Theatre in 2006, exhibiting live stage productions.

# FRANCIS ASBURY STATUE

16th and Mount Pleasant Streets NW
Approximate distance to Metro: 0.5 miles

Francis Asbury is known as the father of the American Methodist Church due to him helping the American Methodist Church grow through his travels and preaching. For D.C., this is a rare example of the commemoration of a religious leader. On October 15, 1924, the bronze, life-sized equestrian statue was dedicated. It was later added to the National Register of Historic Places in 2007. The artists behind the statue are H. Augustus Lukeman for the grouping and Evans Tracy for the marble base. The statue features Asbury wearing a cloak and a wide-brimmed hat with his right arm bent. He is seen carrying a Bible with his forefinger inserted between the pages. The horse's neck is bent toward its left knee in order to lick it.

# BLOOMBARS

3222 11th Street NW
Approximate distance to Metro: 0.3 miles

Open to all, this not-for-profit community arts organization offers dance classes, film screenings and open mic performances. The venue launched in 2008 out of a former two-story print shop. It's hard to pinpoint exactly what BloomBars is. Is it a bar? No, it doesn't serve any alcohol. In an interview with the *Washington Post* in 2011, owner John Chambers said, "It's not a theater, art gallery, studio, music venue. It's all of those things, but more than that. It's an environment created to support people's growth."

# Georgia Avenue–Petworth

## PRESIDENT LINCOLN'S COTTAGE
## (OLD SOLDIER'S HOME, ANDERSON COTTAGE)

140 Rock Creek Church Road NW
Approximate distance to Metro: 2 miles

 This one Petworth cottage has many names and has had many tenants, but it is best known for being a place of solace for U.S. President Abraham Lincoln. Lincoln spent approximately one-quarter of his presidency in this thirty-four-room country house, inhabiting the property most often during the summers from 1862 to 1864. One reason for escaping the White House to this former military asylum was to avoid the heavy heat of the nation's capital. As a place of study, it was also the location where he wrote the final draft of the Emancipation Proclamation.

While the cottage now has the name of Lincoln in its title, it has been the home of three other presidents: Rutherford B. Hayes, Chester A. Arthur and James Buchanan Jr. The only other president to visit this site was President Bill Clinton, who declared the cottage a National Monument in July 2000. Approximately twenty-five years earlier, it was recognized as a National Historic Landmark.

Part of what makes this restored residence-turned-museum so historic is not only its affiliation with U.S. presidents but also its impact on the U.S.

military. In November 1827, Secretary of War James Barbour made the recommendation to Congress that an asylum for old or disabled soldiers should be founded. It wasn't until 1851 that Congress finally passed the bill doing so, allowing three sites in D.C. and branch sites in New Orleans, Louisiana, Mississippi and Kentucky. The three asylum sites in D.C. were known as Anderson Cottage, the Corn-Riggs House and Sherman South.

Anderson Cottage, which would eventually become Lincoln's Cottage, was constructed in 1842 by banker George Riggs, who later went on to form the now-defunct Riggs Bank.

Lincoln's Cottage first opened as a museum in February 2008 after an eight-year, $15 million capital restoration project by the National Trust for Historic Preservation was completed.

## PETWORTH NEIGHBORHOOD LIBRARY

4200 Kansas Avenue NW
Approximate distance to Metro: 0.5 miles

First opened on January 27, 1939, this library was the work of more than ten years of planning by the citizens of Petworth. As early as 1927, community organizations like the Petworth Citizens' Association petitioned for a public neighborhood library. When it opened, it became the sixth neighborhood library to open in the city and the third to be funded strictly through public appropriations. The American architect behind the building was Nathan Wyeth, the same architect behind the D.C. Armory and the White House's Oval Office. The original plans were modified to reduce construction costs, though the overall appearance was unaltered.

In June 2009, a two-phase renovation began that would modernize and refresh the two-and-a-half-story Georgian Revival–style building. When it reopened in February 2011, some of the many new features included a twelve-person conference room, a one-hundred-person community room connected to an outdoor patio, forty computers with free Wi-Fi access and dedicated areas for adults, children and teens. Additional highlights also include two study rooms, improved ADA access and design features like new and restored woodwork, a new terrazzo tile floor mosaic and a new cupola and balustrade constructed according to the original 1938 design. The renovation also resulted in the building becoming more environmentally friendly with a new heating and air conditioning system, energy-efficient lighting and water-efficient toilets and faucets.

Following the renovation, the library received an award from the Washington, D.C. chapter of the American Institute of Architects.

## SHERMAN CIRCLE

Illinois and Kansas Avenues NW and 7th and Crittenden Streets NW
Approximate distance to Metro: 0.8 miles

This grassy area was named after Civil War Union army General William Tecumseh Sherman, who has an equestrian bronze and granite monument located in President's Park, near the White House. Dedicated in 1903, the statue was designed by sculptor Carl Rohl-Smith. Sherman is best known for his 1864 March to the Sea. The reason why his statue is not in the circle named after him is because his supporters wanted the monument to be located in a more prominent place in the city. This is the same reason why the nearby Grant Circle, which is named after Ulysses S. Grant, is statue-free.

In the early 1930s, there were talks of moving the Sherman monument to Sherman Circle, but because the move would have required an act of Congress, the statue remained in place. At one point, there was also a proposal to relocate the Bartholdi Fountain, designed by Frédéric Auguste Bartholdi, on this site. Bartholdi is known for creating the Statue of Liberty. The fountain is instead located on the grounds of the U.S. Capitol.

# Part V

# The Green Line

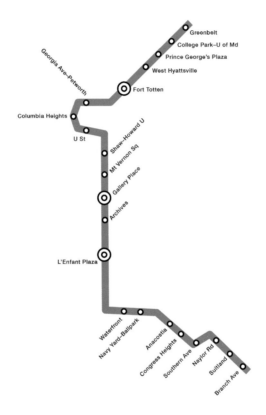

Greenbelt
College Park–U of Md
Prince George's Plaza
West Hyattsville
Georgia Ave–Petworth
Fort Totten
Columbia Heights
U St
Shaw–Howard U
Mt Vernon Sq
Gallery Place
Archives
L'Enfant Plaza
Waterfront
Navy Yard–Ballpark
Anacostia
Congress Heights
Southern Ave
Naylor Rd
Suitland
Branch Ave

## HIGHLIGHTS ON THE GREEN LINE:

> Maine Avenue Fish Market at Waterfront
> Blind Whino at Waterfront
> Nationals Park at Navy Yard–Ballpark
> The Big Chair at Anacostia
> Frederick Douglass Home at Anacostia
> St. Elizabeth's Hospital at Congress Heights
> THEARC at Southern Avenue

# 1

# Greenbelt

## GREENBELT MUSEUM

10-B Crescent Road
Approximate distance to Metro: 2.5 miles

The community of Greenbelt, Maryland, was created in the late 1930s by President Franklin D. Roosevelt's New Deal administration. The museum is a nonprofit organization that is formed by a partnership between the

City of Greenbelt and the nonprofit Friends of the Greenbelt Museum. This neighborhood museum acts as a way for locals and visitors to learn about the town through exhibits, public programs, educational programs and walking tours. The former residence that now houses the two-story museum dates back to 1937.

## OLD GREENBELT THEATRE (ROOSEVELT CENTER)

129 Centerway
Approximate distance to Metro: 3 miles

This Art Deco–style single-screen building first opened in 1938, beginning as a cooperative where members staffed the theater together and made decisions about the film screenings and concessions as a group. Between 2014 and 2015, the theater was remodeled. Now, it is owned by the city and operated by a nonprofit. It offers over 360 seats.

## GREENBELT COMMUNITY CENTER (GREENBELT ELEMENTARY SCHOOL, GREENBELT CENTER SCHOOL)

15 Crescent Road
Approximate distance to Metro: 2.5 miles

Originally, this circa 1937–built community center served as a school and a library with seven teachers and twenty-four students. Eventually, it became a neighborhood hub as both a church and community center. In the early 1990s, the $7.9 million Greenbelt Elementary School replaced this Art Deco–style building, which closed in the late 1970s during a period of decreasing enrollment. After the new school was constructed, the city refurbished the historic building into its present status.

2

# College Park–University of Maryland

## COLLEGE PARK AIRPORT

1909 Corporal Frank Scott Drive<br>Approximate distance to Metro: 0.5 miles

This is the world's oldest continually operating airport and was the site of the training of the first military fliers in the United States. The College Park Airport was established in August 1909 by the U.S. Army Signal Corps with civilian aircraft flying here as early as December 1911. The entire campus spans approximately sixty-six acres of land with a paved 2,750-foot runway. The compass rose has been carefully preserved since it was installed in 1918.

Wilbur Wright was an instructor for Signal Corps officers of the army with the first flight from a government-owned aircraft in October 1909. In June 1912, the site hosted the first firing of a machine gun from an airplane in flight. Other firsts for College Park Airport include the first mile-high flight by a powered airplane and the first controlled helicopter flight. The Signal Corps training school at College Park Airport officially ceased in 1913, though civilian aviation continued.

In order to improve flying in bad weather and "blind" flying, the Bureau of Standards developed and tested the first radio navigational aids that would be the forerunner of the modern Instrument Landing System used today. This testing ran from 1927 to 1933.

The College Park Airport is listed in the National Register of Historic Places and has been since 1977.

## COLLEGE PARK AVIATION MUSEUM

1985 Corporal Frank Scott Drive
Approximate distance to Metro: 0.5 miles

Not too far from the College Park Airport, this museum offers visitors the opportunity to learn more about the local historic airport and other aviation innovations in Prince George's County. The museum spans twenty-seven thousand square feet. From here, be sure to watch out for any pilots taking off or landing from the runway.

## ROSSBOROUGH INN

Rossborough Lane and Baltimore Avenue
Approximate distance to Metro: 1 mile

The Rossborough Inn is the oldest building on the University of Maryland–College Park campus. Over the years, it has served many purposes and been used as a Civil War encampment site for Confederate soldiers, a hostel, a museum, a library, a restaurant and office space. Different sources offer varying dates of when this building was constructed, but it was built sometime between 1798 and 1814, making it older than the University of Maryland itself.

Land speculator Richard Ross constructed the building. The building is named after the Ross family. One past owner of the property is George

Calvert, who left it to his son, Charles Benedict Calvert, who founded the Maryland Agricultural College, a predecessor of the University of Maryland. Charles was also a U.S. representative from the Sixth District of Maryland and an early backer of the telegraph.

# 3

# Prince George's Plaza

## RIVERSDALE HOUSE MUSEUM (CALVERT MANSION)

4811 Riverdale Road
Approximate distance to Metro: 1.6 miles

There are some who believe that U.S. Senator, Secretary of State and Speaker of the House Henry Clay not only often visited this former residence, but also that he wrote a draft for the Compromise of 1850 while in the northeast bedroom. Furthermore, the house's design has been attributed to William Thornton, the architect who designed the U.S. Capitol, but this rumor has not been substantiated. Now, the building acts as the Riversdale House Museum, first opened to the public in 1993 after a restoration. The museum takes a look at federal, state, local, women's and African American history related to the household.

Originally, the building was constructed in the early 1800s, planned by Baron de Stier to resemble his Belgian home, Chateau du Mick. De Stier first immigrated to the United States in 1794 after the French army occupied Belgium. His son-in-law George Calvert later added hyphens and wings to the building around the year 1830. Eventually, the house came under the ownership of Charles Benedict Calvert, who devoted his life to agriculture, served as a U.S. representative from the Sixth District of Maryland and was an early backer of the telegraph. He also founded the Maryland Agricultural

College, a predecessor of the University of Maryland. Eventually, in 1949, the property was purchased by the Maryland-National Capital Park and Planning Commission for its Prince George's County headquarters.

The former Calvert Mansion was added to the National Register of Historic Places in 1973 and designated a National Historic Landmark in 1997.

## VANADU ART HOUSE

### 3808 Nicholson Street
### Approximate distance to Metro: 0.5 miles

Shock your senses by viewing one of the most out-of-place, embellished art houses in the D.C. area. This residence is filled to the brim with antiques, historical objects, mosaics, recycled metal and what might be considered junk. Clarke Bedford, a museum conservator, has also embellished cars as much as his house with items like moose antlers, vases and graveyard spires. The house was completed around the year 2007.

An embellished car at the Vanadu Art House.

The name "Vanadu" is a reference to "Kubla Khan," a poem by Samuel Taylor Coleridge that featured Xanadu, the summer palace of the Mongol ruler and Emperor of China Kublai Khan.

## PRINCE GEORGE'S AFRICAN AMERICAN MUSEUM AND CULTURAL CENTER

### 4519 Rhode Island Avenue
### Approximate distance to Metro: 2 miles

Since 2010, the Prince George's African American Museum and Cultural Center (PGAAMCC) has celebrated the diverse artworks and experiences of the area's African American community through exhibitions and public programs. The museum is thanks to Friends of North Brentwood, a nonprofit organization created in 1998 to develop a museum for the town of North Brentwood. Friends of North Brentwood worked with the Gateway Community Development Corporation (GCDC) as well as state, county and local officials to develop the museum. In January 2007, the Friends group changed its name to the PGAAMCC.

## FRANKLIN'S RESTAURANT, BREWERY AND GENERAL STORE

5123 Baltimore Avenue
Approximate distance to Metro: 1.6 miles

Inside an 1880s-era former blacksmith, carriage shop and eventually hardware store, Franklin's is a community gathering space that includes Prince George's County's first microbrewery. It also claims to be the only combination restaurant, brewery and toy store in the world. While the restaurant is serious, the store is quirky and colorful, filled to the brim with candy, hot sauces, children's toys, trinkets and decorations.

Mike and Debra Franklin purchased the property in 1992 to open Franklin's General Store and Deli. The store was doubled in size in 2002 when the deli closed in order to open a two-hundred-seat brewpub in its place. With this store's success in the community, there are some who credit Franklin's with the wave of redevelopment along Route 1.

4

# West Hyattsville

## ASH HILL (HITCHING POST HILL)

3308 Rosemary Lane
Approximate distance to Metro: 2.6 miles

Around the year 1840, Englishman Robert Clark built this two-story brick house in order to create a space that would allow some peace and quiet away from the city of Washington, D.C. The house was originally constructed on approximately 430 acres of land. The square building measures fifty feet by fifty feet with a five-bay façade with a central doorway. The porch extends around either side with Doric columns supporting an entablature of frieze and cornice.

Frontiersman, diplomat and entrepreneur General Edward Beale purchased the property in 1875, later entertaining President Ulysses S. Grant and President Grover Cleveland in the home. Beale was also an owner of Decatur House.

Ash Hill, originally known as Hitching Post Hill, was listed in the National Register of Historic Places in 1977.

5

# Archives

## NATIONAL ARCHIVES BUILDING

700 Pennsylvania Avenue NW
Approximate distance to Metro: 0 miles

Some of Washington, D.C.'s most precious, revolutionary documents are housed in this building. Constructed in 1935, this limestone-covered property is John Russell Pope's second giant mausoleum in the District with the first being the Masonic Temple, now known as the National Museum of Women in the Arts. This building's function is twofold: to securely protect and exhibit documents, such as the Declaration of Independence, the Constitution and the Bill of Rights; and to allow for research in reading rooms and archival vaults.

In comparison to other federal buildings planned for the Federal Triangle after the 1926 Public Buildings Act, the Archives Building proved to be much more difficult to design and plan. It stalled for a number of years, especially in the site selection, land acquisition and design stages. The site chosen for the National Archives moved twice before the final location was chosen. Before this building was erected, farmers' markets occupied the grounds, starting in 1801 with the Center Market built on this site in 1871. The market was designed by German-born architect Adolph Cluss. To make way for the National Archives, the Center Market was demolished in 1931.

The monumental structure that Pope designed offers seventy-two 53-foot-tall Corinthian columns, 40-foot-tall bronze doors and four large allegorical sculptures. On the Pennsylvania Avenue NW side, the sculptures represent the Future and the Past, while the sculptures on the Constitution Avenue NW side depict Heritage and Guardianship. The 118-foot-wide, 18-foot-tall pediments on the north and south sides of the building are the largest in the city with additional sculptures depicting figures that represent destiny, inspiration, history and guardianship. Inside the building, there are two murals in the exhibition hall, known as the Rotunda for the Charters of Freedom. The artworks were installed in D.C. in 1936, originally painted in New York City by artist Barry Faulkner,

The National Archives Building was added to the National Register of Historic Places in 1971.

## U.S. NAVY MEMORIAL

701 Pennsylvania Avenue NW
Approximate distance to Metro: 0.5 miles

The idea for a memorial celebrating the rise of the U.S. Navy was first envisioned by Pierre Charles L'Enfant, but it wasn't fully realized until the twentieth century. Following the redevelopment of Pennsylvania Avenue NW, spurred by President John F. Kennedy, Admiral Arleigh Burke proclaimed in 1977 that "we have talked long enough about a Navy Memorial, and it's time we did something about it."

This memorial honors those who serve or have served in the U.S. Navy, Marine Corps, Coast Guard and the Merchant Marine. It was dedicated on October 13, 1987, the 212th birthday of the U.S. Navy. This plaza features a round granite ceremonial amphitheater with a one-hundred-foot diameter map of the world. Here, visitors will find fountains, pools, flagpole masts and sculptural panels. There is also a statue, known as the "Lone Sailor," near the edge of the plaza.

Adjacent to the memorial is the Naval Heritage Center, which offers interactive exhibits, a theater and a media resource center with printed, video and audio historical documents on the U.S. Navy. There is also a navy log room for searching for information on Sea Service members and veterans.

# 6

# Waterfront

## MAINE AVENUE FISH MARKET
## (MUNICIPAL FISH MARKET)

1100 Maine Avenue SW
Approximate distance to Metro: 0.8 miles

Located on the banks of the Washington Channel, this fish market is the oldest continuously operating open-air fish market in the nation. Dating back to 1805, the Maine Avenue Fish Market offers a variety of vendors who offer both fresh and cooked seafood. Over the years, the fate of the fish market has been threatened more than once. The Municipal Fish Market that opened in 1918 was demolished in the 1960s during an

urban renewal effort in Washington, D.C.'s Southwest quadrant. Since 2015, there have also been plans to renovate the fish market by restoring the historic oyster shed, relocating the fish cleaning building and adding a distillery building, market hall and two retail additions.

# THE WHARF

1100 Maine Avenue SW
Approximate distance to Metro: 0.8 miles

This ambitious project opened in October 2017 with a first phase that included 3.2 million square feet of mixed-use space, including retail, residential, hotel, music venues and park space. The second phase, which is expected to be completed around the year 2021, will add 1.2 million square feet of mixed-use space, designed by a team of eleven architects. Leading the project is developer Hoffman-Madison Waterfront. The Wharf totals twenty-four acres of land and more than fifty acres of waterfront.

# ARENA STAGE AND KREEGER THEATER
## (THE MEAD CENTER)

1101 6th Street SW
Approximate distance to Metro: 0.2 miles

Before a dedicated space was built, the repertory currently housed at the Mead Center was founded in August 1950 by Zelda Fichandler, Tom Fichandler and Edward Mangum, becoming one of the first nonprofit theaters in the nation. Arena Stage is also the first regional theater to transfer a production to Broadway, the first invited by the U.S. State Department to tour behind the Iron Curtain and the first to receive the Regional Theater Tony Award. Arena Stage was also host to the world premiere of Howard Sackler's *The Great White Hope* in 1967.

Originally, the repertory was located in a converted movie-burlesque house, known as the Hippodrome Theatre, before later moving to the Old Heurich Brewery. Arena Stage opened in 1961, designed by Harry Weese & Architects, the same firm behind the city's Metrorail system. Ten years later, Weese designed the Kreeger Theater, which was placed adjacent to

Arena Stage. Arena Stage was designed as a theater-in-the-round with four tiers of seats placed around the stage, while the fan-shaped Kreeger Theatre offered an intimate setting for experimental productions. Over time, both theaters suffered from issues like undersized lobbies and insufficient back-of-house facilities, leading the repertory to expand to other locations before Vancouver-based Bing Thom refurbished the two original buildings in 2010. Bing Thom's Mead Center, spanning 200,000 square feet, placed both theaters under a cantilevered roof with a centralized lobby.

After Bing Thom designed and opened the Mead Center, Roger K. Lewis of the *Washington Post* wrote that Thom designed an "aesthetically bold, sometimes theatrical, architectural ensemble unlike anything else in Washington." In the *AIA Guide to the Architecture of Washington, D.C.*, this complex is also described as "one of the District's most significant modern cultural institutions."

# BLIND WHINO

### 700 Delaware Avenue SW
### Approximate distance to Metro: 0.5 miles

For almost a century, this former church was home to the Friendship Baptist congregation, but it has been reborn as an edgy, colorful arts and event space. The building dates back to 1886, designed and built by James A. Boyce, making it one of the oldest extant buildings in the city's Southwest quadrant. The congregation closed down the church in 2001, and it remained vacant for more than twenty years. At one point, the building was expected to be demolished for condominiums and office space, but a 2004 Historic Preservation Board designation thwarted these plans.

The nonprofit that is currently located in the space was founded by Shane Pomajambo and Ian Callender. Its exterior was painted by Georgia-based artist HENSE, who spent two weeks covering the building with bold colors. Blind Whino officially opened in 2013.

# THOMAS LAW HOUSE (HONEYMOON HOUSE)

1252 6th Street SW
Approximate distance to Metro: 0.1 miles

This residence wasn't originally built as a forever home. In 1794, land speculator and developer James Greenleaf constructed the Federalist-style mansion for Thomas Law and his wife, Eliza Parke Custis, who was First Lady Martha Washington's eldest granddaughter. The couple only lived here for three months as they awaited completion of their eventual home. Afterward, the "Honeymoon House" saw new use as a hotel during the Civil War and later a hospital and medical clinic. It was also used as an amenity space for the nearby Tiber Island Cooperative Homes. The Thomas Law House is one of the oldest homes in Washington, D.C.

This site was added to the National Register of Historic Places in 1973

# TITANIC MEMORIAL

P Street SW and 4th Street SW
Approximate distance to Metro: 0.5 miles

This lesser-known memorial can be found at the south end of Southwest Waterfront Park on the Washington Channel. It was originally located farther north along the Potomac River and was unveiled in 1931 by Helen Herron Taft, widow of William Howard Taft, with the purpose to remember the men who perished in the wreck of the *Titanic* on April 15, 1912, who gave their lives so that women and children could be saved. It was removed from its original location in 1966 and relocated in 1968.

The design of the approximately fifteen-foot-tall memorial was chosen in a competition that was restricted to female artists. Sponsoring the competition was a group known as the Women's Titanic Memorial Association. The designer was Gertrude Vanderbilt Whitney, who was both an artist and prominent patron of the arts. While the design was chosen in 1914, it took approximately twenty years to gather enough funds for it.

It's worth noting that the resemblance of the statue to the iconic outstretched pose that actress Kate Winslet had in the 1997 film *Titanic* is coincidental.

# 7

# Navy Yard–Ballpark

## WASHINGTON NAVY YARD

Approximate distance to Metro: 0.3 miles

This approximately forty-two-acre area houses some forty-five major historic structures, many of which date back to the nineteenth century. As the first navy yard in the country, the Washington Navy Yard served as the U.S. Navy's first home port and as the center for early nineteenth-century naval operations. Famous individuals who worked here have included Robert Fulton, who tested early torpedoes; Commodore John Rodgers, who built the first marine railway; and John P. Holland, who developed the first submarine formally commissioned by the U.S. Navy. This navy yard has served as a testing ground, laboratory and at one point a gun factory. Today, the Washington Navy Yard acts as a major naval administrative center with the Navy Museum and the presidential yacht.

After the U.S. Department of the Navy was established in 1798, the development of the Washington Navy Yard followed soon thereafter, built under the direction of Benjamin Stoddert, the first secretary of the U.S. Navy, under the supervision of the yard's first commandant, Commodore Thomas Tingey. The original master plan was created by Benjamin Henry Latrobe. One of Latrobe's creations that continues to this day is the heavily stuccoed brick Main Gate, which acts as the principal entrance into the Washington Navy Yard. It was completed circa 1804, making it one of the first structures built at the yard and one of the oldest extant examples of Greek Revival architecture in the country. While in continuous use since 1806, the Main Gate has experienced substantial alterations over the years, especially in 1880 and 1881. Two of the most famous visitors who have passed through the Main Gate have included King George VI and Queen Elizabeth.

The Washington Navy Yard is not open to the public, though the Navy Museum is. The area was added to the National Register of Historic Places in June 1973.

## NATIONALS PARK

1500 South Capitol Street SE
Approximate distance to Metro: 0.4 miles

With a capacity of approximately forty thousand, Nationals Park is more than just a baseball stadium. It is also one of the largest venues in the nation's capital. This property spans more than 55,000 square feet across fourteen indoor spaces and over 240,000 square feet across eight outdoor spaces. Nationals Park opened in 2008, designed by HOK Sport (now known as Populous) and Devrouax & Purnell Architects, the same firm behind the Walter E. Washington Convention Center.

Along with housing the Washington Nationals baseball team, this venue offers additional highlights like being the first major stadium to receive a U.S. LEED certification and being the recipient of the U.S. Green Building Council's Silver Status. Construction of Nationals Park also spurred a wave of development in the neighborhood, catching the attention of major news publications. Eight years after the stadium's opening, Thomas Boswell wrote in the *Washington Post* that "Washington has won. And it has won big." He described Nationals Park as "extremely ambitious" and "an urban development triumph."

# NAVY YARD CAR BARN (BLUE CASTLE, WASHINGTON AND GEORGETOWN RAILROAD CAR HOUSE)

770 M Street SE
Approximate distance to Metro: 0.3 miles

Originally, this circa 1891–constructed building served as a storage and repair facility for streetcars, built for Washington and Georgetown Railroad Company, the first street railway company in the nation's capital. After the city's streetcar industry ceased in 1962, the Navy Yard Car Barn switched ownership to a company known as D.C. Transit. Eventually, its use became a bus garage before 2014 when the National Community Church purchased the historic car barn. Currently, the tenants inside the building are two D.C. public charter schools.

This Romanesque Revival–style building was designed by Kansas City–based architect Walter C. Root and is the only extant structure of the four streetcar-related buildings designed by Root in D.C. proper. It was expanded in 1909 to accommodate a larger fleet of streetcars. It is the only Washington and Georgetown Railroad Company building to survive from the cable car era. Known as both the Blue Castle and the Navy Yard Car Barn, this is also one of the only surviving streetcar facilities in the city.

In 2006, the building was added to the National Register of Historic Places.

# TINGEY HOUSE (QUARTERS A)

East of Main Gate and South of M Street SE in the Navy Yard
Approximate distance to Metro: 1 mile

Constructed in 1804, the Tingey House serves as the residence for the Washington Navy Yard's commandants, including its first, Captain Thomas Tingey. This two-and-a-half-story brick structure is one of the earliest buildings erected at the yard and is one of the few public buildings not seriously damaged in the British invasion of 1814. While remodeled, the house retains much of its original character, though the property has been substantially Victorianized by additions and lengthening of the windows. The architect behind this structure is a mystery.

Tingey, who lived in the house from 1812 until his death in 1829, was very active in the local community, being an organizer of the city's first publicly supported school and Congressional Cemetery, as well as an organizer of President James Madison's first inaugural ball in 1809. Some of Tingey's most famous friends included Madison, John Quincy Adams, Benjamin Henry Latrobe and William Thornton.

# 8

# Anacostia

## FREDERICK DOUGLASS NATIONAL HISTORIC SITE (CEDAR HILL)

### 1411 W Street SE
### Approximate distance to Metro: 0.7 miles

Atop one of the steepest hills in Anacostia stands the former home of African American social reformer, abolitionist and author Frederick Douglass. The residence was once known as Cedar Hill, named after cedar trees that were planted nearby, most of which are gone by now. The property was built circa 1855 by an unknown architect with Douglass living here from 1877 until his death in 1895. In 1962, the federal government purchased the property in order to preserve it and reopen it for public tours. It was declared a National Historic Site in 1988.

One of Douglass's most famous writings is his autobiography, titled *Narrative of the Life of Frederick Douglass, an American Slave*. In his book, he shared details about his life as a former slave, born into bondage in Talbot County, Maryland, in 1817. After escaping slavery, he established the newspaper *North Star*. Following the Civil War, he became the United States' minister resident and consul-general to the Republic of Haiti.

# THE BIG CHAIR

Martin Luther King Jr. Avenue SE and V Street SE
Approximate distance to Metro: 0.5 miles

At one point, this nineteen-and-a-half-foot-tall structure was the largest chair in the United States. This Duncan Phyfe dining room chair was commissioned by the Washington, D.C.–based company Curtis Brothers Furniture as a display outside its showroom at V Street SE and Nichols Avenue SE, now known as Martin Luther King Jr. Avenue SE. Bassett Furniture Industries constructed the replica originally out of wood in the 1950s.

To further boost the chair's fame, Curtis Brothers Furniture hired a glassmaker to build a ten-by-ten-foot glass house on the seat of the chair in order for someone to live in it temporarily. The space was built with an air conditioner, heater, telephone, toilet, bed and shower. The temporary resident was Rebecca Kirby, who went by the name Lynn Arnold and was a model and Washington Junior Chamber of Commerce's "Miss Get Out the Vote 1960." She remained in the glass box for a total of forty-two days.

The original wooden Big Chair was removed in August 2005 and replaced eight months later with an aluminum replica.

# ANACOSTIA COMMUNITY MUSEUM
# (ANACOSTIA NEIGHBORHOOD MUSEUM)

1901 Fort Place SE
Approximate distance to Metro: 1.5 miles

Originally known as the Anacostia Neighborhood Museum when it opened in 1967, this became the first federally funded community museum in the nation. At the time, then–Secretary of the Smithsonian Institution S. Dillon Ripley saw the museum as an outreach effort to the local African American community with exhibitions and educational programming that would be relevant to both their local and national experiences and history.

The name of the museum changed to the Anacostia Community Museum in 2006 as its focus renewed to issues impacting contemporary urban communities.

## ANACOSTIA ARTS CENTER

1231 Good Hope Road SE
Approximate distance to Metro: 0.7 miles

This arts space serves as an incubator for art and new businesses with several located in the center itself. Here, there is a one-thousand-square-foot black box theater, galleries and boutique spaces as well as a café and lounge area. The Anacostia Arts Center opened in 2013 and is owned by parent organization ARCH Development Corporation. Since 1991, ARCH has worked in Anacostia, focusing on small-scale business development and support.

## ANACOSTIA PARK

1900 Anacostia Drive SE
Approximate distance to Metro: 1.3 miles

This recreation area is one of the District's largest, spanning over 1,200 acres across multiple sites. These acres include ballfields, basketball and tennis areas and picnic areas. The site also houses the approximately 3,300-square-foot Anacostia Park Pavilion, which offers a space for roller skating. The development of Anacostia Park is thanks to the appointment of the McMillan Commission by Congress in 1901. Planning for a public park took several decades, which required constructing a seawall on the banks of the Anacostia River and dredging the river bottom. In 1933, the National Park Service took over management and oversight responsibilities for Anacostia Park.

# 9

# Congress Heights

## ST. ELIZABETH'S HOSPITAL
## (GOVERNMENT HOSPITAL FOR THE INSANE)

1100 Alabama Avenue SE
Approximate distance to Metro: 0.3 miles

When St. Elizabeth's first opened in 1855, there were very few private and public mental hospitals in the nation. This federally operated hospital opened on the site of a former farm thanks to the work of psychiatric reformer Dorothea Lynde Dix, who argued for healthier, more humane conditions for patients. Its first name was the Government Hospital  for the Insane. It didn't become known as St. Elizabeth's until 1916, thanks to legislation passed by Congress. Along with treating Civil War soldiers, this hospital even took in animals at one point before the Smithsonian National Zoological Park was created. At its height, St. Elizabeth's housed more than eight thousand patients, one of the most famous being poet Ezra Pound.

The hospital, designed by Thomas U. Walter, is divided into two campuses, the West Campus and the East Campus. The West Campus is owned by the federal government, while the East Campus, owned by the District, will house a sports and entertainment complex for the Washington Wizards and Washington Mystics as well as residential, retail, hotel and office space.

St. Elizabeth's Hospital is a National Historic Landmark and is listed in the National Register of Historic Places.

# 10

# Southern Avenue

## THEARC (TOWN HALL EDUCATION ARTS RECREATION CAMPUS)

1901 Mississippi Avenue SE
Approximate distance to Metro: 0.6 miles

The Town Hall Education Arts Recreation Campus, otherwise known as **THEARC**, encompasses over sixteen acres of land with a campus that totals 110,000 square feet of space. It officially opened in October 2005, built and operated by a nonprofit known as Building Bridges Across the River, or **BBAR**. This multimillion-dollar facility has welcomed President Barack Obama twice  and has featured events hosted by Yoko Ono and NASA. Created as a one-of-a-kind resource for those east of the Anacostia River, THEARC offers dance classes, art classes, music classes, medical and dental care and other community services. The campus also hosts a 365-seat community theater, libraries, a gymnasium, an art gallery and playgrounds.

# JOINT BASE ANACOSTIA–BOLLING (JBAB)

20 MacDill Boulevard SE
Approximate distance to Metro: 3 miles

While not open to the public, this joint base is still worth knowing about, especially when passing it by on Interstate 295. Spanning over nine hundred acres, this military installation was established in October 2010 as one of twelve joint bases formed around the nation as a result of the 2005 Base Realignment and Closure Commission (BRAC). JBAB is the consolidation of the Naval Support Facility Anacostia (NSF) and Bolling Air Force Base (BAFB), which were adjacent to each other but separate. While JBAB is a relatively new installation, the property has been a Department of Defense asset since 1917.

From the start, the installation has served an important role. It was the site where navy seaplanes were first tested and where air force aerial refueling techniques were developed. The air force's first headquarters was established at the installation in 1941. Additionally, President Harry Truman's initial official aircraft, known as the Sacred Cow, and President Franklin D. Roosevelt's only official aircraft retired from service on the installation in 1961.

# 11

# Naylor Road

## CEDAR HILL CEMETERY
## (FOREST LAKE CEMETERY, NONESUCH PLANTATION)

4111 Pennsylvania Avenue
Approximate distance to Metro: 1.3 miles

This plot of land was once part of one of the largest pre–Civil War plantations, known as Nonesuch. It didn't become a cemetery, originally known as Forest Lake Cemetery, until 1901. The name wasn't changed until 1913. Covering 150 acres of land, Cedar Hill Cemetery includes more than sixty-five thousand burials with the oldest known tombstone dating back to 1871. There are also three mausoleums, two of which are from the early 1900s, and a pet cemetery.

# 12

# Suitland

## VINE DELORIA JR. LIBRARY

4220 Silver Hill Road
Approximate distance to Metro: 1 mile

This is the twentieth library of the Smithsonian Libraries, sharing research and collection space with the National Museum of the American Indian Archives. The Deloria Library has been in operation since 1999. Its collection includes over forty thousand volumes of books, microfilm and media, covering a broad range of topics related to American Indians and other Indigenous peoples in the Western Hemisphere. Some of the topics covered include tribal histories, biographies and traditional and modern art.

Vine Victor Deloria Jr. was an American Indian author, theologian, historian and activist. One of his most well-known books was *Custer Died for Your Sins: An Indian Manifesto*, published in 1969. He served as executive director of the National Congress of American Indians from 1964 to 1967 and was a board member of the National Museum of the American Indian in 1977.

# 13

# Branch Avenue

## UH, OH!

You have found a Metro station that is basically in the middle of nowhere. Are there any historical sites nearby worth venturing to? Probably not.

# Part VI

# The Silver Line

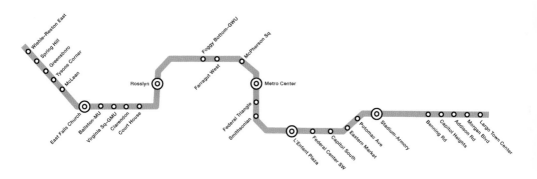

HIGHLIGHTS ON THE SILVER LINE:

> Ash Grove at Spring Hill
> Freedom Hill Park at Greensboro
> Tysons Corner Center at Tysons Corner

# 1

# Wiehle–Reston East

## HERNDON DEPOT MUSEUM

717 Lynn Street
Approximate distance to Metro: 3.5 miles

This simple, one-story wooden structure was constructed in 1857 as a stop on the Alexandria, Loudoun and Hampshire Railroad. It is still basically in its original condition. However, approximately twenty feet of the west end of the building have been removed to allow construction of a road, according to the building's nomination form for the National Register of Historic Places. In the early twentieth century, the Herndon Depot was the center of a large and profitable dairying area. Since a restoration in the early 1970s, it has served as the headquarters of the Herndon Historical Society. The society also offers a museum in the building, which displays artifacts from Herndon, Virginia's history and displays of maritime memorabilia in honor of Virginia-born sea captain and town namesake William Lewis Herndon.

## RESTON HISTORIC TRUST AND MUSEUM

1639 Washington Plaza N
Approximate distance to Metro: 2.5 miles

Local history is celebrated in this museum. The Reston Historic Trust was founded in 1997 as a nonprofit dedicated to sustaining local history.

Here, the museum offers original artworks, crafts and educational programs. The collection of materials spans all the way back to the year 1965 with topics that touch on development, architecture, government and social life. The museum first opened in this space in November 1997. From 2004 to 2009, the museum was overhauled, and an archive system was created.

## HERNDON FORTNIGHTLY LIBRARY

768 Center Street
Approximate distance to Metro: 4 miles

The name of this library is meant to call back to the contributions of the Herndon Fortnightly Club, which was organized in 1889 by eleven local women who met once every two weeks, hence "fortnightly." The purpose of this club was to establish the area's first library, which opened in 1900 in a rented room in the downtown area. By 1927, another library had opened, this time at 660 Spring Street in what is now known as the Herndon Friends Meeting House. The current library at 768 Center Street was constructed in 1995.

## SULLY HISTORIC SITE (SULLY PLANTATION)

3650 Historic Sully Way
Approximate distance to Metro: 8 miles

When it was first built around 1794, this residence was the country home of politician Richard Bland Lee and his wife, Elizabeth Collins Lee. Richard's father, Henry Lee II, was elected to represent Northern Virginia in the first Congress of the United States. Henry was also the grandfather of Robert E. Lee. Richard was a member of the U.S. House of Representatives from 1789 to 1795. Afterward, he was a member of the Virginia House of Delegates.

The Sully house is two and a half stories high and three bays wide with a resemblance to town houses of Philadelphia due to Henry spending much of his time working in the Pennsylvania city. After 1811, the property changed hands numerous times with past owners including U.S. diplomats Walter Thurston and Frederick E. Nolting Jr. The Fairfax County Park Authority has owned the site since 1959.

The site is listed in both the Virginia Landmarks Register and the National Register of Historic Places.

## 2

# Spring Hill

## ASH GROVE

8881 Ashgrove House Lane
Approximate distance to Metro: 0.6 miles

A fire in September 1960 could have decimated the history of Ash Grove, but it was fully restored years later with a new kitchen and a garage addition. The current home was built according to drawings, photographs, recollections of the Sherman family and measurements by the Historic American Buildings Survey in August 1960. The original three-story country estate was constructed circa 1790 by the Fairfax family. Still, two eighteenth-century outbuildings remain on the land.

The site was originally owned by Thomas Fairfax, who later gave Ash Grove and its land to his son, Henry Fairfax. A farmer known as James Sherman purchased Ash Grove in 1850, and his family continued to live here for nearly 150 years until the Fairfax Park Authority purchased several parcels of the land in 1997 and 1998.

# 3

# Greensboro

## FREEDOM HILL PARK

8531 Old Courthouse Road
Approximate distance to Metro: 1 mile

Near this site stood one of Fairfax County's earliest free black communities, which settled near here in the 1840s. It is because of this proximity that this land was named Freedom Hill. According to a nearby historical marker, this site housed one of the Civil War outer defensive lines that encircled Washington, D.C. The redoubt, or temporary fortification, built on Freedom Hill was constructed with a gun platform at the center and ditches ringing the exterior. The hill became a staging point for numerous patrols into western Fairfax County, including portions of the Fifth Pennsylvania Heavy Artillery Regiment. No significant action was seen at this redoubt during its lifetime.

# 4

# Tysons Corner

## TYSONS CORNER CENTER

1961 Chain Bridge Road
Approximate distance to Metro: 0.3 miles

Originally, Tysons, Virginia, was a quiet, rural community. Since the 1950s, the area has rapidly urbanized into a bustling city with an expansive mall, known as the Tysons Corner Center. This major employment and retail center is one of the largest shopping malls in the United States, measuring approximately 2.2 million square feet with nearly three hundred stores. When it first opened in 1968, it was one of the first fully enclosed climate-controlled shopping malls in the D.C. area. Behind the venture was a developer named Theodore Lerner, who later went on to buy the Washington Nationals baseball team.

Across the street from the mall is Tysons Galleria, which opened in 1988.

# 5

# McLean

## FORT MARCY PARK

671 Chain Bridge Road
Approximate distance to Metro: 5.3 miles

The well-preserved Fort Marcy dates to the fall of 1862, when it was constructed to protect Leesburg Pike and Chain Bridge. When it was built, its perimeter spanned 338 feet with eighteen mounted guns, a ten-inch mortar and two twenty-four-pound Coehorn mortars. The hill that it is located on was originally known as Prospect Hill with a fort called Fort Baldy Smith, named after General W.F. Smith, whose brigade helped build the earthworks. The space didn't open as a public park until 1963, four years after the land was deeded to the federal government by the DeLashmutt family, who previously purchased the property from the Vanderwerken family.

This relatively undisturbed fort was named after Massachusetts native Brigadier General Randolph Barnes Marcy, who also served as chief of staff to General George B. McClellan.

## CLEMYJONTRI PARK

6317 Georgetown Pike
Approximate distance to Metro: 3.6 miles

The motto of this park is "where every child can play." Because of this focus, this public park is perfect for families with children of all abilities. Each area is specially designed so that it can be used by children who use wheelchairs, walkers or braces or who have sensory or developmental disabilities. There are lowered monkey bars, swings with high backs and arm rests, rubber surfacing for wheelchair mobility and wider openings for easier access. There is also a carousel and picnic pavilion. The entire space covers two acres.

The name Clemyjontri comes from the donor's four children: Carolyn (CL), Emily (EMY), John (Jon) and Petrina (Tri).

# Further Reading

Anderson, Brian. *Ford's Theatre.* Images of America. Charleston, SC: Arcadia Publishing, 2014.

Cooling, Benjamin Franklin, III, and Walton H. Owen II. *Mr. Lincoln's Forts: A Guide to the Civil War Defenses of Washington.* Lanham, MD: Scarecrow Press, Inc., 2009.

Goode, James M. *Best Addresses.* Washington, D.C.: Smithsonian Institution, 1988.

Jacob, Kathryn Allamong. *Testament to Union: Civil War Monuments in Washington.* Baltimore, MD: Johns Hopkins University Press, 1998.

Kelly, Clare Lise. *Montgomery Modern: Modern Architecture in Montgomery County, Maryland, 1930–1979.* Silver Spring: Maryland–National Capital Park and Planning Commission, 2015, 179.

Luebke, Thomas E., ed. *Civic Art: A Centennial History of the U.S. Commission of Fine Arts.* Amherst: University of Massachusetts Press, 2013.

Scott, Pamela, and Antoinette J. Lee. *Buildings of the District of Columbia.* New York: Oxford University Press, 1993.

Vogel, Steve. *The Pentagon: A History.* New York: Random House Trade Paperback Edition, 2008.

Weeks, Christopher. *AIA Guide to the Architecture of Washington, D.C.* 3rd ed. Baltimore, MD: Johns Hopkins University Press, 1994.

# Index

**A**

Abbot, Merkt & Company  85
Abraham Lincoln Memorial  48,
    146, 175, 176, 178, 189
Ackerman and Ross  252
Adams, John  43, 59, 118, 158, 162,
    167, 175, 197
Adams Memorial  99
Adas Israel Congregation  69
Adas Israel Synagogue  74
Addison Road  215
Adjaye, David  183
AFI Silver Theatre and Cultural
    Center  105
African American Civil War
    Museum and Memorial  263
Agnew, Spiro  45
Aitken, Robert Ingersoll  255
Akamu, Nina  80
Albert Einstein Statue  179

Alexander Crummell School  89
Alexander, Robert  204
Alexandria African American
    Heritage Park  119, 126
Alexandria Black History Museum
    126
Alexandria National Cemetery
    120, 123
Allen, Francis Richmond  41
Alva Belmont House  78
American Red Cross  28, 52, 60,
    68, 166
American University  21, 33, 35
Anacostia  296
Anacostia Arts Center  298
Anacostia Community Museum  297
Anacostia Park  298
Andersen, Henry  52
Archives  286
Arena Stage  289
Arlington Cemetery  135

Arlington House  135, 244
Arlington National Cemetery  136, 137, 138, 140
Arlington Post Office  235
Armistead Boothe Park  115
Army Medical Museum  25, 106, 185
Arthur, Chester A.  180, 271
Arthur M. Sackler Gallery  187
Arts and Industries Building  68, 168, 180, 199
Arts of Peace Sculptures  176
Arts of War Sculptures  176
Ashford, Snowden  89
Ash Grove  310
Ash Hill  285
Athenaeum  117
Atlas Performing Arts Center  80, 100

**B**

Bacon, Henry  48, 176
Bailey, John  47
Bake, Garin  83
Baldwin, Ephraim Francis  12
Ball Family Burial Grounds  234
Ballston-MU  231
Baltimore & Ohio Railroad Station  12
Barracks Row  201
Barry, John  167
Barry, Marion, Jr.  163, 206, 239
Barton, Clara  28, 68
Basilica of the National Shrine of the Immaculate Conception  93
Bayard, George Dashiell  32
Beale, Edward  162, 285

Beall-Dawson Museum  16
Bell, Alexander Graham  41, 68, 98, 143, 168
Belmont-Paul Women's Equality National Monument  78
Benjamin Banneker Park  190, 191
Benning Road  212
Ben's Chili Bowl  264
Berks, Robert  179, 205
Berryman, Clifford Kennedy  95
Bethesda Theatre  27
Bethesda Trolley Trail  20
Bethune, Mary McLeod  50, 204
Big Chair, the  297
Blackburn, Richard  229
Blagden Alley  254
Blind Whino  290
BloomBars  270
Blues Alley Club  156
Bodley, George Frederick  41
Boks, Joost W.C.  144
Boundary Stone  103
Bowman, Alexander H.  169
Bowser, Muriel  156
Boyce, James A.  290
Braddock Road  126
Bradley, William A.  95, 143
Branch Avenue  304
Breuer, Marcel  191
Brooke, Frederick H.  51, 152
Brookland-CUA  92
Brookside Gardens  110
Brooks Mansion  95
Browne, Herbert W.C.  49
Brumidi, Constantino  78, 203
Buberl, Casper  73
Buchanan, James, Jr.  271
Bulfinch, Charles  77

Bunshaft, Gordon  185
Burnham, Daniel  76
Bush, George H.W.  40, 73, 80, 185
Bush, George W.  69, 124, 182, 208

## C

Cabin John Regional Park  23
Cady Lee Mansion, the  102
Cairo Condominiums  54, 107
Calvert, Charles Benedict  281, 282
Campos, Olavo Redig de  52
Capital Crescent Trail  29
Capital One Arena  70
Capitol Heights  214
Capitol South  196
Car Barn, the  209
Carlton R. Sickles Memorial Sky
    Bridge  23
Carnegie, Andrew  101, 252
Carnegie Library  252
Carter G. Woodson Home National
    Historic Site  258
Carter, Jimmy  73, 181, 183
Cassell, Albert Irvin  238, 261
Catholic University of America  92
Cedar Hill Cemetery  302
Center Market  83, 199, 286
Chatelain, Leon, Jr.  34
Cherry Hill Farmhouse  228
Cheverly  242, 243
Christ Church  124, 204, 206, 229
Chung, Chien  37
Churchill, Winston  124
Clara Barton National Historic
    Site  28
Clarendon  235

Clarendon Citizens Hall  235
Clarendon School  233
Clark, Appleton P., Jr.  22, 52, 53
Clark, Robert  285
Clemyjontri Park  313
Cleveland, Grover  44, 73, 285
Cleveland Park  39, 43, 69
Cluss, Adolph  68, 83, 168, 180,
    199, 286
C&O Canal  150
Cohen, Wilbur Joseph  193
College Park Airport  279
College Park Aviation Museum  280
College Park–University of
    Maryland  279
Columbia Heights  269
Confederate Memorial  139
Congress Heights  299
Congressional Cemetery  206, 295
Contrabands and Freedmen
    Cemetery Memorial  120
Cook, Robert E.  57
Coolidge, Calvin  49, 60, 163, 165
Corcoran, William Wilson  160
Courthouse  237
Court of Neptune Fountain, the  198
Crandall, Harry M.  262, 269
Crane, C. Howard  65
Cret, Paul P.  198
Crystal City  131

## D

Daniel, Watha T.  258
DAR Constitution Hall  165
Davis, A.J.  68
Davis, Frank E.  15

Dawson-Bailey House, the  143
D.C. Armory, the  209, 272
D.C. Improv Comedy Club  164
Deanwood  240
Decatur House  161, 285
Deloria, Vine Victor, Jr.  303
Denby, Edwin  48
Dennis and Phillip Ratner Museum,
    the  21
Dessez, Leon  102
Dickens, Charles  66
Dickie, George  179
Dix, Dorothea Lynde  299
Douglass, Frederick  89, 186, 205,
    261, 296
Dumbarton House  152
Dumbarton Oaks  151, 152
Dunn Loring  225
Dupont Circle  41, 48, 51, 53,
    57
Dupont Circle Fountain  48
Du Pont, Samuel Francis  48
Dupont Underground  58


**E**


Eastern Market  68, 168, 199
East Falls Church  228
Ebenezer United Methodist
    Church  202
Eberson, John  27, 105
Edison, Thomas  54, 68
Edwards, Thomas H.  15
Einstein, Albert  179, 182
Eisenhower Avenue  250
Eisenhower, Dwight D.  68, 86, 101,
    141, 163

Eisenhower Executive Office
    Building  159
Elliot, William P.  68
Embassy of Brazil  52
Embassy of Britain  52
Embassy of China  37
Embassy of Finland  53
Embassy of Indonesia  52
Embassy of Syria  22
Embassy Row  33, 49, 51
Emory Grove  13
Engine Company 26  88
Exorcist Steps, the  155
Ezekiel, Moses Jacob  139


**F**


Falls Church Episcopal, the  229
Farragut, David  157
Farragut North  61, 157
Farragut Square  157
Farragut West  157
Farrand, Beatrix  152
Federal Bureau of Investigation
    Headquarters  170
Federal Center SW  192
Federal Triangle  170, 286
FedEx Field  216
Foggy Bottom–GWU  145
Folger, Emily Jordan  198
Folger, Henry Clay  198
Folger Shakespeare Library  198
Ford, Gerald  124, 170
Ford, John T.  62
Ford's Theatre  62, 63, 244
Forest Glen  106
Forrest, Uriah  43, 153

Fort Bayard Park  31
Fort Bennett Park and Palisades
    Trail  142
Fort Marcy Park  313
Fort Reno Park  34
Fort Totten  97
Fort Totten Park  97
Fort Ward Museum and Historic
    Site  127
Francis Asbury Statue  270
Franciscan Monastery of the Holy
    Land in America  93
Franconia Museum  113
Franconia-Springfield  113
Franklin D. Roosevelt (FDR)
    Memorial  187
Franklin School  168
Franklin Square  167
Franklin's Restaurant, Brewery and
    General Store  284
Fraser, James Earle  177
Fraser, John  56
Frederick Douglass National
    Historic Site  296
Freed, James Ingo  132, 183
Freedom Hill Park  311
Freedom House Museum  120
Freedom Plaza  63, 64
Freelon, Phil  183
Freeman Store and Museum  222
Freer Gallery of Art  187
French, Daniel Chester  48, 176
Friedberg, M. Paul  64
Friedlander, Leo  176
Friendship Archway  67
Friendship Firehouse Museum
    121

Friendship Heights  28
*From a Model to a Rainbow*  100


**G**

Gadsby's Tavern Museum  118
Gaithersburg Community
    Museum  12
Gallatin, Albert  78, 169
Gallaudet, Thomas Hopkins  82
Gallaudet University  82
Gallery Place–Chinatown  67
Gandhi, Mahatma  53
Gaye, Marvin  213, 256
General Oliver Otis Howard
    House  257
George Washington Masonic
    National Memorial  118
George Washington University
    148, 149
Georgia Avenue–Petworth  271
Glebe House  231
Glen Echo Park  29
Glenview Mansion  14
Glenwood Cemetery  95
Grant, Ulysses S.  66, 74, 158, 169,
    174, 205, 273, 285
Gravelly Point  129
Greenbelt  277
Greenbelt Museum  277
Greensboro  311

## H

Hansen, Tomas 147
Harry Weese & Architects 289
Hay-Adams Hotel, the 46, 162
Hecht Warehouse, the 88
Herndon Depot Museum 307
Herndon Fortnightly Library 308
Heurich House Museum 53
Hill Center 200
Hillwood Estate, Museum and
    Gardens 37
Hirshhorn Museum and Sculpture
    Garden 185
Hoffman Town Center 250
Holt House 46
House of Sweden 147
Howard Theatre 256
Howard University 260
Howlson, Allan T. 89

## I

Immaculata Seminary 35
InterContinental The Willard
    Hotel 65
Irwin, John N., II 43

## J

Jackson, Andrew 68
James G. Blaine Mansion 56
Jammin Java 224
Japanese American Memorial to
    Patriotism During World War
    II 80

Jefferson, Thomas 53, 103, 118,
    119, 128, 146, 158, 165,
    173, 174, 189, 197, 198,
    204, 266, 267
Jemal, Douglas 69
John Mercer Langston 211
Joint Base Anacostia-Bolling
    (JBAB) 301
Jones, Thomas Hudson 136
Josiah Henson Park 19

## K

Katzen Arts Center 33
Kenilworth Aquatic Gardens 241
Kennedy, Robert F. 94, 136, 208
Kennedy-Warren, the 42
Kentlands Mansion 11
King Street–Old Town 116
Kramerbooks & Afterwords Café 56
Kreeger Theater 289

## L

Lady Bird Johnson Park 139
Lafayette, Marquis de 17, 118
Lamb, Thomas White 269
Landover 244
Langley, Charles Albion 59
Langston, John Mercer 212
Langston Terrace Dwellings 211
Largo Town Center 218
Latrobe, Benjamin Henry 77, 90,
    158, 161, 172, 177, 204, 206,
    292, 295
Latvian Museum 17

Laurel Grove Colored School
	Museum  113
Lee, Robert E.  32, 40, 110, 116,
	124, 135, 143, 308
L'Enfant, Pierre Charles  41, 63, 68,
	136, 154, 167, 172, 190, 199,
	204, 287
L'Enfant Plaza  190, 191
Library of Congress  21, 196, 198
Lincoln, Abraham  48, 62, 63, 68,
	82, 83, 95, 106, 123, 135,
	143, 146, 162, 173, 176, 185,
	200, 204, 271
Lincoln Park  204
Lincoln Theatre  262, 265
Lin, Maya Ying  178
Little, Arthur  49
Liu, Alfred  67
Lloyd House  121
Lockie, James A.  14
Lockkeeper's House, the  177
Long Bridge Park  129
Lovering, William  203
Lukeman, H. Augustus  270
Lyceum, the  122


**M**

MacVeagh, Wayne  52
Magruder, Fielder  243
Magruder Spring Historic
	Landmark  242
Maine Avenue Fish Market  288
Malcolm X Park  263
Manfredi, Michael  137
Mansion on O Street  55

Maples, the  203
Marilyn Monroe Mural  47
Marshall, Michael  38
Marshall Moya Design  38, 256
Marshall, Thurgood  136, 261
Martin Luther King Jr. Memorial
	188
Martin Luther King Jr. Memorial
	Library  70
Marvin Gaye Park  213
Mary Ann Shadd Cary House  265
Mary Church Terrell House  259
Mary E. Switzer Memorial
	Building  193
Mary McLeod Bethune Council
	House National Historic
	Site  50
Masonic Temple  50, 66, 209, 286
Mayfair Mansions Apartments  238
Mayflower Hotel, the  163
McCormick, Cyrus  68
McKim, Mead and White  60, 99,
	152, 159, 184
McKinley, William  73, 162
McLean  313
McPherson Square  167
Mead Center, the  289
Meadowlark Botanical Garden  222
Medical Center  24
Meigs, Montgomery C.  72, 123, 136
Mellon, Andrew W.  181
Meridian Hill Park  148, 153, 203,
	204, 263, 264
Meridian House  266
Mesrobian, Mihran  46, 162
Metro Center  62
Metropolitan Branch Trail  83

Meyers, John Granville 53
Mies van der Rohe, Ludwig 70
Milken Institute School of Public
	Health 148
Milken, Michael R. 149
Mills, Robert 68, 169, 174, 207
Moore, Arthur Cotton 54, 58
Mooseum at King Farm Barn, the
	12
Moretti, Luigi 145
Morgan Boulevard 216
Mosaic District 226
Mount Hope 242
Mount Olivet United Methodist
	Church 231
Mount Vernon Square 252
Mullett, Alfred B. 159, 169
Murray-Dick-Fawcett House 121
Museum of the Bible 194
Museum Resource Center 244


N

NASA Goddard Visitor Center 245
National Air and Space Museum
	182
National Arboretum 78, 90, 91
National Archives Building 165,
	199, 286, 287
National Building Museum 72,
	123, 136
National Capital Trolley Museum
	109
National Gallery of Art 53, 165,
	174, 181, 185, 266, 267
National Geographic Museum 164

National Harmony Memorial Park
	217
National Institutes of Health, the
	24, 25
National Law Enforcement Officers
	Memorial 73
National Mall 44, 134, 172, 173,
	177, 178, 186, 188, 192,
	225, 264
National Museum of African
	American History and
	Culture 182
National Museum of African Art
	186
National Museum of American
	History 181, 184
National Museum of American
	Jewish Military History 55
National Museum of Health and
	Medicine 106
National Museum of Natural
	History 51, 181, 184
National Museum of the American
	Indian 185, 303
National Museum of Women in the
	Arts 66, 286
National Park Seminary 107
National Portrait Gallery 67
National Science Foundation (NSF)
	Headquarters 250
Nationals Park 293
Navy Yard–Ballpark 292
Navy Yard Car Barn 294
Naylor Road 302
Netherlands Carillon 144
New Carrollton 245
Newseum 74

Nixon, Richard 73, 145, 163, 208
NoMa–Gallaudet U 82
Norton, Eleanor Holmes 69, 167
Nourse, Joseph 153
NPR Headquarters 84
Nurses Memorial 138

**O**

Oakley Cabin African American
    Museum and Park 109
Obama, Barack 56, 79, 209, 300
Old Greenbelt Theatre 277
Old Post Office Pavilion 171
Old Stone House 154
Olmsted, Frederick Law 44, 46, 82
Olmsted, Frederick Law, Jr. 90,
    143, 175
Onassis, Jacqueline Kennedy 136,
    148
Original Vienna Little Library 223

**P**

Page, Harvey L. 59
Page, Russell 90
Patterson Mansion 60
Patton, George 64
Peaslee, Horace 153, 203, 204, 264
Pei, I.M. 37, 181, 190
Pei, Li Chung 37
Pei Partnership Architects 37
Peirce Mill 36
Pennsy Collections and Support
    Center 244

Pentagon 128, 133
Pentagon City 132
Pepco's Friendship Heights
    Substation 31
Perry, Roland Hinton 198
Pershing, John J. 64
Pershing Park 64
Petersen House 63
Petworth Neighborhood Library 272
Phillips Collection 51
Phyllis Wheatley Young Women's
    Christian Association 260
Pierce, Franklin 82
Pierce-Klingle Mansion 39
Pink Palace 266
Platt, Charles Adams 187
Polshek Partnership Architects
    75, 186
Pope, John Russell 53, 143, 165,
    174, 181, 263, 266, 267, 286
Porter, Irwin Stevens 14
Post, Marjorie Merriweather 37
Potomac Avenue 206
President Lincoln's Cottage 271
President Woodrow Wilson House
    49
Prince George's African American
    Museum and Cultural
    Center 283
Prince George's Plaza 282
Puławski, Kazimierz 64

**R**

Reagan, Ronald 57, 73, 80, 124,
    128, 132

Red Brick Courthouse 15
Reed, Walter 25, 106, 107
Renwick Gallery of the
    Smithsonian American Art
    Museum 160, 180
Renwick, James, Jr. 160, 180
Reston Historic Trust and
    Museum 307
Rhode Island Avenue 88
Rich, Lorimer 136
Ripley, S. Dillon 185, 297
Riversdale House Museum 282
Robert C. Weaver Federal
    Building 191
Robert F. Kennedy Memorial
    Stadium 70, 208
Robert Llewellyn Wright House 30
Robinson, Hilyard R. 211
Rock Creek Cemetery 97, 98
Rock Creek Park 32, 37, 39
Rogers, Isaiah 169
Rohl-Smith, Carl 273
Ronald Reagan Washington
    National Airport 128
Roosevelt, Eleanor 50, 188, 238
Roosevelt, Franklin D. 50, 124,
    128, 133, 163, 174, 175,
    181, 187, 193, 211, 254,
    256, 277, 301
Roosevelt, Theodore 73, 138, 142,
    143, 158, 159, 162, 205
Root, Walter C. 294
Roscoe the Rooster Memorial
    Statue 102
Rosedale 43
Rossborough Inn 280
Rosslyn 141
Ross, Wendy 22

## S

Saal, Stefan 22
Saint-Gaudens, Augustus 99
Samuel Gompers Memorial Park
    254
Satterlee, Nicholas 59
Schneider, Thomas Franklin 54, 107
Scottish Rite Temple 267
Serra, Richard 64
Sewall, Robert 78
Shady Grove 11
Shaw–Howard U 256
Shaw (Watha T. Daniel)
    Neighborhood Library 258
Sherman Circle 273
Sherman, William Tecumseh 273
Sickles, Carlton R. 23
Signature Theater 131
Silver Spring 29, 83, 104, 105
Silver Spring Baltimore and Ohio
    Railroad Station 104
Simmons, Katheryn 213
Sixth and I Historic Synagogue 69
Sligo Creek Trail 105
Smith, Chloethiel Woodard 73
Smith, Delos H. 15
Smithsonian American Art
    Museum 67, 192
Smithsonian Castle 160
Smithsonian Institution 79, 97,
    117, 179, 180, 182, 184, 185,
    186, 244, 297
Smithsonian National Postal
    Museum 79
Smithsonian National Zoological
    Park 44, 46, 82, 143, 299
Society of the Cincinnati 49

Sonnemann, Alexander H.  43
Sousa, John Philip  202, 204
Southern Avenue  300
Spanish-American War Memorial
    138
Spanish Steps  57
Spite House, the  122
Spring Hill  310
Stabler-Leadbeater Apothecary
    Museum  116
Stadium-Armory  208
St. Aloysius Church  86
St. Anselm's Abbey  94
State Theatre  229
St. Coletta of Greater Washington
    210
St. Elizabeth's Hospital  299
Stoddert, Benjamin  292
Stone, Edward Durell  146, 164
Stone, Edward Durell, Jr.  139
Stonestreet Museum  16
Storck, J. Edward  256
St. Paul's Episcopal Church  98
Strand Theater  240
Strathmore  22
Suitland  303
Sully Historic Site  308
Supreme Court  21, 26, 135, 136,
    150, 153, 196, 206, 230, 261

**T**

Tabler, William B.  57
Taft, William Howard  36, 49, 73,
    136, 175, 196, 291
Tait-Trussell House  32

Takoma  100
Takoma Park Adventist Church  101
Takoma Park Library  101
Takoma Theatre  100
Tenleytown-AU  33
Terrell, Mary Church  50, 71, 259
Terrell Place  71, 89
THEARC  300
Theodore Roosevelt Island  142
Thomas Jefferson Memorial  174
Thomas Law House  291
Thom, Bing  290
Thornton, William  77, 154, 207,
    236, 282, 295
Tingey House  294
Tinner Hill  230
Titanic Memorial  291
Tivoli Theatre  269
Tomb of the Unknown Soldier  136
Torpedo Factory Art Center  117
Totten, George Oakley, Jr.  267
Townes, Charles H.  167
Town, Ithiel  68
Tracy, Evans  270
Treasury Building  159, 169, 174
Tudor Place  154, 236
Twain, Mark  66, 99, 162
Twinbrook  18
Twin Oaks  41
Tysons Corner  312
Tysons Corner Center  312

**U**

Uline Arena  85
Union Market  83

Union Station 76, 83, 171
United States Naval Observatory 45
University of Maryland 16, 280, 281, 283
University of the District of Columbia (UDC) Student Center 38
Uptown Theater 42, 80, 100
U.S. Air Force Memorial 132
U.S. Botanic Garden 192
U.S. Capitol 39, 64, 76, 77, 80, 90, 119, 134, 154, 165, 169, 173, 192, 196, 197, 198, 203, 205, 217, 267, 273, 282
U.S. Holocaust Memorial Museum 132, 183
U.S. Marine Corps War Memorial 141
U.S. National Library of Medicine 25
U.S. Navy Memorial 287
U Street 262

**V**

Vanadu Art House 283
Van Dorn 115
Van Ness–UDC 36
Venturi, Rausch and Scott Brown 64
Venturi, Robert 64
Vienna 221
Vietnam Veterans Memorial 178, 244
Vine Deloria Jr. Library 303
Virginia Square–GMU 233
Vitale, Ferruccio 264

**W**

Walker, Allen E. 163
Walter E. Washington Convention Center 253, 293
Walter Reed National Military Medical Center, the 25
Walter, Thomas U. 68, 77
Wardman, Harry 45, 162
Warner Theatre 65
Warren, Whitney 163
Washington and Old Dominion (W&OD) Railroad Regional Park 225
Washington City Canal 172, 177
Washington, George 14, 118, 119, 124, 135, 148, 150, 154, 158, 165, 173, 229, 267
Washington Grove 13
Washington Hilton 57
Washington Marriott Wardman Park 45
Washington Monument 169, 173, 174, 178, 217
Washington National Cathedral 40
Washington Navy Yard 292
Washington, Walter E. 253, 258
Waterfront 288
Watergate Hotel, the 145, 163
Watkins Nature Center 218
Webb and Knapp 190
Weeks, John C. 59
Weeks, John W. 48
Weinert, Albert 198
Weinman, Adolph Alexander 268
Weiss, Marion 137
Weldon, Felix de 141
West End Library 149

Western Union Tower 34
West Falls Church 227
Wetmore, Charles 163
Wharf, the 289
Wheatley, Phyllis 260
Wheaton 108
Wheaton Regional Park 108
Wheeler, Perry 37
White, Edward Douglas 52
White Flint 19
White House, the 39, 57, 64, 65,
 88, 128, 158, 161, 162, 163,
 167, 168, 169, 175, 203, 209,
 217, 251, 263, 271, 272, 273
White, Stanford 60, 99
Whitman, Walt 68, 143, 205
Whittemore House, the 59
Wiehle-Reston East 307
Wilbur J. Cohen Federal Building
 193
Wilcox, Walter D. 59
Williams, Anthony 69, 71
Wilson, Woodrow 49, 66, 140,
 180, 221
Wingårdh, Gert 147
Winslow, Lorenzo 159
Wolf Trap National Park for the
 Performing Arts 221
Women in Military Service for
 America Memorial 137
Woodlawn and Pope-Leighey
 House 124
Woodlawn Cemetery 212
Woodley Park 44
Woodson, Carter G. 258
Wood, Waddy Butler 49, 52, 66,
 159, 209

Woodward & Lothrop Service
 Warehouse 85
Wright, Frank Lloyd 18, 30, 124
Wright, Robert Llewellyn 30
Wyeth, Nathan 88, 159, 209, 272

**X**

Xiaobo, Liu 38

**Y**

Yixin, Lei 188
Young, Ammi B. 169
Younger, Joseph 42

**Z**

Zeckendorf, William 190
Zink, Atkins and Craycroft 42
Zink, John J. 65
Zink, John Jacob 80, 100
Zuckerman, Shelton 69

# About the Author

Michelle Goldchain is a Washington, D.C.– born journalist, photographer, podcaster, artist and YouTuber. Her bylines have been seen in *Washington City Paper*, *Education Week*, DCist, Curbed, Eater DC, Racked, Recode, Vox, Greater Greater Washington, DC Refined, *Whurk Magazine* and *Tagg Magazine*.

For three and a half years, she worked as editor of Vox Media's Curbed DC blog, where she wrote about real estate and development in the D.C. area. Since September 2017, she has edited the newsletter *Capital Women*, which expanded into a podcast in January 2018. *Capital Women* is focused on profiling successful local women and highlighting news and events geared toward female-identifying people in the nation's capital. Michelle is also the host, writer and co-creator of *Artsplained*, a weekly YouTube comedy show that makes high art more down-to-earth. She has been a guest on WAMU's *Kojo Nnamdi Show*, SiriusXM's *Jennifer Hammond Show* and the *You, Me, Them, Everybody* podcast.

Michelle holds a bachelor of arts in English with an art minor from Longwood University. She currently resides with her fat cat, Harley, in Alexandria, Virginia.

To learn more about her, visit www.michellegoldchain.com.